ISLAND OF HELL

It was Monday morning, the nineteenth of February. A light mist hovered over Iwo Jima as the first sign of light began to show on the horizon.

At 0900 the first troops hit the beaches. The Marines immediately found themselves stumbling ankle deep in sand and volcanic ash. The soft terrain reduced their upward climb to a crawl. To their amazement they encountered very little opposition. What they couldn't know was that they were falling right into Kuribayashi's trap. . . .

When the assault troops moved toward the airfield, the Japanese defenders hit them with everything they had. From concealed pillboxes the Japanese raked the Marines with machine guns and lobbed hundreds of mortar shells. Nevertheless, the Marines continued their bloody step-by-step advance.

As darkness approached, the Japanese continued to rain death on the attackers. During that first day of Iwo Jima, 2,420 Marines became casualties. And that was only the beginning. . . .

THE
GREAT BATTLES
OF
WORLD WAR II
VOLUME I: THE PACIFIC ISLANDS

BY CHARLES E. PFANNES AND VICTOR A. SALAMONE

ZEBRA BOOKS
KENSINGTON PUBLISHING CORP.

ZEBRA BOOKS

are published by

Kensington Publishing Corp.
475 Park Avenue South
New York, N.Y. 10016

First printing: January 1985

Printed in the United States of America

For Peggy:

We all miss you.

Having completed our *Great Commanders* and *Great Admirals* series, we have now contracted to author a *Great Battles* series. Our first volume will feature the Pacific Island battles. Subsequent volumes will cover Pacific naval battles, European land battles, Mediterranean ground battles, and featured sea and air campaigns.

This present volume will study seven Island battles. Two of the battles were Japanese victories, five were American. Chapter one will study the Japanese victory at Singapore: chapter two will examine General Homma's victory in the Philippines. Chapter three will feature America's first offensive in the Pacific, the six-month-long campaign at Guadalcanal. Chapter four will look at the first offensive of the Central Pacific Drive, the assaults on the islands of Tarawa and Makin. The next chapter focuses in upon the difficult and controversial campaign in the Marianas, the islands of Saipan, Tinian and Guam. Chapter six studies the horrid battle for Iwo Jima, the bitterest battle in Marine Corps history that gave rise to the Marines' symbol of victory. The last chapter studies the largest combined invasion of the Pacific War, the battle of Okinawa.

We want to thank Zebra for the opportunity to write this battle series. We want to thank the readers who have faithfully followed our commanders and admirals series. We hope they will equally enjoy our battle books. We again want to thank our wives and children without whom this venture would be useless.

Charles "Chuck" Pfannes
Cold Spring, New York

Victor A. Salamone
Poughkeepsie, New York

May 25, 1984

TABLE OF CONTENTS

Introduction

The Decision to Use the Atomic Bomb: Did It Cause Japan to Surrender?

On August 6, 1945, the United States exploded an atomic bomb over Hiroshima. This event was followed three days later by the dropping of another bomb on Nagasaki. On August 8, the Soviet Union declared war on Japan. The United States Navy, meanwhile, had managed to completely isolate Japan from its empire. American bombers devastated Japan's cities. Any one of these could have led to Japan's surrender.

The decision to use the atomic bomb was made by President Harry S. Truman. Though attuned to the counsel of his chief advisors, the actual decision was his alone. In justifying his decision Truman said that the basic reason for using the bomb was to end the war and avoid having to invade the Japanese homeland, an operation that estimates said would cost countless lives. Was Truman's decision to use the bomb correct? Did it in fact end the war?

The atomic bomb project began as far back as 1939 when a group of scientists approached the U.S. government and apprised it of the vast potentials of atomic energy and the possibility of Germany developing a powerful weapon using this new source of energy. The U.S. government immediately became interested in the project. Thus was born the top-secret Manhattan Project. The sole purpose of this project was:

> To harness the energy of the atom in a chain reaction to produce a bomb that could be carried by aircraft if possible, and to produce it before the Germans could.[1]

From the very inception of the project it was never doubted that if a bomb were successfully produced, it would most certainly be used. Even before the project was completed, the Army Air Force had selected potential targets in Japan. Still, no one was actually certain that if a bomb was produced, it would even work.

By March, 1945, it was possible to predict that the bomb would be ready for testing the following July. Among the top American officials there was no doubt that even at this late date, if necessary, the bomb could be used to end the war. Certain scientists, however, indicated great reluctance to use it.

Following President Roosevelt's untimely death on April 12, 1945, his successor, Truman, was briefed on the Manhattan Project by Secretary of War Henry Stimson. The project was so classified that even as vice president, Truman had no knowledge of it. At this point, the new president approved the appointment of a special committee to review in what manner the bomb should be used if at all. The Interim Committee, as it was known, was chaired by Secretary Stimson. James Byrnes was Truman's personal representative. Byrnes said:

> The President requested me to act as his represent-

ative on the committee . . . [the] interim committee to consider and make recommendations to the
President on such important questions of policy as
the test of the bomb, its use in the war, and the
postwar use of atomic energy.[2]

The committee completed its work on June 1, 1945
and submitted its report to Truman. It recommended
that the bomb be used against Japan as soon as possible,
that it be used against a military target surrounded by
other buildings and that, it be used without prior warning of the nature of the weapon.

Stimson was convinced, as was the committee, that
the only way to persuade the emperor and his military
advisors to surrender was by administering a tremendous shock that would serve to convince them that the
United State possessed the power to destroy the Empire. A number of scientists protested and said that the
bomb should not be used against people. What they recommended instead was a demonstration of the new
weapon. After the demonstration the Japanese could be
given an ultimatum. Only if they rejected the ultimatum should its further use be contemplated.

This recommendation was studied by a group of
high-ranking physicists including Doctors Arthur
Compton, Enrico Fermi, E.O. Lawrence and J. Robert
Oppenheimer. After studying the report these eminent
scientists said that they could see no practical way of
ending the war by a demonstration. What if the demonstration were a failure? What if the Japanese placed
American POWs at the demonstration site? There were
simply too many risks involved in staging a demonstration. Therefore, by the middle of June, Truman found

unanimity among his top civilian advisors regarding the bomb's use.

Meanwhile, the military situation cried out for a new weapon. The bitterly fought campaigns on Iwo Jima and Okinawa, and the *kamikaze* vividly demonstrated the tenacity, determination and fanaticism of the Japanese. An invasion of Japan would be a certain blood bath. Was there an alternative to invasion?

One alternative was to isolate Japan completely and starve it into submission. Admiral King stated:

> that the defeat of Japan could be accomplished by sea and air power alone, without the necessity of actual invasion of the Japanese home islands by ground troops.[3]

General MacArthur, on the other hand, was not convinced that bombing alone was the way to defeat Japan. He pointed to the recently concluded European War where Germany's cities were pounded into rubble. Yet Germany refused to surrender until Allied troops physically conquered the country.

By mid-June Truman had reviewed all the alternatives and had accepted the invasion plan. Kyushu would be invaded in November (Operation Olympic) and Honshu the following March (Operation Coronet). The president was also handed the gloomy casualty estimate.

Truman also reviewed another alternative. Could the war be concluded by political means? Might not the Japanese surrender? Through code-breaking the United States was aware that the Japanese had approached the Swedes in September, 1944. More recently they had approached the Soviets. Truman then knew that the Russians would also enter the Pacific War.

Though the prospect of Soviet participation in the Pacific was something long desired by the Americans, by June of 1945 this attitude had changed drastically. What had once appeared desirable was far less so now that the war in Europe was over and Japan all but defeated. The impasse reached with the Russians in Europe helped to harden the American view of Soviet participation. There were others, however, who felt that Soviet participation was necessary in order to end the war:

> The point in our military progress at which the Japanese will accept defeat and agree to our terms is unpredictable. . . . Like the Germans, their protracted resistance is based upon the hope of achieving a conditional surrender. Presumably, only the conviction that their position is completely hopeless will persuade them to give up their holdings in Asia. Probably it will take Russian entry into the war coupled with a landing, or imminent threat of landing, on Japan proper by us, to convince them of the hopelessness of their position.[4]

For their part, the Japanese were hoping that war weariness in the United States would cause the Americans to agree to a conditional surrender. To them unconditional surrender was something they simply could not accept. There were some who felt that had conditions been offered to the Japanese, particularly ones that included the retention of the imperial system, the Japanese might have surrendered. Was that estimate accurate?

Postwar accounts on Japan do in fact indicate this to be true. The Japanese had been attempting, through channels, since September, 1944 to find out the Allied terms for peace. Obviously the Allied demand for unconditional surrender was the greatest obstacle. In June, 1945, Japan attempted to work through the Soviets. The Japanese wished to end the war but would accept no terms that did not include the preservation of the imperial system. The Russians put the Japanese off.

Meanwhile, some voices in the United States government wanted to use the atomic bomb to end the war before the Russians could enter it. Byrnes said:

> I believed the atomic bomb would be successful
> and would force the Japanese to accept surrender
> on our terms. I feared what would happen when
> the Red Army entered Manchuria.[5]

Some went so far as to state that use of the bomb might become a powerful deterrent to Soviet expansion in Europe. Others believed that the bomb should be used to justify the expenditure of two billion dollars on the Manhattan Project:

> What more striking justification of the Manhattan
> Project than a new weapon that had ended the
> war.[6]

In the interim, President Truman travelled to Germany to participate in the final wartime meeting of the major powers, the Potsdam Conference. The conference opened on July 17, one day after the successful explosion of the bomb. Truman now knew that the experiment was a success and furthermore, had the approval of his political and military advisors to use the bomb.

On July 26, the Big Three presented the Japanese with terms for surrender. This was known as the Potsdam Declaration. No mention of the emperor or of the imperial system was made. They warned the Japanese of dire consequences if they refused to accept surrender. Not once was there any mention of the atomic bomb.

When the Potsdam Declaration reached the Japanese, they decided to await the results of the Soviet overture made earlier in the month, an overture which the Russians conveniently forgot to mention at the Potsdam Conference. On July 28, Prime Minister Suzuki responded to the Japanese press on the Potsdam Declaration. He told the press that Japan would ignore the declaration. The Allies took this as a rejection.

The Americans were now convinced that only a dramatic act could convince Japan's military clique to end the war. Truman waited a few days before issuing his orders. His wait was in vain. No message from Tokyo was forthcoming. All Truman got was silence. The Japanese were waiting for the Russians to get back to them.

On August 6, Hiroshima was bombed. The following day the Japanese ambassador in Moscow received word that Soviet Foreign Minister Molotov wished to see him. On August 8 he went to Molotov's office hoping to receive Russian assurance that they would act as mediator with the Allies. Instead, he was handed the Soviet declaration of war.

What did force the Japanese to finally surrender? Was it the aerial bombardment, the naval blockade, the atomic bomb or the Soviet entry into the war in the Pacific?

The United States Strategic Bombing Survey concluded that Japan would have surrendered by the end of the year, without invasion and without the atomic bomb. Other equally informed opinion maintained that it was the atomic bomb that forced Japan to surrender. . . . Admiral Nimitz believed firmly that the decisive factor was the complete impunity with which the Pacific Fleet pounded Japan and General Arnold claimed it was air bombardment that had brought Japan to the verge of collapse. But Major General Claire L. Chennault . . . maintained that Soviet entry into the Far Eastern War brought about the surrender of Japan and would have done so even if no atomic bombs had been dropped. [7]

Which one actually caused Japan to finally surrender? To pinpoint one or the other is difficult at best. The effects of the naval blockade and the devastating fire bombings of Japan's cities followed by the dropping of the atomic bomb on Hiroshima and Nagasaki along with the Soviet stab in the back had actually acted in unison to convince the emperor to come down from his throne and demand an end to the war. One can only speculate, however, if the Japanese would have surrendered well before August, 1945 had the United States dropped its unconditional surrender formula. In that event, perhaps the bomb might never have been dropped. But, to repeat, that is mere speculation after the fact. There is no one clear answer that will satisfy everyone. As a result the issue will remain a question of debate for centuries ahead.

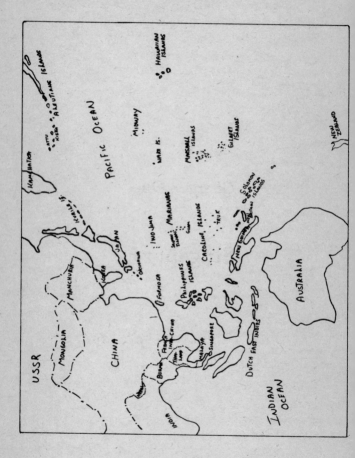

Chapter One

Singapore

In a record-setting time of seventy-three days, Gen. Tomoyuki Yamashita conquered what was considered to be the British bastion of the Far East, Singapore. Using superior tactics, the Japanese commander conducted a successful campaign against a numerically superior force. To the British the loss of Singapore was a devastating blow. It not only humiliated them and made the white man appear less than invincible to the natives, it was the harbinger of the end of the colonial era.

In November, 1941, General Yamashita was summoned to Tokyo. There he was informed that he was to assume command of the Twenty-fifth Army. This unit was already in training for the invasion of Malaya in the event Japan decided to go to war. If war came, Yamashita would be responsible for the capture of the "Pearl of the Orient," the great British naval base on the island of Singapore.

Yamashita accepted his command with mixed feelings for he was well aware that his superiors, Generals Tojo and Sugiyama, did not like him. A highly talented officer, Yamashita had run afoul of the two by backing the Imperial Way Faction. Both Tojo and Sugiyama belonged to the rival Control Faction. During the 1930s the Control Faction felt that Japan needed to expand into China no matter what the consequences, even if that thrust the nation into a war with America and Great Britain. The Imperial Way group, on the other hand, wanted to establish military rule under the emperor. Russia was viewed as the main enemy and this group felt that any Japanese expansion should be at the expense of the Soviet Union. Their contrasting philosophies escalated into rebellion in the 1930s which resulted in Yamashita's banishment to the Manchurian Frontier. With Tojo and Sugiyama in control of the army, Yamashita knew that he would be closely scrutinized and spied upon, and any failure would be punished by dismissal and humiliation.

Even before Yamashita was named commander of the Twenty-fifth Army, both army and navy staffs debated the strategy to be used in the invasion of Malaya and Singapore. The navy felt that in order to ensure the safety of the troop transports, the RAF had to be eliminated.

In contrast, the army staff thought that this method would sacrifice the element of surprise, a factor they considered vital to the success of the operation. The army reasoned that the British would not make any aggressive moves, even if they detected the approaching Japanese armada. Therefore, by the time the enemy realized they were at war, the Japanese air force would have already gained aerial supremacy by having surprise on their side. After much debate, the commander of the Japanese Fleet for the invasion of Malaya, Vice Adm. Jisaburo Ozawa, accepted the army's proposal. Ozawa stated:

I say that the navy should accept the army's proposal even at the risk of annihilation.[1]

This effectively ended all debate.

The actual site of the invasion was also decided prior to Yamashita's assuming command of the attack forces. The narrow neck of land known as the Kra Isthmus, which joins Thailand to Malaya, was the area designated to be attacked. The three main attack points on the isthmus were Singora and Patani in Thailand and Kota Bharu at the mouth of the Kelantan River in northern Malaya. Each of these three ports contained excellent anchorages and nearby airfields. The main landing was to take place at Singora, since it possessed the best beach for exploitation.

What were Yamashita's feelings towards his country's preparation for war?

The cause of this war is fundamentally economic. Fifty years ago Japan was more or less self-sufficient . . . the people could live off the land. Since then the population has almost doubled, so that Japan has had to rely on outside sources of food supply and other economic requirements. In order to buy or import her commodities she has had to pay ultimately in commodities. This effort on her part was prevented for one reason or another by other countries. Japan made attempts to solve the misunderstandings through peaceful methods, but when all her efforts were thwarted or negated she felt it necessary to engage in open warfare.[2]

The general wrote these words shortly after the attack

on Pearl Harbor. Along with the majority of his countrymen, he did not consider war an infamous act, but rather a sacred duty.

For the proposed invasion, the Twenty-fifth Army was allotted five divisions. When Yamashita arrived at his new headquarters on Hainan Island, he reviewed the situation and made a startling suggestion. During an interview with Army Chief of Staff Sugiyama, he stated that three divisions would be more than enough for the operation, instead of the allotted five.

This was indeed surprising since most commanders usually ask for more forces, not less. Yamashita, however, was astute enough to realize that the terrain of Malaya mitigated against the use of large numbers of troops. Fewer troops of superior quality, he felt, could move more rapidly.

A total of sixty thousand men were thus allocated to Yamashita for the operation. These men comprised the Fifth and Eighteenth Divisions, two of the best trained and most experienced units in the Imperial Army. The third division was the Imperial Guards. These formations would be supported by two regiments of heavy artillery and a tank brigade. The army forces would be protected by 450 land-based planes and 150 naval aircraft, along with the combined firepower of a battle-cruiser and 10 destroyers.

Two of Yamashita's divisional commanders were also highly experienced and well liked by their troops. The Fifth Division, veterans of the war in China, were commanded by Lt. Gen. Takuro Matsui. His counterpart in the Eighteenth Division was Lt. Gen. Renya Mutaguchi. Yamashita liked both men but felt a far closer bond of friendship with Mutaguchi, who had served as his chief of staff in 1937 with the Kwangtung Army. The remaining division, the Imperial Guards, was commanded by Lt. Gen. Takuma Nishimura, a man who disliked Yamashita immensely and attempted to be as uncooperative as possible. In addition to being uncooperative, Nishimura was a close friend of the commander of the Southern Area Army and Yamashita's immediate superior, General Terauchi. He was also close to Army Chief of Staff Sugiyama. This friendship was to cause Yamashita many problems during the battle.

Besides Nishimura, another individual who caused problems for Yamashita was his own chief of operations, Col. Masanubu Tsuyi, an austere and sinister looking person. Tsuyi was actually something of a government spy and dutifully reported all his impressions of the army commander to Prime Minister Tojo.

Thus Yamashita was faced with enemies above him, beneath him, and on his own staff. Hardly an ideal situation for a man about to embark on the difficult venture of conquering the "Bastion of Singapore."

The Japanese invasion plan called for the attacking forces to land at three beaches in the north, two in Thailand and one in Malaya. It was a daring plan calling for an assault on Singapore from the north, something the British considered highly unlikely. The defenses of the naval base were designed to protect it from the obvious direction of a potential attack, the sea. The idea of driving a force down the spiny, jungle-covered back of Malaya, although deemed possible, was considered improbable. Yet that was precisely the route the Japanese intended to take.

The Malayan Peninsula is roughly four hundred miles long and varies in width from two hundred to sixty miles. It is joined to Thailand by the narrow Kra Isthmus. Malaya has a spiny backbone, a ridge of jungle-covered hills rising to about seven thousand feet in the north and three thousand feet in the south. On both sides of the mountains lie coastal plains. These contain hundreds of rivers and streams which meander their way from the mountains to the sea, cutting through endless areas of thick jungle and swamps. The great growth of jungle is so dense that in places visibility is reduced to yards. Cultivated areas feature miles of rice paddies or fields where six-foot-high elephant grass, so sharp it can cut a man like a thousand knives, grows wild. This then is Malaya, a land totally unsuited for military maneuver, or so the British thought.

For the invasion, portions of the Fifth and Eighteenth Divisions were to land at the two points in Thailand between Singora and Patani, and at the Malayan Port of Kota Bharu. Once the two divisions had established their beachheads, it was planned to land Nishimura's less efficient Imperial Guards. A reserve division, the Fifty-sixth, would remain on board ship in case help was required. Once the beachheads were consolidated, the Japanese force would move toward Singapore.

Early in December, reconnaissance flights were sent over Thailand and Malaya. These flights confirmed the suspicion that British troops were deployed in defensive positions around Kota Bharu. Opposition could be expected at this point. However, the Thai beaches were undefended.

From his headquarters in Saigon, General Count Terauchi sent a signal to Yamashita confirming the date for the commencement of hostilities, December 8 (December 7, Hawaiian time). At the same time he informed

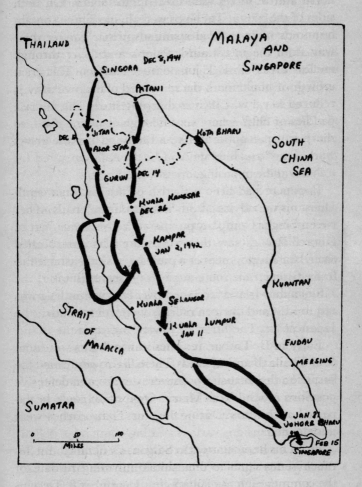

THAILAND

MALAYA
AND
SINGAPORE

SINGORA   DEC 8, 1941

PATANI

DEC 8   JITRA

ALOR STAR

KOTA BHARU

SOUTH
CHINA
SEA

GURUN   DEC 14

KUALA KANGSAR
DEC 26

KAMPAR
JAN 2, 1942

KUANTAN

STRAIT
OF
MALACCA

KUALA SELANGOR

KUALA LUMPUR
JAN 11

ENDAU

MERSING

SUMATRA

0   50   100
MILES

JAN 31
JOHORE BHARU

FEB 15
SINGAPORE

Yamashita that should a negotiated settlement occur in the diplomatic talks then taking place in Washington, the attack would be cancelled.

Yamashita's forces were loaded into ships which then set sail for Malaya. The ships were divided into five separate convoys to avoid arousing suspicion. Two convoys headed for Singora, two for Patani, and the remaining one for Kota Bharu. The landing of Mutaguchi's forces at Singora would mark the spearhead of the invasion.

December 8 was Japan's day of destiny. The men of the Twenty-fifth Army were filled with nationalist fervor. Finally, an opportunity had come to oust the hated "barbarians" and liberate Asia for the Asians.

What of the opposing forces?

Singapore had been a British possession since 1819 when, on the advice of Sir Thomas Stamford Raffles, the East India Company purchased it from the Sultan of Jahore. Raffles saw that Singapore was strategically placed for development as a port. Its position astride the India-China trade route made its possession vital.

Singapore Island stretched twenty-seven miles from east to west and thirteen miles from north to south at its widest point. The Strait of Jahore separates the island from Malaya. The strait varies in width from six hundred to five thousand yards. At its narrowest point the British had constructed a causeway to the mainland.

British control over Malaya itself dated back to the nineteenth century. During the years of the great British colonial expansion, various trading companies negotiated trade agreements with the Sultan of Jahore. By the 1920s Malaya had become part of the vast British Empire even though the sultan continued to rule his own territory.

Malaya and Singapore were both vitally important to the empire. Rubber and tin were Malaya's major products. These brought enormous wealth to British coffers. By 1941 rubber estates covered more than three million acres and produced over one-third of the world's output. Tin mining accounted for fifty-eight percent of world production.

The protection of Malaya and Singapore, however, was not given serious consideration until the 1920s. Up until then Britain had no real rival for the colonies, but with the advent of Japanese expansion and naval growth, the British found themselves forced to pay attention to the defense of their Far Eastern colonies.

Early reports on Singapore's defense stated that an attack from the Malayan peninsula was impossible because of the terrain and the jungle. The only possible attack on the colony would come from the sea.

From the early twenties and on into the thirties debate ensued on the best ways to defend Singapore. The air ministry claimed that bombers protected by fighters could adequately protect the colony at a substantial financial saving over the construction of concrete bunkers with large gun emplacements. The admiralty and the war office, on the other hand, stuck to the gun theory, arguing that the heavy guns were more of a deterrent against attacking enemy ships than planes would be.

In 1926 the Committee of Imperial Defense decided to implement the first stage in the development of Singapore's defense by ordering close and medium batteries along with three fifteen-inch guns installed. Meanwhile, discussions continued between the opposing sides.

In 1929 the Labor government took office in England with its platform of disarmament. Following the London Naval Treaty of 1930, work on Singapore's defenses slowed greatly.

By 1931 the Far Eastern situation had become critical following Japan's attack on Manchuria. Critics of disarmament quickly demanded that the work of Singapore's defenses be continued. Once more squabbles occurred over the best method of defense. Finally, in May 1932, the government ruled that while guns should constitute the main weapons of defense, aircraft could provide valuable assistance. By 1935 the first stage of construction on the naval base at Singapore was complete. The government then gave permission to install heavy batteries along the southern coast.

While a great naval base was being constructed at Singapore, work on airfield development in Malaya proceeded. Two main sites were developed, one at Kota Bharu and the other at Kuantan. These airfields were located in the north so that the RAF would be able to detect the early approach of an enemy convoy. Unfortunately the air forces themselves failed to consult with the army. The result was that the airfields could not be defended from attack. At the same time, the defense of eastern Malaya was completely neglected.

In 1937, Maj. Gen. W.S.S. Dobbie was appointed commanding officer, Malaya. From his new position Dobbie took a fresh look at the entire defensive plan for Malaya and Singapore. He came to the uncomfortable conclusion. that, contrary to earlier studies, landings on Malaya's eastern seaboard were possible, particularly during the period from October to March, the monsoon season, when the enemy could utilize the bad visibility to cloak their advance. Dobbie went on to declare that the enemy would probably establish bases in Siam and make landings along the coast of that country. The general urged London to send additional reinforcements but he was ignored. Dobbie correctly saw what many others failed to. That was:

> the defense of the naval base in Singapore island was bound up with the defense of the whole Malayan Peninsula.[3]

Dobbie's chief of staff was Col. Arthur Percival, a man whose future would be intimately linked with the fate of Singapore. General Dobbie attempted again in early 1938 to get his point across by sending another report to London. In the report he said:

> It is an attack from the northward that I regard as the greatest potential danger to the fortress. Such attack could be carried out during the period of the north-east monsoon. The jungle is not in most places impassable for infantry.[4]

Once more the arguments fell on deaf ears.

Meanwhile, in 1937, the Japanese launched a full scale war with China. Dobbie continued to warn London but all he received in return were assurances and little in the way of funding and reinforcements.

Eventually, the political situation in Europe began to deteriorate. That event caused a greater danger to Britain's Far Eastern colonial empire. Sensing the danger, the government sent an Indian Brigade group, a Mountain Artillery regiment, and two bomber squadrons to

Malaya in August 1939. Even with these reinforcements, however, the defensive situation in Malaya and Singapore remained pitiful. Only fifty-eight aircraft were available, not one tank was to be found and the number and quality of the troops left a great deal to be desired. If Japan attacked in 1939, the best the British would be able to do was to make a token defense.

In 1940 Lieutenant General Bond was appointed G.O.C., Singapore. He was horrified at the state of the defenses there and wanted to recruit the local labor force to construct additional defenses. The civilian governor, Sir Shenton Thomas, was dead set against this proposal since the local laborers were required in industry.

The Labour Controller in Singapore, however, advised against this on the ground that their formation would be detrimental to the production of rubber and tin and the completion of civil defence projects. He pointed out that local labour would be difficult to recruit for service in military units, for they would be required to leave their homes.[5]

Thus Singapore went about its business just as if the dark shadow of war was not hovering over it. The locals continued to work the fields and mines while the defenses went ignored. In reality, Shenton Thomas was not oblivious to the danger of war and in fact did cable London requesting more planes, but business and commerce were his first priorities.

Throughout 1940, although the debate on Singapore's defense continued, very little was physically accomplished. Then, by the end of the year, the critical situation in the Middle East moved to the fore. In Winston Churchill's words:

> First, the defense of the Island . . . secondly, the struggle in the Middle East and Mediterranean, thirdly, after June, supplies to Soviet Russia, and last of all, resistance to a Japanese assault.[6]

In October of that year, Gen. Arthur Brooke-Popham was appointed commander in chief, Far East. Upon assuming command he quickly concluded that Singapore could not be held unless all of Malaya were also held. Brooke-Popham asked for further reinforcements. The Middle East priorities precluded any chance of this. The following February some reinforcements did arrive in the form of the Eighth Australian Division. These were followed a month later by yet another Indian Division.

In March 1941, Lt. Gen. Arthur Percival was named G.O.C., Malaya. One historian described Percival as "not the man for a crisis and certainly not the man for a desperate campaign . . . a colorless character, more a staff officer than a commander and certainly not a natural leader."[7]

Although this assessment was highly accurate, Percival was not undistinguished. During World War I he had won the Distinguished Service Order and the Meritorious Conduct Medal. Between the wars he served in Ireland and Malaya and attended advanced courses at the Staff College. In Ireland, Percival earned a well-deserved reputation for being a ruthless murderer. He was so brutal in his dealings with the Irish that the IRA placed a price on his head and those of his troops. Percival was unable to move about freely without a bevy of bodyguards. Based on his prior service in Malaya, though, at the time of his appointment Percival was considered the ideal man for the job.

Within a week Percival formed the conclusion that Malaya was indefensible unless it could be reinforced further. He boldly informed the British War Office that at least six additional divisions, two regiments of tanks, and more antitank and antiaircraft units were urgently required. In addition, he urged that the strength of the RAF be increased. These demands fell on sympathetic but deaf ears, since as already stated, British commitments to North Africa took precedence.

Thus Percival had to make do with what he already had. His total force numbered 88,000 men; 19,000 British, 15,200 Australians, 37,000 Indians, and 16,800 local volunteers. Since he accepted the principle that the defense of Singapore meant the defense of Malaya, forward airfields were developed in northern Malaya. Unfortunately, these airfields lacked the necessary number of planes to defend the area. In addition, the airfields themselves required Percival to scatter his forces to protect the fields from attack.

So the British commander faced many obstacles. First, he did not have enough troops for adequate protection. At the same time he had no tanks, and other military essentials were in short supply. What troops Percival did have were inadequately trained, most notably the Indian units. The only defense Singapore itself possessed were the mighty guns that faced seaward and two capital ships, the battleship *Prince of Wales*, veteran of the epic battle against the Bismarck, and the old battlecruiser *Repulse*. The two ships had been sent to Singapore in October, 1941 in an effort to raise morale. The population was elated at the arrival of the huge ships and a sense of relief settled over the naval base. The effect of the arrival of the two warships was not unlike the effect of the Maginot Line* on the French populace.

Meanwhile, try as he did to quickly construct defenses, Percival's efforts proved too little, too late. In December, 1941, the British force remained totally inadequate to protect the prize colony. Singapore's major defenses still pointed seaward, the troops were understrength and ill-trained, and there were precious few planes and no tanks. Although there were two capital ships available neither of them was an aircraft carrier.

On December 4, Yamashita's convoy set sail from Hainan, arriving off the invasion coast on the moonlit night of the seventh. Shortly after midnight the British beach defenses at Kota Bharu were systematically shelled by Japanese warships. Then the amphibious forces struck. The RAF did manage to bomb the convoy and cause some initial confusion but the Indian troops defending Kota Bharu were easily overwhelmed by the superior Japanese forces.

The Indian positions were situated a mere hundred yards from the water, placing them in an excellent position to rake the invading forces. Quick action saved the day for the Japanese. By driving hard into the Indian fire, the invaders circled their positions and fired into the hapless Indians from all sides. Panic swiftly spread among the defenders as the word went around

*Defensive line constructed on the French-German border and thought by the French to be impregnable.

that the Japanese had broken through. In fact, the Japanese were experiencing a difficult time.

Percival's misfortune of having to rely on such poorly trained troops was a boon to the Japanese. As panic spread through the ranks of the defenders, the Indians evacuated their positions, including those around the airfields, leaving behind valuable equipment and supplies. Besides the undestroyed airstrip, the defenders left behind bombs and fuel, all intact and ready for Japanese use. Kota Bharu was in Japanese hands in a matter of hours.

The landings at Singora and Patani were routine. Initially there was light resistance from patrols of the Thai army and local police but it failed to amount to anything significant. At 0520 Yamashita came ashore at Singora and established his headquarters. It was there that he first received word of the attack on Pearl Harbor.

Within a few hours, a compromise was reached with the Thai government that allowed the Japanese troops to pass through the country uncontested. Of course the Thais had little choice. Either they complied or their country would be devastated.

Percival had developed a defensive plan, Operation Matador. Basically, it called for British forces to advance to wherever the Japanese landed. But when word was received of the landings at Kota Bharu the British decided that it was useless to initiate Matador, so the order went out for the their forces to fall back from the Thai border to a defensive position then under construction around Jitra. This position was the key to the entire campaign. With only five hundred men and a mere ten tanks, General Matsui reached the Jitra line like a burst of thunder. The fighting was heavy but thanks to the popular Japanese hook tactic in which troops infiltrated through the jungle and moved behind the enemy positions, the British position fell rapidly. The Jitra line was easily breached and the Japanese were on the way toward the next immediate objective, Aloi Star.

Arthur Swinson said of the action at the Jitra line:

As for the action at Jitra itself, this had proved possibly the biggest disgrace to British/Indian armies since Chillianwala in the Second Sikh War of 1848.[8]

What was even more humiliating to the defenders was that the Japanese captured the line without having to deploy the entire Fifth Division. The task had been accomplished by the advance guard only. Japanese losses were a mere fifty men.

Not only had the Japanese easily captured an important defensive position, the panic-ridden Indians left food, ammunition and large quantities of guns and trucks behind. In their haste to retreat the Indian troops neglected to carry out the prescribed demolitions. Yamashita was overheard to remark that if Indian troops comprised the bulk of the British forces defending Malaya then the rest of the job would be easy.

In defense of the Indian troops it must be stated that they had been handed a difficult assignment without benefit of the proper training or heavy weapons. In fact, it wast the first time many of the Indian troops had even seen a tank.

Having breached the Jitra line, the Japanese rolled south. Yamashita exuded confidence but continued to caution that speed was of the essence during the advance. The further south the Japanese advanced, the more confident they became. The troops quickly adapted themselves to fighting in the jungle and their confidence was bolstered by the recent victories. Fattened on captured food, strengthened with captured fuel, vehicles and ammunition, the Japanese became convinced that their opponents were inferior. The steamroller was unstoppable. "The keynote of Yamashita's campaign in Malaya," wrote A. J. Barker, was "advance breakthrough, pursuit, consolidation."[9]

The tactic used at the Jitra line became the basic model for the balance of the campaign. Infiltrate the enemy line, hit them with tanks and always apply pressure. By maintaining constant pressure the Japanese never allowed the defenders the time needed to consolidate a new position. Yamashita's infantry even used bicycles to speed themselves along. They would pedal their way along roads and paths and carry the bikes across the rivers and streams, always maintaining the pressure on the retreating enemy.

In advocating the hook tactic, Yamashita found himself in disagreement with Tsuyi, his operations officer, who wanted to keep the pressure confined to the main roads. Tsuyi considered Yamashita's encouragement of wide encirclement along the jungle paths to be expensive in terms of manpower. In a heated debate, Tsuyi was no match for the army commander. This caused him to lose face. He offered to resign but Yamashita refused to consider it. From that time forth, however, Tsuyi became an implacable enemy who began to conspire against his commander. This vilification campaign was enthusiastically encouraged by Prime Minister Tojo who would ultimately manage, at the end of the campaign, to deny Yamashita the fruits of the great victory he was about to win. Despite the disagreement, Yamashita continued to stick with the proven hook tactic, even utilizing seaborne flanking operations.

For the British, one disaster followed another, even at sea where the twin "saviors" of Singapore moved out to destroy the Japanese landings.

Shortly after noon on the eighth, Vice Adm. Tom Phillips, the commander of Force Z comprising the *Prince of Wales*, *Repulse*, and four destroyers, called a conference aboard the flagship to decide what action he would take regarding the enemy landings. The admiral decided to take Force Z north to the landing beaches and there to blast the Japanese transports.

At 1735 the force left Singapore roads. Phillips was hoping for RAF cover but was informed that none was available for the ships. Nevertheless, the dauntless admiral decided to proceed. If by the ninth the force had not been sighted by the enemy, he would attempt to carry out the mission.

Throughout the ninth the sky was overcast and raining, affording Phillips the necessary cover. Unfortunately, late in the day the sky cleared and exposed Force Z to enemy reconnaissance aircraft. The force was quickly sighted by three Japanese planes thereby ending all hopes for surprise.

Realizing that the element of surprise was lost and that no air cover was forthcoming, that evening Phillips decided to turn back for Singapore.

Shortly afterward the admiral received information regarding a Japanese landing at Kuantan. Without informing Singapore, Phillips decided to make for Kuantan and attack the enemy landing force. Unfortunately, a Japanese submarine sighted Force Z at 0210 and quickly radioed its position and course.

On the morning of the tenth, Japanese reconnaissance aircraft were up looking for the British ships. As Phillips moved closer to Kuantan, thirty-four high-level and fifty-one torpedo planes were making for Force Z.

When the British fleet arrived off Kuantan they found the area devoid of enemy ships. Phillips decided to make a sweep of the waters to the north in hopes of locating the landing barges. Meanwhile, the radar aboard the *Repulse* picked up the approaching Japanese planes. Around 1100 the planes were within visual range. The attack was on.

Wave after wave of planes attacked the unfortunate British force as the ship's captains tried valiantly to avoid the deadly torpedo wakes. After many hits, Captain Tennant of the *Repulse* gave the order to abandon ship. Captain Leach of the *Prince of Wales* was forced to follow suit a few minutes later. An observer from one of the destroyers commented on the attack:

It was the most impressive pattern we have ever seen. It horrified us, destroying all misconceptions in its thunder, for in that brief instant *Repulse* had disappeared, had disappeared completely, in a forest of cascading bomb-bursts which merging together, were replaced in seconds by a giant wall of water. It was a fantastic, near-incredible spectacle.[10]

Captain Tennant described the loss of his ship in these words:

Men were now pouring up on deck. They had all been warned twenty-four hours before to carry or wear their life-saving apparatus. When the ships had a thirty-degree list to port I looked over the starboard side of the bridge and saw the commander and two or three hundred men collecting on the starboard side. I never saw the slightest sign of panic or ill discipline. I told them from the bridge how well they had fought for the ship and wished them good luck. The ship hung for at least a minute and a half to two minutes with a list of about sixty or seventy degrees to port and then rolled over at 12:33 p.m.[11]

514 men lost their lives on the *Repulse* and 337 more on the *Prince of Wales*. Admiral Phillips and Captain Leach were not among the survivors plucked from the sea by the destroyers *Electra*, *Express*, *Tenedos* and *Vampire*.

The destruction of Force Z was one of the greatest disasters in the history of the Royal Navy. To the British in Malaya who had placed so much hope in the capital ships, it was as a devastating blow and shattered the myth of British invincibility. The action announced to the world in abrupt fashion that the day of the capital ships was over. Ships without aircraft protection were sitting ducks.

Winston Churchill was greatly affected by the loss of the two ships.

In all the war I never received a more direct shock. The reader of these pages will realize how many efforts, hopes, and plans foundered with these two ships. As I turned over and twisted in bed the full horror of the news sank in upon me. There were no British or American capital ships in the Indian Ocean or the Pacific except the American survivors of Pearl Harbor. . . . Over all this vast expanse Japan was supreme, and we everywhere weak and naked.[12]

The news of the victory brought great jubilation to the Japanese. Their aircraft, operating four hundred miles from base, had sunk two of England's most prized ships. This accomplishment, following so close on the heels of the great victory at Pearl Harbor, helped foster the myth of Japanese invincibility. The British in Malaya were deeply shocked while many wondered if their ground forces would be able to stop the Japanese advance.

Questions on Admiral Phillips' conduct off Malaya have cast a shadow on his reputation. Unfortunately he did not survive the battle and so was unable to come to his own defense. Why had he proceeded with the operation without air cover? Why didn't he inform Singapore of his change of plan to proceed to Kuantan? Then, after he had been located on the tenth, why hadn't he notified Singapore immediately? These and other questions will continue to haunt historians as they attempt to unravel the last days of Force Z.

Meanwhile, following the fall of the Jitra line, the British forces retreated southward. Within six weeks the capture of Malaya was complete. The British routine during this period followed a distinct pattern: retreat, halt and dig a defensive position, come under attack by Japanese forces, and take a further step backward. Over and over again, step by step, down the entire length of the peninsula, the routine was repeated. In the course of the retreat, over twenty thousand Indian troops surrendered. Percival's only remaining hope was the Eighth Australian Division at Jahore in southern Malaya.

Thus far the Australians had done relatively well against the Japanese. Though they too had been forced to retreat, they had given the enemy a bloodletting thus making the victory more costly. Unfortunately for the British, these better trained troops were few in number. When Yamashita's forces made an amphibious landing on the west coast of Jahore and launched a frontal assault against the inexperienced Forty-fifth Indian Brigade, Percival was left with no choice but to fall back on Singapore, to the disappointment of the Australians who felt they could have held the enemy. The remnants of the Indian troops were withdrawn across the stone causeway connecting Singapore with the mainland, British and Australian troops forming the rear guard. On January 31, 1942, the last of the rear guard crossed the causeway. When the last troops had crossed, the link to the mainland was blown sky high.

Meanwhile, in Japan, the press were already making a national hero of Yamashita. Unhappily for the general, the adulation had an adverse effect on his career thanks to Tojo's animosity and jealousy.

The Japanese forces began massing for the final drive of the campaign, the attack on Singapore. The actual city of Singapore is in the southernmost part of the island. The rest of the island is comprised of jungle and swamps interspersed with rubber and coconut plantations. The major defenses were located at the naval base. Unfortunately, the massive guns there still faced seaward and would prove useless during the forthcoming battle.

The defense of Singapore was in the hands of eighty-five thousand men including six recently arrived British battalions. Percival actually had numerical superiority so in theory should have been able to thwart any Japanese attack. There were, though, some deep seated problems.

The northern portion of Singapore was literally defenseless. General Wavell, Percival's theater commander, had recently inquired as to why no defenses had been constructed in the north. Percival replied to the astonished ABDA* commander that the construction of defensive works would have a negative impact on morale. Whereupon Wavell angrily responded that the impact on morale would be even greater when retreating troops began to cross the causeway from the mainland. Churchill ordered that Singapore be turned into a citadel. On January 20 he signalled Wavell:

> I want to make it absolutely clear that I expect every inch of ground to be defended, every scrap of material or defenses to be blown to pieces to prevent capture by the enemy, and no question of surrender to be entertained until after protracted fighting among the ruins of Singapore city.[13]

For the attack Yamashita had the services of only sixty thousand troops. His heavy artillery was severely

*American, British, Dutch, Australian Defense Area.

reduced, his ammunition in short supply, and his line of communication long and tenuous. Only in the air did the Japanese have the advantage thanks to the support of some two hundred aircraft compared to the single squadron of Hurricane fighters remaining to the British. Yamashita knew that he had to strike quickly before the British realized the inferiority of the Japanese force. If British morale revived and they managed to put up a staunch defense, Yamashita knew that he lacked the tools for a long, drawn out campaign.

While the Japanese prepared for the attack, their planes flew over the city and subjected it to tremendous punishment. Approximately two hundred people perished daily in the city from the effects of the bombing.

Yamashita was a troubled man. In addition to the shortages of critical supplies he was barraged by an interfering commander, Count Terauchi, commander of the Southern Area Army. From his headquarters in Saigon Terauchi issued orders to the Twenty-fifth Army on how to conduct the assault on Singapore. Yamashita deeply resented the Monday morning quarterbacking. He was further incensed when Terauchi sent his own chief of staff to Yamashita's headquarters with voluminous notes and instructions on how to organize the assault. Yamashita dealt with the notes by tearing them to shreds.

By February 4 the Japanese were ready to begin the attack. Yamashita assembled two hundred collapsible launches powered with outboard motors and a hundred larger landing craft. He then moved his three divisions into position along with three thousand vehicles.

On the sixth he met with his divisional commanders

and gave them their final orders. Nishimura's division would make a feint to the east on the evening of the seventh in an effort to draw the British in that direction. Then, after dark on the eighth, the Fifth and Eighteenth Divisions would cross to the northwest corner of the island. Once these divisions were established the Imperial Guards would follow. Nishimura, who already felt that the army commander had slighted him, added this to his list of grievances against Yamashita.

Yamashita was depending on Percival to fall for the feint. To add to the deception the Japanese commander had erected dummy camps on the mainland opposite the invasion area. Each day, trucks headed eastward under the watchful gaze of the British. What the British failed to see were the trucks doubling back at night. All this activity confirmed what Percival already suspected, that the Japanese would invade the northeast sector. Accordingly, he sent more ammunition to that sector.

From the glass-domed tower on the grounds of the sultan of Jahore's palace, Yamashita watched the beginning of the assault on the morning of February 8. The attack was preceded by a heavy artillery bombardment and massive air strikes. Although British machine gunfire raked the Japanese ranks, by the morning of the ninth thousands of the attackers were on the island and moving south. Yamashita then moved his headquarters to a rubber plantation on Singapore Island.

Just before noon on that day, with the Fifth and Eighteenth Divisions already across the strait, it was time for the Imperial Guards to make their crossing. Nishimura deferred because he felt he had lost face. In reprisal for what he considered humiliation, the Guards commander brutally ordered the beheading of two hundred Australian and Indian troops who had been trapped in Jahore. Nishimura used every method at his disposal short of outright insubordination to make things difficult for Yamashita. He questioned orders and made excuses. Yamashita said of his subordinate's attitude:

> I ordered the Imperial Guards to cross the strait. Then their commander asked for further orders from me. I received a message from him that his troops were hesitating to cross because of oil flames on the surface of the water. It looked to me as if he was still upset about not being able to lead the attack. I ordered him to do his duty.[14]

Yamashita could ill afford this internal opposition because he was being pressured from above. Terauchi had promised Tokyo that Singapore would be captured on February 11, Japan's National Foundation Day. This only served to increase the pressure on Yamashita.

The fighting was intense and in many places was hand to hand. Percival had decided to establish a perimeter defense line around the city, reasoning that it was essential to hold the vital reservoirs supplying the city with water. In the meantime, Wavell made one final visit to Singapore on the tenth. He ordered an immediate counterattack but was realistic enough to realize that it would have little chance of success. Wavell then left for his headquarters in Java.

By the twelfth the vital road junction leading to the

city was in Japanese hands. As a result, panic ensued in the city. But Yamashita was beginning to feel apprehensive. His chief supply officer had warned that he was critically short of fuel and artillery ammunition. If the capture of Singapore required a lengthy siege, the Japanese would not have the tools necessary to carry it out.

That evening, Yamashita held a conference at Mutaguchi's headquarters. The army commander explained that unless further supplies were forthcoming the guns would fall silent within six days. At the same time, Yamashita knew that he had to continue the battle without letup for if he so much as briefly allowed the British the opportunity to contemplate the situation, their morale might revive. Thus it was important to continue the attack just as if the situation was well in hand and hope that the British would capitulate before the ammunition ran out. To nudge the British in this direction, Yamashita had a note dropped onto Percival's headquarters demanding an immediate surrender while at the same time promising leniency. On the other hand, the note threatened reprisals should resistance continue. The message read:

Your Excellency

I, the High Command of the Nippon Army, based on the spirit of Japanese chivalry, have the honor of presenting this note to your Excellency advising you to surrender the whole force in Malaya. My sincere respect is due to your army, which true to the traditional spirit of Great Britain, is bravely defending Singapore, which now stands isolated and unaided. Many fierce and gallant fights have been fought by your men and officers, to the honor of British warriorship. But the development of the general war situation has already sealed the fate of Singapore, and the continuation of futile resistance would only serve to inflict direct harm and injuries to thousands of noncombatants living in the city, throwing them into further miseries and horrors of war, but also would not add anything to the honor of your army. . . . In closing this note, I pay again my sincere respects to your Excellency.

(signed) Tomoyuki Yamashita

1. The Parliamentaire should proceed to the Bukit Timah Road.
2. The Parliamentaire should bear a large white flag and the Union Jack.[15]

Percival had no intention of complying. That same day, however, the Japanese advance overran a vital British ammunition dump and a large military hospital. When the medical officers at the hospital attempted to surrender, Japanese troops swarmed into the hospital and savagely bayoneted 230 patients and 93 of the staff to death. A handful of survivors fled to the city carrying word of the atrocities. The rumor quickly spread that this same treatment was in store for everyone if Percival continued to refuse to surrender.

Morale in the city had already deteriorated at a rapid rate. Now the deterioration accelerated like wildfire as news of the slaughter at the hospital spread. It appeared as if Yamashita's bluff would succeed even though he was not a party to the atrocity.

My attack on Singapore was a bluff, a bluff that worked. . . . I knew that if I had to fight long for Singapore I would be beaten. That is why surrender had to be at once.[16]

From where Percival stood, surrender now seemed the only alternative. Wavell finally authorized him to make the decision once Percival was completely satisfied in his own mind that continued resistance was no longer feasible. Wavell had reached his conclusion the day before, after receiving a wire from Churchill:

You are of course sole judge of the moment when no further results can be gained in Singapore and should instruct Percival accordingly. CIGS concurs.[17]

By the fourteenth, the only water reaching the city came from a pumping station only half a mile from the nearest Japanese position. Some parts of the city were already without water and there was concern that disease might hit the city. Percival was informed that within forty-eight hours there would probably be no water available at all.

On Sunday the fifteenth, Percival called a conference of his subordinate commanders to solicit their opinion. He left the meeting convinced that the situation was hopeless. At 10:00 that morning, a party of British soldiers carrying a large white flag approached the advance units of Mutaguchi's division. A few hours later Yamashita was notified that the British were ready to discuss truce terms. The bluff had paid off. On hearing the news Yamashita commented, "I prepared myself against being deceived, and ordered the British commander to come in person."[18] The British delegation returned to their lines and reported that Percival would have to personally go to the designated meeting place. The British commander arrived late that afternoon at the slope of Bukit Timah carrying a white flag. The hapless Percival, attired in a light tropical shirt and shorts, and Yamashita, dressed in the tunic of a Kwangtung Army officer complete with leggings and boots, sat down to the table.

Yamashita asked Percival if he wished to surrender unconditionally. The British commander replied in the affirmative. The next question to them was did they have any Japanese prisoners of war? Percival said no. Then Yamashita placed the document of surrender on the table. Percival read the document, then asked permission to wait until the next day before signing.

Yamashita could not afford any further delay. Feeling that perhaps the British might discover his shortages, the Japanese commander wanted an immediate surrender. Therefore, he told Percival that he had to either sign right then or the fighting would resume. The Japanese interpreter at the conference was not particularly adept, and Yamashita was rapidly losing patience. In a loud voice he shouted to the interpreter, "Is the British Army going to sign or not? Answer yes or no."[19]

At this, the dejected and startled Percival said yes. The surrender document was signed at 1810.

With the surrender official, Yamashita had gained the greatest victory of any Japanese general. The heralded bastion of Singapore had fallen to him in a mere seventy-three days. The loss of Singapore sent shock waves throughout Asia and dramatically demonstrated that the stature of all white men in the East would never again be the same. Yamashita's forces had captured 130,000 British, Australian, Indian and Malay troops at a cost of 9,823 Japanese casualties.

Without a doubt, Yamashita rightfully earned the nickname, "Tiger of Malaya." Lacking adequate strength and short of critical supplies, he conducted a brilliant campaign. His "hook" tactic had proven immensely successful and his ability to coordinate amphibious and ground operations was masterful. The bluff during the final days of the campaign saved Japan from a long, drawn out attritional campaign. Granted, Yamashita faced a number of inferior forces, but there were enough British formations available to have inflicted heavy losses. It was primarily Yamashita's forcefulness that brought about a successful conclusion to the campaign.

On the other hand, the British had to fight an uneven struggle. The Malayan command suffered from shortages because of British Middle East commitments. Those forces that could be spared were of poor quality and lacked such essential war equipment as tanks. Force Z was a tragedy. Two capital ships were sent to defend a country that lacked the ability to protect the ships once the battle began.

As for Yamashita, after his great victory, Tojo saw to it that he did not receive the honors due him. He was sent into exile in Manchuria, only to be brought back after Tojo's fall and given command of the Philippines. Though he managed to put up an excellent defense there, problems with his superiors prevented him from fighting the Philippine campaign in his own way. After the war, Yamashita was executed for crimes he had not committed.*

Percival remained in a Japanese prisoner of war camp until the end of the war. On September 2, 1945, the emaciated general was present on the battleship *Missouri* to witness the signing of the Instrument of Surrender. General Douglas MacArthur gave Percival one of the pens used to sign the document.

*See *The Great Commanders of World War II, Volume IV: The Japanese*, by these same authors.

Chapter Two

The Philippines

Because of their strategic location, the Philippine Islands became a focal point for the Japanese. If it were to fulfill its divine mission and establish the Greater East Asia Co-Prosperity Sphere, Japan needed control of the Philippines to protect her shipping lanes.

By 1941 Japan found itself denied many essential raw materials vital to an industrial nation. Because of the war with China, the United States and other nations embargoed precious resources as a punitive measure. In July, 1941, as a protest against Japan's occupation of French Indochina, the United States ceased exporting oil. Without oil Japan's industry would be helpless. However, oil was available in Borneo, Java and Sumatra; tin and rubber existed in Malaya. Why could Japan not take what it needed?

Cut off from the essentials for existence and with its rights as a nation challenged, Japan concluded that it had no option but to seize what it needed even if this led to war against the United States, Great Britain and the Netherlands. The Philippines were directly astride the sea lanes between the Dutch East Indies, Malaya and the Japanese homeland. Therefore, their strategic location made them a necessary target for conquest.

Faced with the prospect of war, Admiral Yamamoto, commander in chief of the Combined Fleet, proposed that a decisive attack be made on the American fleet based at Pearl Harbor. If this fleet were destroyed, the Philippines could be attacked without fear of the intercession of the American fleet.

The invasion of the Philippines came under the jurisdiction of General Count Terauchi's Southern Army. Beneath him was the Fourteenth Army commanded by Gen. Masaharu Homma. The Fourteenth Army was comprised of two infantry divisions, two tank regiments, a battalion of artillery, three engineering regiments, and five anti-aircraft battalions. This army was handed the task of capturing the Philippines.

The Philippine archipelago is made up of over seven thousand islands of which Luzon is the most important. This island is almost forty-one thousand square miles and is largely mountainous with many peaks reaching six thousand feet; some soar as high as ten thousand feet. Between the mountains are large plains. The most populous of these stretches from the coast at Lingayen Gulf southward to Luzon's principal city, Manila.

The Philippines became an American colony as a result of the Spanish-American War of 1898. Since that time the United States had run the colony in a benign, paternalistic manner. Promises of independence had been made repeatedly but in the 1930s the Filipino people were given the promise of total independence by 1946. Their political hopes centered upon an ex-lawyer, Manuel Quezon, who became the first president of the Philippine commonwealth in 1935. It was his job to prepare the country for independence.

In 1935 the new commonwealth's president went to

Washington to invite the American chief of staff, General Douglas MacArthur, to come to the Philippines after his retirement and help build the country's defense force so that when full independence did come in 1946, the islands would have a proper defense force. MacArthur readily accepted the challenge.

MacArthur began to tackle the objective of making the Philippines militarily capable of defending itself from any aggressor immediately. He advocated the formation of a flotilla of swift, hard-hitting PT boats, an air fleet of some 250 planes, and a large conscripted army of forty divisions built around a force of professional career officers and enlisted men.

The Filipino people quickly came to love and revere MacArthur but the Americans resented his aloofness. Nevertheless, he and his chief of staff, Col. Dwight D. Eisenhower, worked relentlessly. Their main obstacle was the same one they had encountered in the states during the 1930s: money. The Philippine government lacked the funds to provide the forces needed.

Monetary obstacles were not the only problems. The conscripted troops spoke eight distinct languages and no less than eighty-seven different dialects. In addition, virtually one quarter of them were illiterate which hindered their ability to work together.

Yet another problem was naval defense. Any serious attempt to defend the islands would have to rely on assistance from the United States Navy. The drawback here was the tremendous distance of the Philippines from America as opposed to its relative nearness to Japan.

MacArthur was insistent, however, that any attack against the Philippines could be met at the water's edge and thrown back into the sea. He approached the defense problem with an air of optimism, secure in the knowledge that U.S. air power could turn the enemy back and that American superiority was more than capable of dealing with Japanese inferiority.

Quezon and MacArthur both expected heavy American support but priorities caused Washington to default on many of its promises. This led to a strain in relations between Washington and Manila. In July, 1938, MacArthur resigned his army commission and became a full-time employee of the Philippine government.

After the termination of his affiliation with the U.S. Army, MacArthur's status with President Quezon began to decline. The general was now simply another government employee. Quezon also had second thoughts about MacArthur's war plans. He saw how rapidly the Japanese were destroying the reputedly strong Chinese Army. This frightening turn of events caused Quezon to propose to Roosevelt that the Philippines be granted their independence in 1939 instead of waiting until 1946. Aware that in any conflict between Japan and America the Philippines would become a battle zone, Quezon reasoned that by becoming an independent nation he could declare neutrality and possibly save his country. Quite naturally, Roosevelt was cool to the suggestion. Quezon's opinions were on a collision course with those of MacArthur. In the meantime, the budget for the country's armed forces dwindled.

Meanwhile, the Asian situation continued to deteriorate. The Japanese had seized the whole of the Chinese coast and were making menacing gestures against French Indochina. After the rapid fall of France to the German blitzkrieg in June, 1940, Japan viewed the

French colony as a piece of fruit ripe for the picking. As a result, they simply occupied the northern portion of the country. In addition to their aggression in Asia, the Japanese also signed the Tripartite Pact in September of the same year, linking the destiny of the Sons of Nippon to that of Nazi Germany and Fascist Italy.

As Japan continued to creep southward, MacArthur prepared against strong odds. While he planned, so too did the Washington strategists who, along with the British, were even then conducting secret talks and drawing up a future strategy for the time when America finally entered the war. In June, 1941, a joint war plan was adopted known as the "Rainbow Five" plan. This plan stated that in the event of a two-ocean war, the European enemy would be dealt with first, leaving the forces in the Pacific to simply hold on until that was accomplished. This plan effectively wrote finis to the plan MacArthur originally expected to adopt, "War Plan Orange." That plan postulated the abandonment of Manila and the withdrawal of the defenders to the Bataan Peninsula. From there, and from offshore fortresses like Corregidor, Manila Bay would be defended until the American Pacific Fleet could come to the rescue. With the adoption of "Rainbow Five," however, the Philippines were abandoned to their fate.

In the meantime, MacArthur sought complete command of all American and Filipino forces in the islands. This was made possible when he was officially recalled to active duty on July 26, 1941. General Marshall wrote MacArthur:

Stimson and I have decided that your outstanding qualifications and vast experience in the Philippines make you the logical selection for the Army in the Far East should the situation approach a crisis.[1]

The situation had indeed reached the critical stage. That same month, Japan occupied the rest of Indochina. Roosevelt reacted by freezing all Japanese assets in the United States and embargoing all shipments of materials, particularly oil, to Japan on the same day that MacArthur returned to active duty.

The action of the president, especially the oil embargo, made war between the United States and Japan inevitable. The Japanese had to choose between withdrawing from Indochina and the Chinese mainland (which was unlikely) and invading Malaya and the Dutch East Indies to secure their own resources.

American codebreakers followed the belligerent tone of messages as they flowed between the Japanese prime minister, Hideki Tojo, and the foreign embassies around the world. The Japanese felt justified in their anger since both Britain and Holland declared similar embargoes. Consequently, they felt strangled and held the United States responsible.

MacArthur faced an enormous challenge. He had twenty-two thousand American troops and Phillipine Scouts together with a commonwealth army of about eighty thousand Filipinos of dubious quality. Besides the problems of illiteracy and different languages, many of the reservists were poorly trained and some divisions were drastically understrength. Shortages were acute, particularly in the areas of light artillery and machine guns. The troops even lacked uniform replacements and the all-important steel helmet.

In most respects, they were a levee-en-masse rather than an army. The only units which showed any signs of discipline and cohesion belonged to the Philippine Scouts, a mixed American and Filipino force.[2]

With this force MacArthur faced a potential force of at least 6 million men. Nevertheless, he knew that he must accomplish all he could with the little time available and the shortage of funds. MacArthur did not, however, know of the existence of the Rainbow Five plan. General Marshall announced that it was the policy of the United States to defend the Philippines. Therefore, he did dispatch some token aid, but it was pitifully slow in arriving. From July through December, 6,083 regulars arrived even though thousands more had been promised.

Not until October did the War Department finally decide that MacArthur should be made privy to Rainbow Five. Predictably, he did not approve of it. Yet he remained optimistic that he could successfully keep the Japanese out of the Philippines altogether. The islands could then be used as a base from which enemy shipping could be attacked. Some revisions to the American plan were made as Marshall and Stimson approved many of MacArthur's defense plans.

MacArthur was convinced of his ability to stop the Japanese on the beaches and proceeded to plan in that vein. He stored supplies in strategic places throughout the islands. The only drawback to this plan was that if the Japanese managed to land successfully, the defenders would be forced to retreat to Bataan just as every feasibility study of Philippine defenses since 1909 had emphasized. The islanders would then be left short of supplies, particularly food.

The plan was not surprising since MacArthur was never one to prefer a purely defensive posture. Even though he might find his troops forced back into Bataan, it was still his intention to fight on the beaches. But he completely underestimated the ability of the Japanese and overestimated the ability of his own forces.

The United States reinforced MacArthur's command with B-17 bombers and P-40 fighters. It was erroneously believed that the Japanese would not dare attack if they knew that the Philippines were defended by a large array of war planes. The presence of these aircraft gave an euphoric sense of false security. Even Marshall felt confident about the Philippines:

He felt the U.S. position in the Philippines was highly favorable. Our strength in the islands, he said, was far larger than the Japanese imagined. We were preparing not only to defend the Philippines but to conduct an aerial offensive from these islands against Japan. . . . If war did start, B-17s would immediately attack the enemy's naval bases and would set the "paper cities" of Japan on fire.[3]

This comment was made a mere three weeks prior to the attack on Pearl Harbor. Such false confidence and underestimation of the ability of the Japanese would later exact a heavy toll of the Americans and their command.

Last-minute negotiations between Japanese and American diplomats in Washington proved futile. All the while, Yamamoto was preparing his forces for a surprise raid on Pearl Harbor. In late November, while MacArthur pontificated that no attack could possibly come before spring, General Homma was ordered to conquer the islands within sixty days of the opening of hostilities.

Meanwhile, MacArthur concluded that Lingayen Gulf would probably be the beach chosen by the Japanese for their main landing. Besides its proximity to Manila and the natural corridor to the city via the plain, Lingayen also had areas suitable for the deployment of large forces. Accordingly, MacArthur deployed the greatest number of his forces on Luzon.

The island was divided into two groups. The North Luzon force was under Lt. Gen. Jonathan Wainwright, West Point, 1906. This force was made up of four infantry divisions and the Twenty-sixth U.S. Cavalry Regiment. The South Luzon Force under Brig. Gen. George Parker was smaller than Wainwright's and was responsible for the defense of southern Luzon. A third command was established, the Virayos-Mindanao Force under Brig. Gen. William Sharp. This force was responsible for the defense of the other major islands of the Philippines.

On the naval side, the American Asiatic Fleet was under the command of Adm. Thomas Hart. This fleet should not be confused with the Pacific Fleet based in Hawaii. The Asiatic Fleet contained only a half dozen cruisers, some destroyers, and a small force of submarines in addition to the PT boats. Hart and MacArthur did not see eye to eye on the best strategy to adopt for the defense of the Philippines. MacArthur considered the admiral to be a pessimist lacking in aggressiveness whereas Hart believed himself to be a realist and was aware of the limitations of his small fleet.

Meanwhile, General Homma readied his army. At forty-seven, the general had a wealth of experience behind him including time as military attache in London and India and as a student at the Military Staff College. Homma quickly earned a reputation as a military genius. In the 1930s he found himself in London for a second time. When he returned to Tokyo in 1933 he was given command of the First Infantry Regiment.

Homma was known as a moderate who opposed war with the United States and Great Britain. This pro-Western philosophy led to his making a number of influential enemies, among them Generals Tojo and Sugiyama. His hostility toward Tojo forced Homma out of Tokyo to a posting in China. The Sino-Japanese War was already in full swing when he took command of the Twenty-seventh Division. While commanding this division Homma cemented his reputation as a brilliant and courageous leader. His failure to get along with the army leaders, however, resulted in his remaining in China.

In December, 1940, Homma was transferred to Formosa as head of the Japanese forces there. In November of the following year General Sugiyama notified him that he was to receive command of the Fourteenth Army whose task was the conquest of the Philippines.

Homma was shocked to find that only two full divisions were assigned to the Fourteenth Army. Yet he was expected to complete his task in only fifty days. Naturally he stated that he had too few troops and too short a time. Sugiyama was upset by Homma's questioning of his authority and quickly shot back:

The fifty-day period is an integral part of the strategic pattern for the entire Pacific campaign. The figure is firm and you will have to accept it.[4]

Still not convinced, Homma continued to question his superior. Sugiyama boiled with rage and did not forget the heated debate. Back at his headquarters in Formosa, Homma continued to fume. His staff informed him that if MacArthur decided to make a stand in the Bataan Peninsula, the allotted forces would be totally inadequate for the task at hand. Homma sent a message to Sugiyama emphasizing his staff's assessment. In response he received a curt reply:

The main purpose of the attack on the Philippines is the occupation of Manila, which is not only the political capital but a place of military importance. The troops opposed to you are third class and unworthy to face in battle. If therefore they retreat to Bataan, there is no reason why you should not blockade them.[5]

Rebuffed, Homma and his fellow commanders then drew up their plan for the attack. They correctly decided that the American Far Eastern Air Force had to be eliminated before the invasion could begin. Once this was accomplished, the seaborne landing had a chance for success.

The Japanese hoped to coincide the destruction of the American air fleet as near as possible with the attack on Pearl Harbor. They designated two air forces, the Fifth Air Group and the Eleventh Air Fleet for the attack. With a three-to-one advantage in aircraft,

71

they planned to hit the Americans hard.

As a further preliminary to the attack, the Japanese planned the seizure of Batan Island, midway between Formosa and the Philippines. The express purpose of this was to utilize an airstrip there for the support of the air assault. Once it was determined that air superiority had been gained, the way would be open for the main attack scheduled for Lingayen Gulf with the main objective being the capture of Manila.

To protect the flanks of his main force Homma added landings at Aparri on Luzon's northern coast, Vigan on the northwestern coastal strip and another at Legaspi on the southern tip of the island to the plan. With the final plan drawn up, Homma waited for the final word that would send his forces into the attack.

"Air Raid Pearl Harbor! This is no drill!" Admiral Hart was the first American commander to hear the shocking news of the Japanese attack. Unfortunately, he neglected to pass this information along to Mac-Arthur who heard the news from his chief of staff, Sutherland. The latter was given the word by a duty officer who had been listening to a California radio station. In this roundabout way, MacArthur received word at 0340. Shortly afterward he received a call from Washington. On the other end of the line was Gen. Leonard Gerow, chief of the army's War Plans Division, confirming the news bulletin.

What transpired next is in many ways a puzzle. Why was MacArthur's air force destroyed on the ground a full nine hours after receipt of the news about Pearl Harbor? A great deal of confusion cloaks this particular disaster. The Japanese pilots could hardly believe their eyes when they flew over Clark Field and saw their prey bunched together just waiting to be destroyed. What had happened? Who was to blame?

General Lewis Brereton had earlier proposed that the B-17s be sent into the air immediately to strike at Japanese bases on Formosa. Three times that fateful morning Brereton approached Sutherland and each time the latter dismissed him. Meanwhile, the bombers were in the air, but without any bombs. Finally, MacArthur himself ordered an attack on Formosa but he scheduled it for the afternoon because of reports of fog over the target. Thus, at half past eleven, the bombers were back on the ground at Clark Field being rearmed and refuelled.

The P-40 fighters were also down, leaving the field completely unprotected. Just at that point Japanese aircraft, delayed by the fog from taking off from Formosa, arrived overhead and proceeded to destroy the air base. If the B-17s had been dispatched earlier, as Brereton had suggested, the outcome might have been entirely different. MacArthur later denied ever hearing of Brereton's proposals and shifted the blame to Sutherland. Nevertheless, MacArthur was the overall commander and his failure to order the attack condemned the air fleet. He should have reached the decision to have the planes up and out against the Formosan air bases on his own. If this was not feasible at the time, then he should have at least sent them out of range of the Japanese. For all his apparent brilliance, this costly error proved that the general was not infallible.

There can be no doubt that MacArthur completely

underestimated the enemy. In fact, he initially thought the Japanese had suffered a serious reverse at Pearl Harbor. When the truth became known, it was already too late. It has also been stated that Mac-Arthur was under strict orders not to initiate any action until the Japanese opened fire. But could not the attack on Pearl Harbor be interpreted as the opening act of war? However, to say that this mistake resulted in the loss of the Philippines is too broad. The final outcome would probably have been the same, but the Japanese conquest might have been made more difficult. With his air arm all but destroyed, MacArthur was forced to face an enemy who controlled the skies over the battlefield.

The next day Manila received its first of many air raids. On December 10 it was the turn of O'Neill and Nichols Airfields and the navy yard at Cavite. Admiral Hart watched sadly as Cavite was pounded into rubble. Then came word of the loss of the *Repulse* and *Prince of Wales* by the British. Hart justifiably feared for his fleet and was determined to bring his ships to a safe port. MacArthur was startled by the naval commander's attitude since he was counting on Hart to keep the sea lanes open for the support vessels bringing in troops and supplies from America.

Hart told MacArthur that the Japanese had the Philippines completely blockaded. The general responded that it was a mere paper blockade. Hart disagreed. MacArthur then cabled Washington stressing the absolute necessity of the United States putting every effort into the defense of the Philippines. Naval support, he went on, was crucial to the defense. Unfortunately, the chief of naval operations, Adm.

Harold Stark, had already written the islands off. Consequently, MacArthur found himself confronted by a seemingly impossible situation. With its air power destroyed and the navy about to abandon it, the Philippines faced a grim future.

The Japanese ground offensive began on December 10 at Aparri and Vigan. The landings were made without any opposition. The Eleventh Division of the Philippine Army was responsible for that area of Luzon but this division had no artillery, no transportation, and was understrength making it totally inadequate for the defense of such a large invasion area. The greatest problem faced by the Japanese was the adverse weather. Heavy surf made transferring from transports to landing barges hazardous.

Upon learning of the enemy landings MacArthur dispatched those P-40s and B-17s that had survived the initial Japanese attack. The planes did manage to cause some damage to the Japanese transports, particularly those bringing in supplies. Nevertheless, the landings at Aparri and Vigan were completely successful. These air attacks represented the last coordinated effort of the Far Eastern Air Force.

After establishing their beachhead, the Japanese began moving south. The forces at Aparri were called the Tanaka Detachment after their commander, Colonel Tanaka, while the Vigan forces were named for their commander, Colonel Kanno. By December twelfth the Tanaka Detachment had moved more than fifty miles inside Philippine territory and had taken three airfields. The Kanno Detachment moved northward. It too managed to take three airfields.

MacArthur had correctly guessed that the twin

landings were merely preliminaries to a major assault and prepared his forces accordingly. He was determined to stop the Japanese when the main attack did hit. Meanwhile, Homma, no longer fearing a counterattack against Tanaka and Kanno, grouped the two detachments together and sent them southward towards Lingayen Gulf where they were to link up with the main landing force scheduled to land on December 22.

During the southward advance the Japanese were attacked by the Philippine Eleventh Division. The more skillful Japanese outflanked the Filipinos and quickly foiled their valiant attempt. Then the Japanese pushed on relentlessly.

Two days after the Aparri and Vigan landings, the Japanese landed at Legaspi. The purpose of this landing was the acquisition of an airfield in the south that could protect the southern flank against an American attack from that direction (Map 3).

The Japanese landing was without incident. After quickly establishing their beachhead they moved to occupy the airfield and started the movement northwest. Five days later they met their first determined resistance. On December 22, the Japanese force confronted the South Luzon Force. In one attack the Japanese sustained such heavy casualties that they actually turned and ran. It was the first, though short-lived, victory of the South Luzon Force. Despite the setback, the landings served their purpose. Luzon was isolated.

That same day the Japanese began their main landings at Lingayen Gulf. From seventy-six army and nine naval transports, the Fourteenth Army,

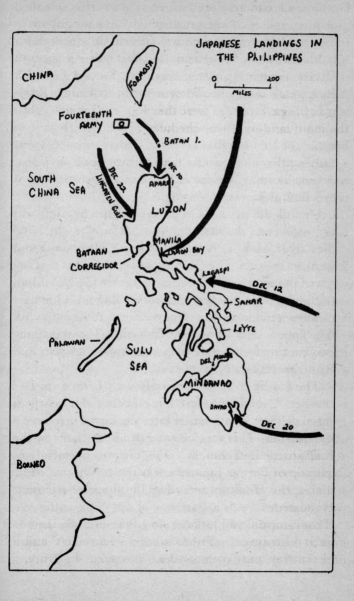

JAPANESE LANDINGS IN THE PHILIPPINES

0   200
MILES

CHINA

FORMOSA

FOURTEENTH ARMY

BATAN I.

DEC 10

APARRI

DEC 22

LINGAYEN GULF

LUZON

SOUTH CHINA SEA

MANILA

LAMON BAY

BATAAN

CORREGIDOR

LEGASPI

DEC 12

SAMAR

LEYTE

PALAWAN

SULU SEA

DEL MONTE

MINDANAO

DAVAO

DEC 20

BORNEO

equipped with artillery and a hundred tanks, crashed ashore. Escorting the invasion fleet was the Japanese Third Fleet under Admiral Takahashi. The main landing force was General Tsuchibashi's Forty-ninth Division made up of the First and Second Formosa Regiments and the Forty-seventh Infantry Regiment. The Japanese plan called for the forty-seventh infantry, accompanied by a detachment of tanks, to make the first landing at Agoo. Thirty minutes later, the First Formosa would land further north at Caba. A third landing, by the Kamajima Detachment, was to follow at Bauang (Map 4).

One of the primary objectives of the landing was the capture of the main highway, Route 3, which led directly to Manila. A spur of Route 3 left Bauang and went to Baguio. The Kamajima Detachment was ordered to move along the spur and seize the Naguilian Airfield before moving on towards Baguio. One part of the detachment was to move north to link up with the Tanaka and Kanno detachments. The remaining two landing forces were to head toward Damortis and Rosario and other points south.

The landings began precisely on schedule on December 22 with the first force hitting the beach at Agoo at 0517. Ten minutes later the First Formosa hit the beaches. This was followed two hours later by the Kamajima Detachment. The biggest obstacle encountered by the Japanese was the heavy surf. The high spray of salt water ruined the signal equipment. Homma, who was aboard one of the ships, suffered a communications blackout and was literally in the dark regarding conditions ashore. Thanks to the skill of the transport commanders, however, the landing

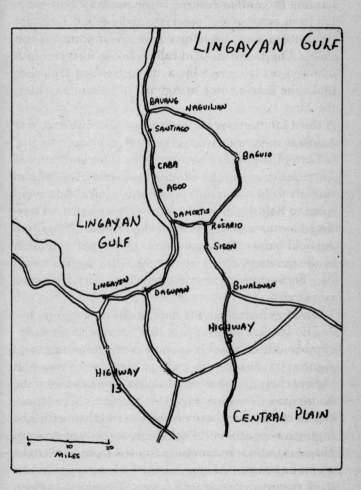

LINGAYAN GULF

Bauang
Naguilian
Santiago
Baguio
Caba
Agoo
Damortis
Rosario
Sison

LINGAYAN
GULF

Lingayen
Dagupan
Binalonan

HIGHWAY

HIGHWAY
13

CENTRAL PLAIN

0   10   20
MILES

forces were saved from floundering.

Opposition was light despite MacArthur's anticipation of landings at Lingayen. With no early warning system, no mobile reserve, little artillery and even less in the way of air forces, the defense was negligible. At Bauang, when the Kamajima Detachment landed, they were met by Filipino troops who put up a wall of fire. Despite heavy casualties, the Japanese advanced inland and forced the Filipinos to withdraw.

The U.S. Navy retaliated with a submarine attack that managed to sink one transport, but that was the extent of the naval opposition. The most spirited defense was provided by the few remaining B-17s that took off from Mindanao. Even this attack, however, failed to halt the invasion. Throughout that first day the Japanese moved steadily inland toward their objectives against little opposition. Units that were sent to oppose them either lacked the spirit for the task, were badly trained, or arrived too late. All were easily swept aside.

But Homma was in the dark about how rapidly his forces were actually moving. Still without communications his fears that his units were meeting heavy opposition increased with each passing hour. Weather reports indicated that there would be no decrease in the high surf the next day so there was little prospect that the Japanese would be able to land their artillery and heavy equipment. Therefore, fearing an American counterattack, Homma decided to shift anchorage. At 1730 he ordered the convoy to move further south during the night, to a point off Damortis, where the landings could continue the next day.

In the interim Wainwright ordered his forces to move on Damortis to keep the vital road from falling into Japanese hands. The attempt failed. Damortis fell as did Rosario and Sison. By the twenty-fourth the Japanese reached Binalonan. Not before meeting stiff opposition, however, from the Twenty-Sixth Cavalry.

While the Japanese consolidated their hold on the Lingayen area, a further landing was made on Christmas Eve at Lamon Bay, south of Manila, by a force under General Marioka. This area was not suited for an advance on Manila because the way was blocked by the Tayabas Mountains. Morioka was counting on surprise to make the landing a success. The landings were made at three points, Mauban, Antimonan and Siain. The choice of landing beaches worked in favor of the Japanese only because the commander of the South Luzon Force, General Parker, had positioned the majority of his armor on the western beaches. Because of their proximity to Manila and better landing conditions, the latter beaches were thus considered the more obvious location of an attack.

The Japanese ran into stiff opposition at Mauban where Philippine Army regulars provided a determined defense. At Siain the Japanese landed with little opposition. After establishing their position, this force split in two with one following the rail line towards Manila and the other advancing south to link up with Colonel Kimura's force moving up from Legaspi. En route, the Japanese ran into fierce resistance. As a result it took them three days to link up with Kimura.

By the evening of the twenty-fourth the Japanese

had completed the final part of their landing operations. Their casualties were a mere 84 dead and 180 wounded. By now the invaders were firmly entrenched north and southeast of Manila and ready to close the arms of a giant pincers on the capital where Homma expected the final battle to take place. MacArthur had failed to prevent the invasion.

Homma wanted the jaws of the pincers drawn shut quickly in order to catch the defenders in the open on the central plain. MacArthur realized that the only hope remaining was to order a retreat into Bataan. Manila, he told President Quezon, would be declared an open city and turned over to the Japanese. The Orange III Plan was dusted off and made ready for implementation. At the same time, MacArthur informed General Marshall that he proposed to defend Bataan and hold on to Corregidor. Marshall approved and replied that he would try his best to send aid. In light of the Japanese mastery of the air and sea, however, it was hard to see how Marshall intended to carry out his pledge. Nevertheless, he did order supplies to the Philippines via Australia and Java.

On December 24 MacArthur gave the order for the withdrawal to Bataan to commence. Now his entreaties to the Filipinos to fight where they stood began to work against the general. Loyal to their orders to hold on, no preparations had been made to withdraw, particularly in terms of supplies (Map 5).

Despite the enormous odds, the sidestep into Bataan was a masterpiece. Even the Japanese marveled at the execution of the retreat. For Homma, the move was one thing he wanted to prevent since he was anx-

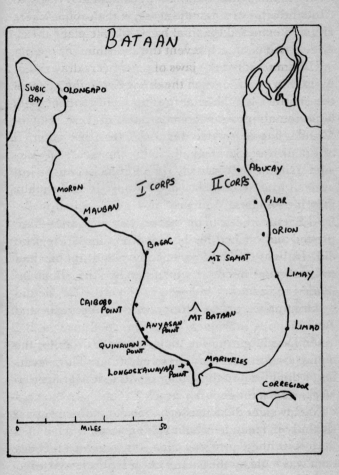

BATAAN

SUBIC BAY

OLONGAPO

MORON

MAUBAN

I CORPS

II CORPS

ABUCAY

PILAR

ORION

BAGAC

MT SAMAT

LIMAY

CAIBOBO POINT

MT BATAAN

ANYASAN POINT

QUINAUAN POINT

LIMAO

LONGOSKAWAYAN POINT

MARIVELES

CORREGIDOR

0   MILES   50

ious to seek a decisive battle near Manila.

The actual retreat was not an easy accomplishment by any means. In fact, even under normal circumstances it would have been considered difficult. Under the prevailing conditions, with the enemy closing in, it appeared to be an impossible feat. Thanks to MacArthur's superb strategic mind, though, the maneuver was a distinct success.

Taking a map, the general drew five delaying lines. He pointed out the vital bridges which either had to be held or blown up. Abandonment of these delaying lines had to be carried out with expert precision. In short, it was a strategy of "stand and fight, fall back and dynamite. It was savage and bloody, but it won time."[6] MacArthur placed the effort in the capable hands of General Wainwright.

Once the wheels of the retreat were in motion MacArthur established his headquarters on Corregidor. Manila was declared an open city and the blackout was discontinued. Unfortunately, the Japanese bombing was not.

Homma began to receive disquieting reports of MacArthur's movement into Bataan. Since he had anticipated fighting the major battle at Manila, this news was received with mixed emotions. The prevailing feeling among the Japanese was that MacArthur's army was "a cat entering a sack."[7]

Wainwright did a masterful job of holding back the Japanese. Though forced to give ground and fall back to newer lines, precious time was bought. His basic aim was to delay the enemy but it took a heavy toll of his forces.

By December 31 the Japanese had approached to

within thirty miles of Manila. At the same time thousands of defenders were pouring into Bataan. To gain additional time MacArthur decided to make a stand in the area around the Calumpit Bridge. He placed every available unit along a line five miles south of Pampanga in the Baliuag-Plaridel area. The defenders held on long enough to allow thousands to use the bridge to cross into Bataan. Finally, on New Year's Day, at 0500, after making sure that the last units had crossed the bridge, Wainwright ordered the Calumpit Bridge blown up. One wonders why the Japanese, with their aerial supremacy, failed to blow the bridge themselves. There is no doubt that this would have trapped many of the defenders and hindered the retreat.

Although Manila was declared an open city on December 26, the commander of the Forty-eighth Division, General Abe, did not receive authorization to enter the city until January 2. Two days later, Homma established the Japanese Military Administration. The purpose of this organization was to totally supervise the life of the citizens of Manila. A curfew was announced, blackouts were reintroduced, and martial law was enforced. The Filipinos were presented with a long list of dos and don'ts. Violations were punished severely depending on the gravity of the act. Homma also established a new Philippine government and staffed it with Filipino collaborators.

On the same day that Japanese troops entered Manila, Imperial General Headquarters in Tokyo informed Homma that the timetable for the invasion of Java had been moved up a month. This necessitated a transfer of the Forty-eighth Division from Homma to

Sixteenth Army which was tabbed to carry out the invasion. In addition to this division, the Fifth Air Group was also taken away. In the place of the Forty-eighth Division Homma received the Sixty-fifth Brigade, a force of sixty-five hundred poorly trained troops. Thus on the eve of his most critical battle, Homma suddenly found his strength reduced drastically.

Meanwhile, the American and Philippine forces continued their systematic withdrawal to defensive positions in Bataan. By January 2 the retreat was largely complete. It was a success. For the first time since the outbreak of hostilities, the Japanese had been outmaneuvered. Though they occupied the strategic city of Manila, access to the vital Manila Bay was denied them as long as the Americans held Bataan and Corregidor.

Into Bataan swarmed some eighty thousand combat troops accompanied by twenty-six thousand civilians. The hasty retreat resulted in severe shortages of all basic essentials. There was food enough for one-hundred thousand men for thirty days. Therefore, if a lengthy defense was to be made, food rationing would have to be introduced. Quinine was also in short supply. This magnified a problem that had already wreaked havoc on the defenders, malaria.

Bataan is a peninsula twenty-five miles long and twenty miles across at its widest point. Down its length, like a spinal cord, run two mountain ranges with peaks rising over forty-five hundred feet, covered with thick jungle. Between the twin mountain ranges is a narrow valley inundated by streams. Narrow coastal plains are found on both coasts.

For the defense of Bataan MacArthur split his forces into two corps. The I Corps under Wainwright was responsible for the left side of Bataan with Parker's II Corps on the right. On Bataan's southern tip a service command was formed and manned with two divisions.

The terrain of Bataan favored the defenders. By utilizing its natural contours MacArthur was able to form solid lines of defense across the length of the peninsula. The first main line ran from Mauban to Abucay. Six miles in the rear was a reserve line. Further south was a line along the Mariveles Mountains, Bataan's highest peaks. Integral to the entire defense was the island of Corregidor which served not only as a supply base, but dominated the entrance to Manila Bay.

Morale was high among the men. This stemmed from a false rumor that massive reinforcements were en route from America. Success, the defenders believed, was simply a matter of holding on until these reinforcements arrived. And what better place to hold on was there than Bataan?

Homma hoped that he would be able to take Bataan quickly. Japanese intelligence estimated that he was opposed by only twenty-five thousand defenders. In reality, the Japanese forces faced more than three times that amount.

On January 9, at 1500 the Japanese assault on Bataan commenced with an intensive artillery barrage on the II Corps front. Following the barrage the Japanese infantry moved forward. They were surprised by the fury of the counterbarrage put up by the defenders. Although the infantry made some progress that day, it was only because they had not reached the main defensive positions.

On the tenth MacArthur and his chief of staff crossed from Corregidor to view the situation first hand. This was his only visit to the beleagured troops during the entire campaign and lasted a mere five minutes. Without question his absence from the front lines was out of character for the man. Why he remained closeted on Corregidor instead of visiting the troops is a mystery. The troops began to call him "Dugout Doug." One critic has said:

> If MacArthur's motto had been to lead from the front in the First World War, his reputation was that of one who led from the rear and deserted in the face of the enemy when the chips were down at Bataan[8].

The "Dugout Doug" tag would remain with him all the way to Korea. A derogatory song originated there on Bataan and remained in vogue for years afterward. The lyrics were sung to the tune of the "Battle Hymn of the Republic."

> *Dugout Doug MacArthur lies ashakin' on*
> *the rock*
> *Safe from all the bombers and from any*
> *sudden shock*
> *Dugout Doug is eating of the best food*
> *on Bataan*
> *And his troops go starving on.*[9]

Some historians have speculated that it was his

acute embarrassment at having promised reinforcements that he was unable to deliver that caused MacArthur to shun the front lines. Whatever the reason, his action was unquestionably a serious mistake. It demonstrated a marked lack of respect for the caliber of men doggedly fighting under him. How could they blame him if help was not forthcoming? In fact, they probably would have felt a closer bond with the man had he shown himself more often and convinced them that he shared their plight. He could have still continued to cling to hope of reinforcements in order to maintain morale, but his presence would have given the men even more, a leader in whom they had faith and who cared about their welfare. If only they knew just how much MacArthur really did care it might have ended the derogatory comments.

On the night of January 10 the Japanese struck the main line of defense. At midnight they began a blood-curdling banzai attack with one wave after another surging forward. The fighting was desperate, at times hand to hand. By dawn the attack was over but both sides had suffered heavy casualties. To Homma the failure of the attack was a bitter pill to swallow since he was certain that the enemy line would fold. As a consequence he painfully concluded that the capture of Bataan was not going to be as easy as originally anticipated.

For the next few days the Japanese regrouped and licked their wounds. On the thirteenth they tried again. This time they directed their attacks towards Abucay. The Philippine Twenty-first Division successfully halted this offensive before it was even launched.

Then Parker asked for reinforcements which came as no surprise. MacArthur sent the Philippine Division, one of the finest units in the army, to reinforce the inland flank, the weakest spot in the entire defensive line.

On the sixteenth Parker attempted to surprise the Japanese by counterattacking. The enemy anticipated the move and resisted fiercely. Once Parker's attack failed, the Japanese swung over to the attack. The Ninth Regiment hit the inner flank of the Philippine Fifty-first Division and made such significant gains that it threatened to envelop the entire II Corps.

On the twenty-second, Sutherland arrived on Bataan to get a first hand appreciation of the situation. After meeting with Parker and Wainwright he realized that the Abucay-Mauban line would have to be abandoned and the troops pulled back to a new position that already existed south of the Bagac-Pilar Road. MacArthur approved the maneuver and reported the latest setback in a pessimistic dispatch to Washington.

Unlike the withdrawal into Bataan, however, the latest retreat was disorderly. The operation took two days with the Japanese in hot pursuit all the way. The rear guards were hard pressed to buy the necessary time for the retreating forces. On the twenty-fifth Japanese aircraft bombed and strafed the troops causing many casualties.

By that evening the troops of the II Corps were settled in their new positions. Thus far the Japanese had been made to pay dearly. Since January 9 the Sixty-fifth Brigade had incurred 1,472 casualties out of a force of 6,651. The brigade commander, General

Nara, wrote on January twenty-fifth that his brigade had reached the "extreme stage of exhaustion."[10]

Homma suggested to his commanders that in order to disperse the American and Philippine forces, landings along the west coast of Bataan might be attempted. Major General Naoki Kimura of the Sixteenth Division therefore decided to attempt landings at three points behind the I Corps front. The first attempt was made on the twenty-second with the Second Battalion, Twentieth Infantry Regiment. Kimura's plan called for his force to leave Moron and land at Caibobo Point. Lack of accurate maps and heavy seas caused this force to miss their landfall. They became divided into two groups. One landed at Longoskawayan Point, ten miles south of its destination, while the other landed at Quinauan Point. But the landings were made against undefended beaches.

As they moved inland from their beachhead, the story was different. Stiff opposition forced them to fall back to the beach and set up a defensive perimeter. On the night of the twenty-sixth the Japanese attempted to send reinforcements from Olbongapo to Quinauan Point. This party also missed their landing point and came ashore two hundred yards short of their objective.

On February 1 another larger force was sent to the Quinauan beachhead. This force was sighted while still aboard their landing craft. Four remaining American P-40 fighters began a deadly attack on the invasion force and caused them to retreat. On the whole, the amphibious operations did not accomplish their intended purpose but instead caused the Japanese to suffer heavy casualties.

Meanwhile, the defenders had established themselves in a new defensive line that ran from Orion on the east coast to Bagac on the west, with Mount Samat in the center. Despite all types of shortages, the morale of the troops remained high. Every Japanese attack thus far had been repulsed with the attacker incurring heavy losses.

General Nara was not ready to be undone and ordered his troops to continue the offensive. Then, on February 8, he was ordered by Homma to stop all preparations and to stand by for new orders. The defenders of Bataan, "the battling bastards of Bataan," as they were called, had done a brilliant job of stopping the Japanese attack. The poorly trained Filipinos and hungry, battle-fatigued Americans, had foiled Homma's chances for a swift victory.

The defenders, however, were suffering from a variety of problems, shortage of food being the greatest. They were reduced to eating dogs, monkeys, bamboo shoots, roots, inguanas, and python eggs. Disease was a major concern. Because of the rapid evacuation to Bataan very few mosquito nets were brought along. Coupled with the shortage of precious quinine, malaria reached epidemic proportions.

On Corregidor, MacArthur found himself dealing with more problems other than the military situation. With him on "the Rock" was President Quezon. He was constantly criticizing America's apparent abandonment of the Philippines and applied pressure on MacArthur to prod Washington into a positive response. For his part the general hoped to use the prestige of the Philippine president to elicit more aid from America. The world situation, however, boded ill for the Philippine forces as United States commitment to the Rainbow 5 Plan placed emphasis on the European situation.

Meanwhile, Homma was under a great deal of pressure to complete the campaign. General Sugiyama directed him to clear the peninsula rapidly and threatened to remove Homma from command if the task were not accomplished in short order. On February 8, a great blow struck Homma in the form of a message from Imperial Headquarters. His chief of staff found him at his desk in tears holding a copy of the message stating that the emperor was very concerned at his lack of progress. This was the most humiliating thing a Japanese officer could hear. Homma knew, however, that it was Sugiyama who had sent the message, using the emperor's name. It was only this knowledge that prevented Homma from committing suicide. The message was Sugiyama's way of covering up his own strategic blunder that had directed Homma to concentrate on the capture of Manila instead of slamming shut the gates to Bataan. Once a stalemate was reached, Sugiyama was eager to pass the buck. Poor Homma was the scapegoat.

In response to the message Homma dictated a letter to Imperial Headquarters questioning the wisdom of continuing the attack on Bataan. Sugiyama burst into a fit of rage upon receiving the letter. He immediately called a meeting of the general staff and urged Homma's recall. The members of the general staff argued against such a rash decision and the meeting ended in a compromise. Homma would remain in command but his chief of staff would be replaced. To fill this position Sugiyama was directed to appoint a "more aggressive" man, Maj. Gen. Takaji Wachi, a close personal friend. In addition, Homma's antagonist appointed Col. Masanobu Tsuji to the general's staff. Tsuji was a noted fanatic, responsible for numerous atrocities in China and Malaya.

In spite of everything Homma could see one ray of hope on the horizon. Reinforcements were also dispatched. When they reached the Philippines, however, Homma looked aghast at them. The units were made up of total misfits who were poorly trained and equipped. Once more Homma vented his rage at the man who was out to sabotage his career. Nevertheless, preparations proceeded.

On February 20, MacArthur was able to overcome a potential disaster, that of Quezon falling into enemy hands. The president, his wife and Vice President Osmena were taken aboard a submarine and transported to Australia. By now General Marshall was also worried about losing his Far East commander. MacArthur was much too experienced an officer to sacrifice. Not only had he proved that he knew how to fight the Japanese, he had become a national hero in America. To lose him might result in serious repercussions. It would give the Japanese an enormous psychological victory if they managed to capture or kill MacArthur. The general had to be saved and Roosevelt agreed.

For many weeks prior Roosevelt had been under pressure from various special groups and influential people clamoring for the general's safe return. The press, the Republican Party, and even Sir Winston Churchill, to name but a few, begged for MacArthur's evacuation to Australia where he could mollify the frightened Australians who feared a Japanese invasion of their own country.

MacArthur was visibly shaken when he received the presidential message ordering his evacuation to Australia. He had no desire to leave his men, but then again, as a dedicated soldier he had no wish to disobey the president's direct order. Consequently, the general threatened to resign and return to Bataan as a common soldier but his staff convinced him that the only reason he was being sent to Australia was to lead a relief expedition back to the Philippines. After weighing all factors, MacArthur realized that the staff's arguments made sense. Every indication pointed to Australia being built up as the base for a great counteroffensive. Accordingly, MacArthur agreed to the order but cabled Roosevelt a few conditions. He informed the president that he would go only if he were allowed to select the right psychological moment to leave lest a total collapse occur. Roosevelt and Marshall concurred.

The days passed and MacArthur still showed no inclination of leaving. Roosevelt sent another message on March 6, insisting on the general's swift departure. Three days later, yet another reminder was sent. In fact, MacArthur had already made up his mind to leave and needed no further prodding. The problem was how to successfully accomplish a breakout through the Japanese naval blockade. Naval officers on Corregidor gave him a one-in-five chance of successfully eluding the enemy patrols. As a vehicle of escape, MacArthur finally selected PT boats and set March 11 for his departure.

As the date drew nearer, MacArthur summoned

General Wainwright to his office and invested in him the command of all forces on Luzon until he could return. Then MacArthur said:

> Jonathan, I want you to understand my problem very plainly. I'm leaving for Australia pursuant to repeated orders of the president. Things have gotten to such a point that I must comply with these orders or get out of the army. I want you to make it known throughout all elements of your command that I'm leaving over my repeated protests.[11]

MacArthur concluded by ordering Wainwright to hold out. Wainright responded, "I told him that holding Bataan was our aim in life."[12]

Actually, MacArthur intended to coordinate the defense of the Philippines from Australia. He made it clear that Wainwright was to command on Luzon only, and then only under his personal direction. In this way MacArthur felt that even if Bataan and Corregidor fell, the balance of the country could continue fighting. Unfortunately, he never communicated the command structure to Washington. Later, the Japanese assumed that Wainwright was the overall commander with authority to surrender all the islands if it came to that.

The story of MacArthur's escape from Corregidor is an epic in itself. John Buckeley, the young commander of the PT boat flotilla, was a swashbuckling sort of commander, just the type suited for so daring a mission. Once at sea danger lurked over every horizon. On more than one occasion the small flotilla came within a few feet of being discovered by Japanese destroyers. In addition, they were nearly sighted by Japanese coastal artillery batteries the huge guns of which could easily blast the general, his wife, child, and staff to smithereens. Finally, on Friday, March 13, the group reached Cagayan on the island of Mindanao, thirty-five hours and 560 miles from Corregidor. From there the party boarded B-17s for the final leg of the journey to Australia. Immediately upon reaching his destination MacArthur made his now famous statement: "I came through and I shall return."

Meanwhile, the Japanese had received welcome reinforcements in the way of heavy artillery. These guns were quickly trained on Corregidor.

The troops on Bataan, though hungry, disease-ridden and besieged, still managed to keep their morale up. In fact, MacArthur's departure was looked upon by some as a sign of hope rather than hopelessness. The general, they felt, would not let them down and would return with a relief force.

Wainwright's first action upon assuming command was to change the name of his forces from United States Forces, Far East (USAFFE) to United States Forces in the Philippines (USFIP). At the same time he appointed Bridg. Gen. Edward King to act as his representative on Bataan.

The latest defense line on Bataan stretched between Orion and Bagac. It was thirteen miles long and manned by the I Corps under General Jones with a total of thirty-two thousand men and the twenty-eight thousand men of Parker's II Corps.

During a lull in the fighting, the American and Filipino forces improved their defensive positions by digging trenches and dugouts and by laying mines. The lack of sufficient food and the ever-present diseases, however, were their greatest concern and took a greater toll on the defenders than did the enemy. By March, what little quinine there was had been used up and the number of malaria cases rose dramatically. In mid-March over three thousand men were hospitalized. By the end of the month between seventy and eighty percent of the troops were ill.

Meanwhile, Homma planned to renew the offensive but his own troops were not immune to the same problems affecting the defenders. Between January 1 and March 31, thirteen thousand Japanese troops were treated for a variety of tropical illnesses. Fortunately for Homma, the latest group of reinforcements, though not the number or quality he desired, had arrived and were welcomed.

Because of its strategical position and excellent observation points on its summit, Homma planned to send a force against the Americans positions on Mt. Samat. At the same time, additional forces would advance down the east coast towards Limay.

The Fourth Division, supported by the Sixty-fifth Brigade, was designated to lead the attack on Mt. Samat. The Twenty-first Division would provide flank cover. The air forces and the artillery battalions were directed to bombard the American line just prior to D-day, which was set for April 3.

Good Friday, April 3, dawned hot and dry. American observers atop Mt. Samat could plainly see the Japanese moving into position. At 0900 the largest bombardment of the campaign thus far began. In the afternoon the infantry began to advance. Nara's

Sixty-fifth Brigade sliced into the left side of the II Corps and pushed aside the feeble Filipino resistance easily. It appeared that the preliminary bombardment had accomplished its purpose.

Homma had ordered the attack on Mt. Samat to commence on the fourth. Parker had no option but to call up his reserves. The Japanese attack was repeated behind another intensive bombardment. The heavy artillery fire stunned the front line defenders. As a result, the Japanese advance continued relentlessly as the defenders were forced back.

Parker hoped to counterattack on Easter Monday and for that very purpose moved all available units up from reserve. Their immediate objective was to re-take the recently lost slopes of Mt. Samat. Constant Japanese pressure, however, foiled any chance for an effective counterstroke.

The II Corps now found itself in a precarious position. The enemy had captured Mt. Samat and were threatening to turn eastward into the corps' flank. As Louis Morton has written:

The story of the last two days of the defense of Bataan is one of progressive disintegration and final collapse. Lines were formed and abandoned before they could be fully occupied. Communications broke down and higher headquarters often did not know the situation on the front lines. Orders were issued and revoked because they were impossible of execution. Stragglers poured to the rear in increasingly large numbers until they clogged all roads and disrupted all movement forward. Units disappeared into the jungle never to be heard from again. In two days an army evaporated into thin air.[13]

On the east coast the story was the same. The Twenty-sixth Cavalry attempted to halt the Japanese advance, but to no avail. Wainwright was besieged with nothing but reports of retreat.

General King, although under orders from Wainwright not to surrender, knew that further resistance was suicidal. Food was virtually exhausted and the troops were barely able to continue. Therefore, King took it upon himself to surrender his forces. At 0330 on April 9, he sent two staff officers under a flag to make contact with the Japanese commander.

Unfortunately, King was not to meet with Homma. Instead, he met with the general's representative, Colonel Nakayama. King was in a difficult position for Nakayama demonstrated an obvious contempt for the American. Nakayama thought that King was actually Wainwright, there to surrender all of the Philippines. The American commander had all he could do to convince the Japanese that he was simply the commander of the forces on Bataan and as such was only empowered to surrender that area. Nakayama was visibly annoyed and refused to listen to any terms King proposed, particularly those regarding the treatment of prisoners of war. King did all he could but was unable to secure a pledge from the Japanese that all prisoners would be well treated.

Homma had already made plans for the disposition of prisoners. He intended to stick closely to the guidelines of the Geneva Convention regarding the conduct toward prisoners of war, even though he was not obliged to since Japan was not a signer of the treaty. Nevertheless, Homma wanted the prisoners treated properly. As early as March, a few weeks prior to the April 3 offensive, he had held a conference during which he broached the subject of future prisoners of war. Homma felt the need to evacuate all prisoners as quickly as possible so that his own forces could concentrate on the campaign. He therefore assigned five officers the task of planning for the movement of prisoners.

On March 23 the five officers completed their plans and submitted them to Homma. They were relatively simple in concept. The chore of handling the POWs was divided into two phases, the first covering the assembling of all the captives, the second the actual journey to the prison camp. Balanga in the east of the Bataan peninsula was selected as the assembly point for all POWs. From there, they were to proceed to their final destination.

For the first phase of the operation no provision was made for transportation since the distance to be travelled was relatively short, the longest being twenty-five miles. The Japanese Army did not pamper its own soldiers in any manner. Vehicles and fuel were far too precious commodities to waste on men capable of walking. The Japanese soldier was therefore accustomed to marching. It was a daily routine during his training. Thus the relatively short distances the prisoners would have to walk to Balanga were not considered excessive by Japanese standards. At any rate, the POWs would have little choice in the matter. Balanga was the food depot. If they wanted to eat, the prisoners would have to walk to the source of food.

Colonel Takatsu was assigned to command the first phase of the operation, General Kawane, the second. It was the latter's job to feed the prisoners, care for the sick and wounded, and provide transportation to the permanent prisoner-of-war camp.

Kawane planned to provide the same quality and quantity of food to the prisoners as was issued to his own troops. In anticipation of the imminent fall of Bataan he designated four towns along the proposed route and assembled rations there. The first of these towns was Balanga. From there it was sixty-five miles to the final destination. En route the POWs would pass through Orani and proceed along Route 7 to Lubao in central Luzon where once more they would be fed. The final leg of the journey was to San Fernando where the prisoners would receive their final meal before reaching the internment area, Camp O'Donnell, a short train ride further north. Kawane also planned to establish field hospitals along the way to care for the sick and wounded. Ideally it was hoped that all prisoners could be transported in vehicles, but given the fact that the Japanese Army was not overly mechanized, it was expected that large numbers of prisoners would have to march. But Kawane felt there would be sufficient food to provide for the marchers (Map 6).

This then was the plan submitted to Homma and the one he accepted. The general added an order of his own stating that all captives were to be treated with a friendly spirit. Tragically, neither the plan nor Homma's order were carried out resulting in the horror known as the Bataan Death March.

A number of fatal errors turned the march into one

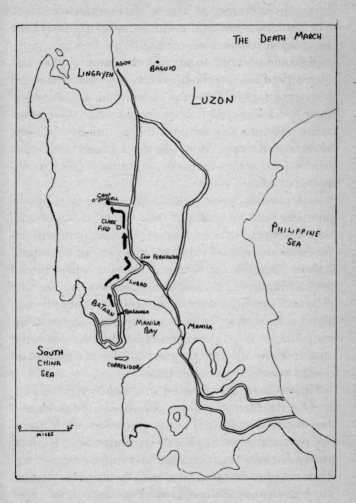

THE DEATH MARCH

LINGAYEN   AGOO   BAGUIO

LUZON

CAMP
O'DONNELL

CLARK
FIELD

SAN FERNANDO

LUBAO

BATAAN

BALANGA

MANILA BAY

MANILA

PHILIPPINE
SEA

SOUTH
CHINA
SEA

CORREGIDOR

0   25
    MILES

of World War II's greatest atrocities. The two phases of the march were under the command of two different officers. No one person was responsible for coordinating the entire operation. There was also a fatal miscalculation regarding the number of prisoners that had to be accommodated. The Japanese estimated the potential number of prisoners to be somewhere between twenty-five and forty-five thousand and never dreamed that the actual total would exceed seventy-five thousand. They compounded their error by underestimating the physical condition of the defenders of Bataan. The Japanese labored under the misconception that the enemy was adequately fed and in decent health.

Another serious miscalculation on the part of the Japanese was the length of time the defenders would hold out after the launching of the April 3 offensive. When the surrender came far sooner than expected, Colonel Takatsu and General Kawane found themselves unprepared to deal with the prisoners. The fall of Bataan one week after the offensive took them completely by surprise. They were then faced with double the number of prisoners anticipated and these were underfed and ill. The preparations for accommodating the prisoners were incomplete.

Since Homma's offensive was considered secondary to the primary Japanese objectives in Malaya and the Dutch East Indies, the general was given a low priority in troops, supplies and equipment. He had barely enough transportation and supplies to accommodate his own troops, let alone a horde of the enemy. Food and medical supplies were in short supply and many Japanese soldiers died needlessly for lack of proper medical attention. Thousands were suffering from malaria and a wide variety of other tropical diseases. Suddenly responsible for over eighty thousand Filipino and American troops, the Japanese found their resources overstretched.

For days after General King's surrender the prisoners poured into Balanga. Some, the fortunate ones, came by truck, but for the most part they were on foot. Along the path to Balanga no food was available. After all, why should it be? The longest one might have to travel was twenty-five miles. That was not an impossible task, of course, if one were healthy. Because of the poor state of the prisoners, however, the journey to Balanga was a horror. It took some groups over two days to make the journey. Food and especially water became an obsession. The first phase of the march thus proved a complete failure. It was totally disorganized, uncoordinated, inadequately supervised and excessively brutal as the merciless Japanese soldiers vented their vengeance and hatred on their captives. They viewed the POWs as something less than human and treated them as such. Thousands of individual horror stories can be recounted. The brutal behavior seemed arbitrary, almost at the whim of the group leader. Some Japanese were relatively kind to the captives but many others were just the opposite. Slowly, the POWs made their painful way to Balanga.

Once the prisoners reached Balanga, the second phase of the Japanese plan was scheduled to commence. Transportation was supposedly to be available for at least one quarter of the POWs. The remainder were expected to walk, but with rest stops along the route. Unfortunately, like phase one, this part of the plan also proved a failure. The result was the Bataan Death March.

As the prisoners assembled at Balanga, the area quickly became a cesspool of filth. During the subsequent march brutality was the rule of thumb. Occasionally a compassionate guard mitigated the tragedy but cruelty seemed to be the order of the day. By the time the horrible event was over, nearly 650 Americans and almost 10 thousand Filipinos had perished needlessly.

When Americans found out about the death march nearly two years later, they viewed it as a deliberate Japanese policy of torture and murder. In reality, however, the death march was not an organized policy, nor was it consciously and maliciously directed. It was "rather, the confused result of a tragic combination of circumstances, attitudes and events."[14] The majority of the atrocities were perpetuated by relatively junior officers or private soldiers, not by the senior commanders.

The causes of the death march can be broken down into five major categories: the deteriorated physical condition of the captives; the total Japanese unpreparedness to care for so many prisoners in such poor condition; the cultural background of the Japanese soldier who, during training, was taught to be cruel particularly to those no longer worthy to be treated as human, i.e., prisoners; the desire for revenge; and finally, the failure of the Japanese leadership to adequately supervise and restrain the hostility toward the prisoners. Thus the death march occurred.

While the death march was in progress Homma

was preoccupied with the critical task of capturing Corregidor and eliminating the enemy forces in the outer islands, most notably at Cebu and Mindanao. Corregidor was the most important objective for without it, Manila Bay was virtually useless to the Japanese.

Corregidor possessed many characteristics similar to a medieval castle. A two-mile strip of sea formed a moat. The island contained solid defenses and was honeycombed by a labyrinth of tunnels. The defenders gave it the nickname "The Rock" for it appeared that its defenses were as hard as rock.

The Rock had been a target of Japanese air forces from late December onward. By mid-January the top of the island was in ruins. By April, the fifteen thousand inhabitants were subjected to the full might of the Japanese bombardment. Then, with Bataan's fall, the punishment intensified as Japanese artillery was positioned on the southern tip of the peninsula. Eye witnesses describe the horror of the deadly bombardment, noting that by midday the island was totally ablaze. The shock of the bombardment made the island tremble. The concussion from the explosions caused many people to suffer ear and nose hemorrhages.

On the evening of May 5, the main Japanese attack began. The core of resistance on Corregidor was Malinta Tunnel and Homma was well aware of this. As the landing barges moved across the narrow strip of water, a sharp current swept them toward the eastern end of the island. A bright moon helped the defenders to see the Japanese. The invaders suffered heavy casualties (Map 7).

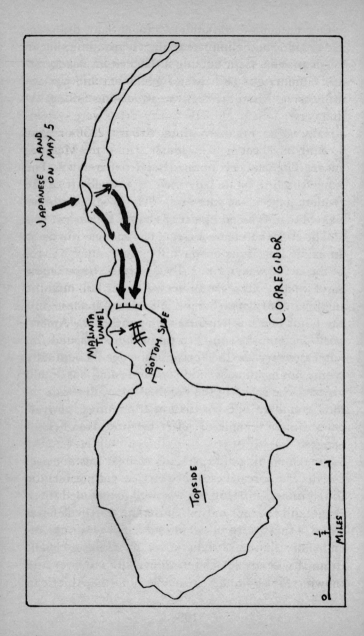

JAPANESE LAND
ON MAY 5

MALINTA TUNNEL

BOTTOM SIDE

TOPSIDE

CORREGIDOR

MILES

0   ½   1

One unit, however, under Colonel Sato, did manage to land successfully and, after regrouping, began to advance on Malinta Tunnel. Back at his headquarters Homma was unaware of Sato's feat and was apprehensive, believing that the attack was failing. At that very moment, though, Sato's forces were systematically advancing on Malinta. Around 2230 on May 6, with the enemy perilously close to Malinta, Wainwright saw no option but to surrender. The many sick and wounded, the horrid stale air of the tunnel coupled with the rapidly deteriorating military situation, convinced him that further bloodshed was senseless. He therefore ordered a white flag run up to the top of the highest flagpole.

Along with two fellow officers, Wainwright made his way to the Japanese lines on Denver Hill near the entrance of Malinta Tunnel. The first Japanese officer they met was a lieutenant who passed the Americans on to a colonel. Wainwright insisted on surrendering only to Homma, however. Eventually the Japanese colonel called for a landing barge and took Wainwright over to Bataan. There, he was escorted to a white house to await Homma's arrival. Even though he spoke perfect English, Homma insisted on speaking through an interpreter. He had the latter explain to the Americans that he was not prepared to consider any surrender that did not include all the forces in the Philippines. This included those troops still holding out in Mindanao under General Sharp. Wainwright responded that he was only responsible for those troops on Corregidor itself. Homma was suspicious of Wainwright's answer and knowing the command structure, told the American general that in that case hostilities would continue until the Americans were ready to accept his terms. With that Homma rose from the table.

Wainwright was in a bind. If he refused to surrender according to Homma's terms, hostilities would continue and probably result in a massacre. Consequently he took the only road open, the general surrendered in the name of all Allied Forces fighting in the Philippines including those of General Sharp. Corregidor had fallen and with it, the Philippines.

Sharp, however, ignored the surrender order and held out for three more days. After that he too had no option but to surrender as well. But some Americans were not so eager to surrender. They melted away into the jungle where they joined up with Filipino guerrilla bands who harassed the Japanese right up until the time of liberation.

General Wainwright took some consolation from a message received only a few hours before he had gone forward to surrender. President Roosevelt said:

> In spite of all the handicaps of complete isolation, lack of food and ammunition you have given the world a shining example of patriotic fortitude and self-sacrifice. The American people ask no finer example of tenacity, resourcefulness, and steadfast courage. The calm determination of your personal leadership in a desperate situation sets a standard of duty for our soldiers throughout the world.[15]

With his forces surrendered, Wainwright now faced more than three years of harsh captivity.

With the conquest of the Philippines the Japanese gained one of the finest harbors in the Orient and excellent bases from which to stage and supply their garrisons to the south and east, in addition to a large population to contribute to the Greater East Asia Co-Prosperity Sphere. They had driven the United States from its Far East stronghold, destroyed a combined American and Philippine army, and forced the Far East Air Force and the Asiatic Fleet back to the line of the Malay Barrier. In Japanese hands, the Philippines constituted a formidable barrier to any Allied thrust from the east aimed at severing the line of communications between Japan and the vast wealth of the East Indies.

For America, on the other hand, Bataan became a symbol, a symbol of American determination to return and right the wrong. That day finally came in October, 1944 when General MacArthur waded ashore at Leyte with the combined weight of two fleets and thousands of fighting men at his back. We had returned.

Chapter Three

Guadalcanal

Once the Japanese steamroller was checked by the naval battles of Midway and the Coral Sea, the latter forestalling the invasion of Port Moresby, New Guinea, American planners began casting about for ways to strike back and begin paving the long road to eventual victory and Japan itself. They were aided in their quest by Japan's seizure of the island of Tulagi in the lower Solomons. The Japanese constructed a seaplane base in the area from which they planned to observe and harass the Allied supply line between Australia and Hawaii. After establishing the base the Imperial High Command concluded that the Allied communications line was vulnerable to attack by aircraft stationed in the lower Solomons. They therefore directed the Tulagi garrison to occupy the neighboring island of Guadalcanal. This island was ideal for the construction of an air base from which to launch attacks against Allied convoys en route to Australia. The location of the two islands also made them ideal staging areas for a projected invasion of Australia.

In Washington, meantime, debate raged regarding the first retaliatory step against Japan. General MacArthur, whose headquarters were in Australia, proposed an immediate operation aimed at the seizure of

Rabaul, the great enemy naval base on the island of New Britain in the Bismarcks. Admiral King reviewed MacArthur's plan and concluded that it was far too ambitious. Because of its significance, Rabaul was too heavily defended. Logistically, an attack on Rabaul from bases in Australia and New Guinea would be next to impossible. Besides, King said, any amphibious assault in the South Pacific would have to be a naval one and he was vehemently opposed to MacArthur commanding naval forces. Instead, the Navy countered with a proposal of its own calling for an indirect approach to Rabaul via the eastern Solomons where it was felt the Japanese were weaker. A naval officer under Nimitz, not MacArthur, would command the assault. Quite naturally, General Marshall, chairman of the Joint Chiefs of Staff, supported MacArthur.

The Pacific command in 1942 was a complicated one. The Joint Chiefs had divided the theater into two spheres. The Southwest Pacific Command under MacArthur encompassed everything west of longitude 159 degrees. East of that line was Admiral Nimitz's Pacific Ocean Area. The admiral's area who so vast that he split his command in three, the Central Pacific, North Pacific, and South Pacific areas. Of the three, the last was potentially the most active. Therefore, Nimitz appointed Adm. Robert Ghormley to act as his deputy and command the South Pacific. Nimitz retained the other commands himself.

As the debate raged about the merits of the opposing Army and Navy views, King grew impatient. He took the bull by the horns and ordered Nimitz to make plans for the seizure of Tulagi even though it was west of the 159 degree boundary thus placing it in MacArthur's operational area. On June 25, the plan was ready and King presented it to the Joint Chiefs. Having already promised MacArthur the command, Marshall found himself in a bind.

It was MacArthur himself who tipped the scales in favor of the Navy. He backed down from his direct approach plan and accepted the indirect approach to Rabaul which King's planners had submitted. But MacArthur did not agree to relinquish the command.

The controversy over command reached a climax on June 29 when King and Marshall met face to face. At this meeting a compromise was reached. Three objectives were adopted for the overall Pacific strategy. The first involved an assault on Guadalcanal and Tulagi. The other two tasks, to be commanded by MacArthur, included the capture of the Western Solomons, Eastern New Guinea, and the Bismarcks that would include the seizure of Rabaul. As a result of the compromise the South West Pacific boundary was shifted westward thus placing Guadalcanal and Tulagi in Nimitz's sphere. MacArthur could no longer claim that he should command all naval forces in that area since the objective no longer lay there. Instead, Vice Admiral Ghormley, Nimitz's deputy, would be responsible for the operation.

On July 4, Nimitz and King met in San Francisco to discuss the forthcoming attack. Rear Adm. Richmond Kelly Turner was also present at this meeting. Turner, fresh from the war plans staff, was slated to command the amphibious phase of the operation.

On the fifth it was learned that the Japanese were constructing an airfield on Guadalcanal. This news emphasized the need to accelerate the Solomons attack if the line of communication between Hawaii and Australia was to be protected. Thus, "Operation Watchtower," the assault on Tulagi and Guadalcanal, took shape. The attack was scheduled for August 1.

Turner assumed command on July 18, just two weeks prior to the projected date of the first American amphibious operation of the war. His first problem was assembling a staff. Hardly any of the officers selected by the Bureau of Navigation had any amphibious training whatsoever. Therefore, Turner would have to rely on the amphibious oriented Marines. General Alexander Vandergrift's First Marine Division was chosen to make the attack.

Turner's plan called for the capture of Tulagi, Guadalcanal and a few smaller islands in the area. The importance of Guadalcanal increased daily as construction of the Japanese airfield progressed. Turner knew that it would be virtually impossible to meet the August 1 target date. There was simply not enough time to assemble the necessary shipping and to train the troops. King agreed to a week's postponement and established the new target date of August 7. Any further delay and the enemy airfield would be completed and operational.

Turner's amphibious force was officially designated Task Force 62. For his flagship the admiral comandeered the merchant ship *McCawley*. Though this ship was deemed adequate for his needs, subsequent experience proved that the *McCawley* lacked too many essentials for the successful conduct of a large-scale amphibious operation.

After leaving Auckland, New Zealand, Task Force 62 headed for Fiji where it was scheduled to undergo a dress rehearsal for the invasion. En route, Turner and his staff composed an eighty-seven page plan by which the operation would be governed.

On Sunday, July 26, Vice Adm. Frank Fletcher, commander of the American carrier force slated to protect the operation, held a conference aboard his flagship, the carrier *Saratoga*. Fletcher announced that his three carriers, *Saratoga, Wasp* and *Enterprise,* along with their escorting warships, would remain in the area for only two days in support of the landings. After that, the amphibious forces would be on their own. Fear of enemy attacks on his precious carriers dominated Fletcher's thinking. He had already lost two carriers: *Lexington* in the Coral Sea and *Yorktown* at Midway.

Turner's chief of staff, Captain Peyton, recalls the conference as a very stormy one. Fletcher, he said, criticized the operational plan saying that it was put together too hastily and therefore not thoroughly planned.

Enraged, Turner shot back condemning Fletcher's decision to pull the carriers out after forty-eight hours. Admiral Ghormley was not present at the meeting. Instead, he was represented by his chief of staff, Rear Adm. Daniel Callaghan. If Ghormley had been present, Turner felt that he would have sided with him and ordered Fletcher to remain in the vicinity longer.

In his view then, the conference was less than satisfactory. Fletcher could not be dissuaded. Turner turned his attention to the all-important rehearsal scheduled for the twenty-eighth through the thirty-first.

The dress rehearsal proved totally inadequate. Koro Island in the Fijis lacked the proper beach conditions and proved hazardous to boats, the very landing craft that Turner could ill afford to risk because of the critical shortage. As a result, only one-third of the Marines who needed the benefit of a rehearsal for the forthcoming attack actually took part in the practice session. Nevertheless, the experience was not totally without value. The gunfire support ships and the supporting aircraft did gain needed experience. General Vandergrift, the Marine commander of the invasion force, complained bitterly that the rehearsal was unsatisfactory.

Following the dress rehearsal, Task Force 62 sailed for the Solomons, eleven hundred miles away. Careful to maintain radio silence, the force glided around the western side of Guadalcanal and through the twelve-mile wide channel separating the island from the Russell Islands.

In no way did Guadalcanal resemble the tropical paradise of travel brochures and story books. The Solomons lie a few degree south of the equator. The climate is wet and hot with an average temperature in the high eighties. The heat and frequent rains make the island a steamy, jungle-covered, pestilential hell. Averaging twenty-five miles in width, Guadalcanal has a spiny ridge of mountains running through the center. The jagged peaks are covered with a tropical rain forest. Numerous rivers flow from the mountains to the coast on the northern side of the island. With the exception of a handful of coconut plantations, the jungle grew right down to the water's edge. The occasional grassy open ground was covered with kunai grass, taller than a man and sharp as a razor (Map 8).

The foul, smelly swamps and humid jungles abound with huge insects, lizards and snakes. At the mouths of the rivers crocodiles lived. The most dangerous inhabitants were the large mosquitos. These insects infected the invading Americans and Japanese alike with den-

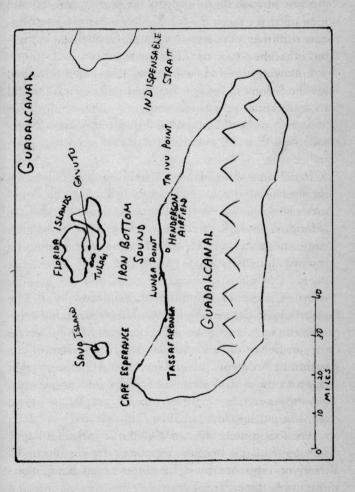

gue, malaria and numerous other tropical diseases. In addition, the tropical humidity caused numerous and frequent fungus infections.

The weather on the morning of the assault was all that an invading force could ask for. After passing Cape Esperance on the northeast corner of Guadalcanal, the American force split up. The lead transports, Group Yoke, headed north of Savo Island toward Florida Island. The larger of the two forces, Group X-Ray, made for Lunga Point on Guadalcanal.

The first sight of Guadalcanal inspired Marine correspondent H.L. Merrilant to comment:

> Guadalcanal is an island of striking beauty. Blue-green mountains, towering into a brilliant tropical sky or crowned with cloud masses, dominate the island. The dark green of jungle growth blends into the softer greens and browns of coconut groves and grassy plains and ridges.[1]

Despite a week's softening up bombing by B-17 bombers from Espiritu Santo, the Japanese did not appear to be anticipating an invasion. Immediately after dawn on D-day, planes from the American carriers began hitting targets on Tulagi, Gavutu and Guadalcanal. Cruisers and destroyers lobbed shells into suspected Japanese positions. Eighteen enemy seaplanes were caught like sitting ducks in Tulagi's harbor and were destroyed at their moorings. At 0800 the First Raider Battalion hit Tulagi's beaches supported by the Second Battalion, Fifth Marines. In just over an hour, one thousand Marines were ashore.

On Tulagi the Marines got their first taste of the Japanese defensive strategy that was encountered all too frequently on other islands later on. The defenders held up in caves that provided immunity from aerial and naval bombardment. Only the direct hit at the mouth of the cave was effective.

The attackers moved quickly inland and began to task of clearing the island. The Second Battalion moved towards the northeastern part of the island and encountered little resistance. By the end of the day the entire northern portion of Tulagi was secured.

Meanwhile, the Raiders had driven across the island and cut it in two. When they pivoted and began advancing southeast, however, Japanese resistance increased dramatically and the attack slowed to a crawl. Using grenades and explosive charges the Marines concentrated on clearing the enemy dugouts and bunkers but progress was slow. It was obvious that Tulagi could not be secured in one day.

As night began to fall the Raiders set up a defensive perimeter. The Second Battalion moved down from the other end of the island and settled into line alongside their comrades. During the night the Japanese wasted the bulk of their manpower attempting to storm the American positions. The line held. The following morning the Marines advanced against the few remaining enemy positions. By 1500 the entire island was in American hands. The Japanese lost about five hundred men on Tulagi. A handful escaped by swimming to nearby Florida Island but only three surrendered. American casualties were thirty-six killed and fifty-four wounded.

Because of the shortage of landing craft, the D-day landings on the twin islands of Gavutu and Tanambogo were scheduled for 1200. The 350 defenders of these two islands, connected by a causeway, put up a bitter defense. The American plan called for this objective to be overrun in one day, but with the enemy holed up in caves and strong bunkers, the task proved impossible. The Marines were compelled to reinforce the original landing force. Gavutu and Tanambogo were not secured until 2100 on August 9, D + 2. In contrast to Tulagi, American casualties were relatively heavy on the twin islands, with 108 killed and 140 wounded.

On the primary objective, Guadalcanal, the Marines hit the beach at 0910 on August 7. The landing point, Red Beach, was located about a mile east of Lunga Point. The attackers expected a hostile reception and were amazed when not one Japanese was found. The First Marines, landing in the second wave, moved quickly inland and established a defensive perimeter. Meanwhile, the Fifth Marines advanced along the coast towards the Ilu River. The Marines stumbled across Japanese barracks and camps with food still on the table, abandoned in haste by the surprised Japanese who fled into the jungle. By nightfall the American perimeter was thirty-five hundred yards deep. One battalion reached the Ilu and dug in for the night. Not a shot was fired in anger that first day. The quiet was ominous.

Thanks to the lack of enemy interference, while the Marines moved steadily inland tons of supplies were deposited on the beaches. The main landing area became so congested that Vandergift was forced to establish another one, known as Red Beach extension, a few hundred yards nearer Lunga Point. By nightfall, over eleven hundred Marines were ashore along with their artillery and equipment. Huge piles of supplies sat on

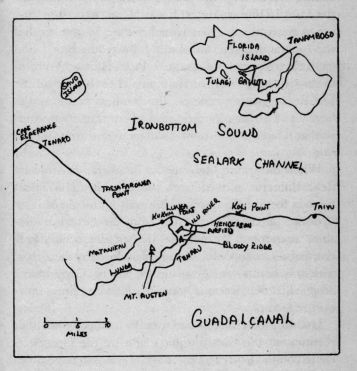

FLORIDA ISLAND

TANAMBOGO

TULAGI GAVUTU

SAVO ISLAND

IRONBOTTOM SOUND

SEALARK CHANNEL

CAPE ESPERANCE

TENARO

TASSAFARONGA POINT

LUNGA POINT

KUKUM POINT

ILU RIVER

KOLI POINT

TAIVU

HENDERSON AIRFIELD

BLOODY RIDGE

MATANIKAU

LUNGA

TENARU

MT. AUSTEN

GUADALCANAL

0   5   10
MILES

the beaches and landing craft hovered offshore waiting to be unloaded.

It did not take the Japanese long to wake up. At the mighty base in Rabaul a flight of bombers was being readied for an attack on Milne Bay, New Guinea. When word of the American landings was broadcast by a radio operator on Tulagi the pilots were ordered to change their targets and roared off toward Guadalcanal.

On Bougainville, Coastwatcher Paul Mason spotted the Japanese formation heading down "the Slot"* and got off a hasty radio message to Pearl Harbor. Word of the sighting was immediately passed to Turner on the *McCawley*. Turner ordered the landing craft off the beaches. The invasion fleet moved out into open water so that it would have room to maneuver during the air raid.

When the twenty-four enemy bombers, escorted by Zero fighters, arrived over the beachhead, Wildcat fighters from the *Enterprise* were waiting for them. The Wildcats and anti-aircraft fire from the escorting warships accounted for twenty-three of the twenty-four bombers. Eleven Wildcats were shot down by the Zeros. The only bomb damage sustained was to the destroyer *Mugford*. Three precious hours of unloading time, however, was lost.

No saga of Guadalcanal can be complete without mention of the contribution made by the Coastwatchers. When the British colonialists evacuated the Solomons in the face of the Japanese invasion, a handful of men, mostly Australian and New Zealander plantation overseers or workers, elected to remain behind and join

---

*The body of water dividing the twin chain of the Solomon Islands.

the natives in offering whatever resistance they could to the invaders. These men established observation posts overlooking the Slot and monitored Japanese ship and plane movements. This information was passed by radio to Allied receiving stations. It was a hazardous occupation at best. Constantly hunted and pursued by the Japanese, the Coastwatchers were forever on the move, forced to establish new observation posts. Many of them were eventually captured. Countless American soldiers, Marines, and sailors owe their lives to the dedication and bravery of this handful of men.

As for the natives, they too were hostile to the foreign invaders. Instead of treating them decently, the Japanese tortured and enslaved the inhabitants of the Solomons, who consequently took advantage of every opportunity to strike back. Lone Japanese and small patrols were ambushed in the jungles and killed. Many of those who abandoned their breakfast on the morning of August 7 and beat a hasty retreat into the jungle met with this fate. No one will ever know just how many Japanese were killed by the natives on Guadalcanal during the six-month long struggle. On the other hand, the British had treated the natives rather well. Therefore, when the white-faced Americans invaded the Japanese-held islands, the Solomon Islanders were more than willing to assist in whatever manner they could.

On the morning of D + 1 the Fifth Marines continued their advance towards Lunga Point. One battalion crossed the Lunga River, reached the west coast of the point, and established a defensive perimeter around Kukum. At 1600 another battalion reached the main objective, the nearly completed airfield, and found it completely deserted.

The airfield was christened Henderson Field in honor of Maj. Loften Henderson, a Marine pilot killed during the battle of Midway. During the advance the Marines at Lunga Point ran into their first hostile fire. Enemy resistance was sporadic, however, and failed to slow the advance. By the end of the second day, the Marines had captured Kukum, secured Lunga Point, the airstrip, and held a large perimeter. Because of the small number of troops available, the American line was not continuous. Large gaps separated the Marine units.

Another air raid during the day resulted in the torpedoing of the destroyer *Jarvis*. A blazing Japanese bomber crashed into the transport *George F. Elliot* setting it on fire. The transport continued to blaze offshore for hours. Air raid alarms, false or real, played havoc with the unloading operation. At each alarm the transports were forced to weigh anchor and make for safer waters. Precious time was lost and, since Fletcher would not be dissuaded from his forty-eight-hour promise, this lost time proved critical.

That night the emperor's admirals struck back. A force of cruisers and destroyers under Admiral Mikawa left Rabaul shortly after the first reports of the American landings. By late evening the Japanese squadron was approaching the waters around Guadalcanal. Admiral Turner had positioned three patrols of warships to guard the transports off Lunga Point. Between Savo Island and Tulagi was a northern force consisting of the cruisers *Astoria*, *Quincy* and *Vincennes*. A southern force made up of the cruiser *Chicago* and the Australian cruisers *Australia* and *Canberra* patrolled back and forth between Savo and Guadalcanal. Both forces were under the tactical command of Rear Admiral Crutchley, RAN. A southern force containing the cruisers *San Juan* and the Australian *Hobart* watched the other end of the sound.

Around 0100 on the ninth Mikawa's forces entered the waters between Savo and Guadalcanal. Two hours earlier Turner had summoned Crutchley to a conference aboard the *McCawley*. Thus the *Australia* was not present when the Japanese opened up on the Allied force with torpedoes and gunfire at 0136. *Canberra* quickly took two torpedoes and over two dozen shell hits. Within minutes the cruiser was a burning, drifting hulk with a large portion of her crew dead or wounded. Another Japanese torpedo blew the bow off *Chicago* and the cruiser drifted out of control and out of the battle.

Mikawa then ordered a ninety-degree turn to port and pointed his ships towards the northern force. Incredibly, events had happened so fast that no one in the southern force thought to get off a report that they were engaged with the enemy. Thus the three unsuspecting ships of the northern force were taken completely by surprise. At 0150 the Japanese ships opened fire again.

The three American cruisers were quickly smothered in a hail of gunfire and torpedoes. The *Quincy* sank at 0235, *Vincennes* fifteen minutes later. *Astoria* lasted until the following noon before slipping beneath the waves. The burnt-out hulk of the *Canberra* was scuttled by her crew around 0800.

The destruction of both Allied naval patrols left the helpless transports at the mercy of Mikawa's warships. Unbelievably, the admiral failed to follow up his victory. Satisfied that he had achieved a great victory, and indeed he had, Mikawa headed back up the Slot. The primary objective, the helpless transports, were left unscathed. Throughout the Solomons campaign this

Japanese trait was in evidence. Almost inevitably they failed to follow up their successes.

Turner's forty-eight hours were fast running out. Throughout the morning a frantic last-minute effort was made to land as many men and supplies as possible. At 1330 the word was passed for the ships to weigh anchor. As the Marines on shore stared in amazement, the invasion fleet moved out to sea, their holds still crammed with ammunition and food. Turner had no choice.

Unable to persuade Fletcher to keep the carriers in the vicinity any longer, he simply could not leave the transports at the mercy of the Japanese air force and navy.

By the time Turner sailed away over ten thousand Marines had been put ashore on Guadalcanal with six thousand more on Tulagi. A thirty-seven-day supply of food was available to sustain operations but without warships, the American rear was completely unprotected. Vandergrift and his men were on their own.

The Japanese command responsible for the Solomons was the Seventeenth Army commanded by Lieutenant General Hyakutake. At the time of the American invasion the general was directing the New Guinea campaign from his headquarters at Rabaul. On August 13 Hyakutake was ordered by Imperial Headquarters to evict the Americans from Guadalcanal. The only force immediately available was a combat team of the Thirty-fifth or Kawaguchi Brigade, named for its commander Major General Kawaguchi. This force, the Ichiki detachment, had originally been slated to occupy Midway but the disastrous turn of events there found Colonel Ichiki and his troops at Rabaul awaiting transportation back to Japan.

On the sixteenth the Ichiki detachment was loaded aboard six destroyers of Adm. Raizo Tanaka's reinforcement force. The force set sail for Guadalcanal. After dark on the eighteenth, Ichiki and nine hundred of his men landed safely at Taivu Point, twenty-two miles east of Lunga. This event marked the first of many "Tokyo Express" runs bringing reinforcements and supplies down the Slot. For his exploits Tanaka earned the respect of his colleagues and was grudgingly nicknamed "Tenacious Tanaka" by the Americans.

August 19 was an active day. An American patrol ambushed a group of Japanese near Koli Point. Thirty-two of the enemy were killed in the action. An examination of the bodies revealed documents indicating that fresh troops (Ichiki's) had just arrived on Guadalcanal.

That same day a raid was carried out against Japanese positions near Matanikau and Kokumbona. Two companies of Marines travelled overland and attacked Matanikau from the west and south. A third company made an amphibious landing at Kokumbona. This attack yielded little but during the other attack, sixty-five Japanese were killed.

The next day the escort carrier *Long Island* sailed to within two hundred miles of Guadalcanal. Nineteen fighters and twelve dive bombers lifted off the carrier's flight deck and landed safely at Henderson Field. Vandergrift's men had worked tirelessly to make the field operational. At the same time, three fast transports brought 120 tons of supplies to the island. These ships lingered long enough to ferry the Second Battalion, Fifth Marines over from Tulagi. With their mission accomplished, the swift little ships hightailed it out of range of enemy planes from Rabaul.

Although a force of ten thousand Marines seemed formidable, it was in fact barely large enough to form an adequate defensive perimeter around Henderson Field. Even then the perimeter was not continuous. Vandergrift positioned his troops so as to protect the airstrip from the most obvious avenues of attack. Elsewhere, gaping holes loomed in the American line. The security of Henderson Field, however, was Vandergrift's foremost responsibility. This, coupled with the fact that the prospect of resupply seemed remote, prevented the Marines from taking the offensive.

Based on the reports from his patrols and the resident Coastwatcher, Martin Clemens, and his native scouts, Vandergrift sensed that a Japanese attack was imminent and that it would probably be made by those fresh troops at Taivutu. The general ordered his troops to dig in on the bank of the Ilu River. Thanks to the inadequacy of their outdated maps, what the Marines thought was the Tenaru River was actually the Ilu. This fact was not discovered until weeks later. Therefore, the forthcoming battle became known as the Battle of the Tenaru.

Although Ichiki detachment was but the leading element of the Kawaguchi Brigade, the colonel was contemptuous of the Americans and decided to attack without waiting for the Tokyo Express to deliver the rest of the brigade. When the Japanese attack came the First Marines were waiting for it.

At the mouth of the Ilu (Tenaru) was a sandpit that formed an ideal ford across the river. There the Marines placed barbed wire and dug in along the west bank of the river. Riflemen and machine gunners waited in foxholes for the impending attack. Just before midnight on August 21 Marine listening posts in the jungle reported large enemy movements. Around 0130 sporadic Japanese rifle and mortar fire began peppering the Marine lines. A few minutes later a howling screeching mob of Ichiki's erupted from the jungle. All along the line the Marines opened up with a withering fire. Grenades and mortars fell in the ranks of the attackers. Anti-tank guns spewed canister shot. The Ichiki ranks were decimated. A few Japanese managed to clamber over the backs of their fallen comrades and reached the Marine lines where they were beaten back with bayonets and rifle fire leaving almost five hundred dead behind them.

If nothing else Ichiki was determined. For the next few hours Japanese artillery fire was directed at the Marine positions. Then, around 0500, the Japanese surged forward again. As Robert Leckie described it:

Running erect and with no attempt to get below the American fire, the Japanese soldiers were cut down by Marine machine guns. Artillery strikes came whistling and crashing down upon them. Balked by the wire, struck from the side by bullets and from the sky by shells, the Japanese perished almost to a man . . . falling upon one another until they lay three deep in death for the tide to bury them in the morning.[2]

Ichiki, and his few remaining troops cowered in the jungle while the Marines continued to pour fire into the position. Then the First Battalion of Marines, which had been held in reserve, launched a counterattack into the jungle. Vandergrift sent a company of tanks to reinforce the attack as the right wing of the Marine line swung around in a broad arc to the sea. The tanks clanked across the piles of enemy dead spewing death and destruction until their tracks resembled meat grinders.

Over eight hundred of Ichiki's shock troops lay dead along the banks of the Ilu. Many of the survivors were badly wounded and later perished during the retreat. Humiliated, Colonel Ichiki burned his colors and shot himself.

Thus the first Japanese attempt to retake Guadalcanal ended in total disaster. At the same time it destroyed the myth of Japanese invincibility as jungle fighters. At the Battle of the Tenaru the United States Marines clearly demonstrated that they were more than the equal of the vaunted Japanese Army.

Even while the Marines were finishing off the remnants of Ichiki's command, the Tokyo Express was making ready to transport the rest of Kawaguchi's force to Guadalcanal. Halfway down the Slot Tanaka's force was sighted by reconnaissance patrols from Henderson Field. Using discretion, Tanaka turned around and headed for the Shortlands.

Meanwhile, in order to mask Tanaka's movement, Admiral Yamamoto attempted to lure Fletcher's carriers away from Guadalcanal. The effort succeeded since Fletcher's force was far out to sea at any rate and in poor position to intervene at Guadalcanal. In the Battle of the Eastern Solomons on August 23, the Japanese lost the light carrier *Ryujo* but the *Enterprise* was badly damaged.

During the great carrier battle Tanaka's superiors, confident that the American carriers were engaged, directed him to reverse course again. One hundred miles north of Guadalcanal the Japanese ships were attacked by a squadron of *Enterprise* dive bombers. The *Enterprise* squadron had been sent to Henderson Field after their ship became inoperable. The Americans hit the cruiser *Jintsu*, Tanaka's flagship, and wounded the admiral. One transport was also hit and sunk with the loss of many troops. Shortly thereafter a flight of B-17s from Espiritu Santo arrived. Bombing from a high altitude they managed to sink two of Tanaka's destroyers. The reinforcement effort ended in failure as Tanaka's mangled force limped back to the Shortlands.

Nevertheless, Tenacious Tanaka was equal to his name. During the last week in August his destroyers managed to land the rest of Kawaguchi's force at Taivu. Harassed by Henderson's planes, the naval force lost four hundred more of Colonel Oka's brigade but over six thousand of Kawagushi's troops were safely put ashore.

In the meantime, General Hyakutake received orders from Imperial Headquarters directing him to go over to the defensive in New Guinea and concentrate all available resources of the Seventeenth Army on the recapture of Guadalcanal.

At the same time the plight of the stranded Marines on the island caused President Roosevelt to prepare for the worst so that the announcement of a defeat in the Solomons would not come as a shock to the nation. In a Labor Day address Roosevelt said:

> We must not overrate the importance of our successes in the Solomons. Though we may be proud of the skill with which these local operations have been conducted.[3]

But even though an air of pessimism hung over Ghormley's headquarters on Noumea, Vandergrift was not ready to throw in the towel. A battalion of the Fifth Marines landed behind Japanese lines near Kokumbona on the night of August 27. After encountering heavy resistance the Marines drove eastward the following morning and made their way back to the Lunga perimeter. Vital information regarding enemy strength and dispositions were gathered during the raid.

The success of the raid bolstered Vandergrift's confidence and caused him to plan another, more ambitious foray. Knowing full well that for two weeks the Tokyo Express had been depositing reinforcements at Taivu, the general sent the First Raider Battalion under Col. "Red Mike" Edson to conduct a raid on Taivu Point itself. Edson was just the type of commander the Marines admired. When asked by one of his troops what could be done about the rapidly dwindling supply of food on the island, Edson replied, "There's lots of chow. The Japs have it. Take it away from them."[4]

Take it away from them they did. Reinforced by the First Parachute Battalion, the Marines went ashore at Tasimboka on the morning of September 8. The Japanese, convinced that a major landing was in progress, fled the scene. Edson's troops failed to kill many of the enemy but they uncovered huge quantities of supplies. There was too little time to load the supplies on the transports so Edson's men jabbed their bayonets into tins of food while others dragged bags of rice into the surf. Kawaguchi's supply base, including a powerful transmitter, was destroyed. The Marines then re-embarked and sailed back to Lunga Point, their pockets brimming with tins of Japanese meat and bottles of sake, and General Kawaguchi's dress white uniform flying from the masthead, the same dress uniform that Kawaguchi planned to wear to the American surrender ceremony.

While Edson was raiding Kawaguchi's base, the latter's men were hacking their way through the jungle toward Henderson Field. One of Edson's patrols had blundered into the Japanese rear guard and reported their findings. When the Raiders arrived back at Lunga this news was quickly given to Vandergrift who immediately began to prepare for another full-scale Japanese attack.

As previously mentioned, there were not enough Marines on Guadalcanal to allow for a continuous perimeter. All Vandergrift could do was defend the more obvious approaches to Henderson Field. The only continuous line that did exist was along the beaches of Lunga Point stretching from the Ilu to Kukum. From Kukum the Marine line bent inland in a wide arc for about two thousand yards. A second line began a thousand yards up the Ilu and continued inland for another twenty-five hundred yards broken in the middle by a bend in the river. The remaining, the shortest, line was about three thousand yards directly south of the airfield along a humpbacked bare stretch of land. This fifteen hundred yard long line was entrusted to the care of Edson's men and the First Raider Parachute Battalion.

Meanwhile, Kelly Turner had arrived on Guadalcanal for a meeting with Vandergrift. Turner promised that somehow he would manage to bring the Seventh Marines up from Samoa. Unfortunately, the two men could not agree on the best method of utilizing these troops. Turner was extremely fond of playing soldier and wished to have the seventh Marines establish an entirely new perimeter. Vandergrift, on the other hand, wanted to use the reinforcements to defend that territory already in American hands.

While the two were conferring, Vandergrift was handed a message from Ghormley that in summary stated he could provide nothing further in the way of reinforcements. Too many ships had already been lost including another carrier. The Marines were being abandoned to their fate. Turner promised to change Ghormley's mind.

During the two nights that Turner stayed on Guadalcanal the Japanese obliged with their nightly show. Destroyers sailed into Ironbottom Sound and lobbed shells into the American positions. But instead of bombarding Henderson Field as per usual, the firing was directed at Edson's positions on the ridge.

Two unremitting nocturnal visitors also paid their nightly visits. "Louie the Louse," a plane that usually managed to drop a bomb or two on the airfield, and "Washing Machine Charlie," another plane whose engine seemed out of synchronization, treated Turner to a display of their antics. Usually neither visitor was able to cause much damage except to keep the Marines awake with the bombing and whining drone of their engines.

Turner left on the twelfth a few hours before a forty-plane raid arrived from Rabaul. For the loss of one aircraft, American pilots shot down sixteen of the enemy. Those that did get through dropped five-hundred-pounders and fragmentation grenades on the ridge. More Marines were killed and wounded.

Around 2100 Louie the Louse showed up again and dropped a flare. A short time later four Japanese warships offshore opened fire. As Edson's men sought cover once more, Vandergrift knew from what direction the next Japanese attack would come. They were paying too much attention to the positions on the ridge.

General Kawaguchi planned a textbook operation calling for a three-pronged attack. The main body of his troops would attack northward across the ridge thereby pinning down the bulk of the Americans. At the same time a second force would attack across the Ilu simultaneously with Colonel Oka's attack against the western perimeter. With the main American force pinned down the latter two Japanese forces would break through and capture Henderson Field. The entire operation relied on precise timing and coordination of effort.

Oka's force, moving overland from Matanaikau, got lost in the jungle and did not arrive in position on time. Nevertheless, Kawaguchi decided to attack as planned. Rabaul had directed him to launch the offensive on the twelfth and with his communications destroyed during the raid on Tasimboka he could not request a postponement. In addition, not all of this force had reached their assembly point. Many units were still strung out behind in the jungle. Consequently, Kawaguchi had only enough troops available for a probing attack.

At 2200 on the night of September 12 a horde of Japanese, shrieking "Banzai" and "Marine, you die," dashed out of the jungle and hit Edson's line head on. The paratroopers' position was overrun and pushed back. Some units were cut off. But the impetus of the Japanese attack was too swift even for them. Leaderless, they milled around behind the Marine lines until they were driven back with rifles and grenades. On the left of Edson's line the enemy swarmed over Marine foxholes. Bayonets, swords and rifle butts flashed in the eerie light of battle and the Japanese attack broke. Edson called for a counterattack and by morning all lost territory was regained.

Even though the ridge had been held Edson knew that the Japanese would be back. Kawaguchi was regrouping and wondering why Oka's attack in the west and Ishitari's attack on the Ilu had not occurred. Despite the loss of a few hundred men, however, Kawaguchi was supremely confident that the next night would bring victory.

Kawaguchi planned for two battalions to blow a hole in the American line. Once this was done a fresh force under Colonel Watanabe would dash through the gap and head directly for the airfield. Around 2130 the attack surged forward again. The brunt of the attack fell on the parachutists on the right of Edson's line. Despite the rain of artillery and mortar fire and the fearsome canister shot, the Japanese came fanatically on. The Marine line bent and broke. Using grenades, machine guns and small arms fire the parachutists eventually restored the line.

A short time later another strong attack struck the Raiders on Edson's left. This attack was much stronger and drove the Marines back. Edson called down artillery fire onto the forward positions of the ridge. Screaming Japanese troops dove into American foxholes to escape the hail of death. The Marines stabbed or bludgeoned them to death and hurled the bodies back again.

Despite the hail of fire Kawaguchi's men continued to swarm out of the jungle, platoon after platoon moved forward. Finally, Edson gave the word to pull back to a shorter line. There the Marines stood their ground as the enemy, climbing over the backs of their dead and dying comrades, broke and ran. Two more weaker attacks were hurled against Edson's troops before Kawaguchi decided to call it quits. Vandergrift then committed his few remaining reserves and drove the enemy back into the jungle. As an effective fighting force, Kawaguchi's brigade no longer existed.

While Edson's men were up to their ears in Japanese,

Ishitari's battalion finally attacked along the Ilu. Attacking across an open field his men ran headlong into the deadly fire of the Third Battalion, First Marines. Hung up on barbed wire or caught in the open by 75mm howitzers, they were slaughtered. A second attack suffered the same fate as the first. Only a handful managed to break through. These were easily dealt with. During the height of the battle one company commander radioed battalion headquarters: "Some Japs just got inside my barbed wire."

After a short pause he resumed: "There were twenty-seven of them."[5]

Oka's tardy attack in the west was easily repulsed by the Third Battalion, Fifth Marines later that afternoon. The colonel was not eager to prove that his troops could die just as easily as Kawaguchi's or Ishitari's. Once he realized that there was no chance of breaking through, Oka called off the attack.

Kawaguchi now began the humiliating task of withdrawing from the scene of the battle. Because of Edson's earlier raid against his supply base the general decided to head west and link up with Oka's force making for Matanikau. Leaving over seven hundred dead for the Americans to bury, he loaded some five hundred wounded on litters and began the trek through the pitiless jungle. En route most of the wounded died or were left behind to perish by their hunger-weakened comrades. A week later the starving survivors of Kawaguchi's once-proud force stumbled into the Japanese lines at Matanikau. But conditions there were little better. Food was at a premium and the Japanese felt the pangs of starvation.

As for Edson his losses were only 59 dead and 204 wounded. However, the Parachute Battalion was decimated and would shortly leave Guadalcanal for good. Red

Mike and his Marines had achieved an enormous victory at a relatively light cost. As was their wont the Marines gave their position an appropriate name: "Bloody Ridge." The struggle for Bloody Ridge would go down in Marine Corps annals as one of the corp's finest moments. More importantly, Henderson Field remained in American hands.

The improvement of the airstrip had been ongoing almost from the day the Marines landed. The runway was enlarged and steel matting laid down so that the mud would not hinder takeoffs and landings. With the improvement of the airstrip came Marine fighter squadrons to man the airfield. Thus was born the "Cactus Air Force."

If the Japanese had failed in their attempts to destroy the Marines, the conditions on Guadalcanal were trying their best to do the job for them. For weeks the Marines had been subsisting on two meals a day, much of those consisting of captured Japanese rice and other provisions. Then there were the diseases. Dysentery, fungus infections (jungle rot) and malaria ravaged the troops. Exhaustion and malnutrition joined hands with the torrid humidity to take their toll. William Manchester has written:

The typical Marine on the island ran a fever, wore stinking dungarees, loathed twilight, and wondered whether the U.S. Navy still existed. He ate moldy rations and quinine. He alternatively shivered and sweated. If he was bivouacked near Henderson, he spent his mornings filling in craters left by enemy bombers the night before. If he was on his way back to the line, he struggled through shattered, stunted coconut trees, scraggy bushes, and putrescent jungle, clawing up and down slopes ankle-deep in mud, hoping he could catch a few hours of uninterrupted sleep in his foxhole.[6]

At dawn on September 18 tearful Marines stared seaward at a welcome sight. Unloading at Lunga Point were transports carrying the Seventh Marines. In the next twelve hours vast quantities of supplies were also brought ashore. Kelly Turner had kept his word to Vandergrift. Once the decimated Parachute Battalion was safely on board, the transports hoisted anchor and sailed away.

Meanwhile, Vandergrift had been sending patrols into the jungle in an effort to ascertain the enemy's intentions. Once the Seventh Marines moved into line the perimeter was almost continuous. Therefore, Vandergrift began to consider taking the offensive.

Flushed with the success of Bloody Ridge and the arrival of reinforcements the general decided to launch a limited offensive aimed at driving the Japanese away from Henderson Field. One battalion of the Seventh Marines, commanded by a colorful character, Maj. Lewis "Chesty" Puller, moved out to attack enemy positions near Mt. Austen while the Raiders advanced along the coast in the direction of Matanikau. Neither of the attacks met with much success.

Even less successful was an amphibious attack west of Point Cruz by three companies of the Seventh Marines. This force was ambushed and lost over sixty men killed with one hundred wounded. The death toll might have been much higher were it not for the guns of the destroyer *Ballard.* Firing from as close inshore as it dared to stray, the destroyer covered the Marines' evacuation and carried them back to Lunga Point.

In the first week of October Vandergrift decided to

have another go at the enemy concentration near Matanikau. Elements of the Seventh Marines would cross the
river upstream and attack the Japanese from the south. At
the same time the Fifth Marines would launch an attack at
the mouth of the river.

On the ninth the Seventh crossed the river and turned
ninety degrees toward the coast. At that point one of the
most successful and bloody actions of the entire campaign
occurred. Puller's First Battalion stumbled upon the Japanese Fourth Regiment taking cover in a ravine. What followed next was almost like a comic opera but with far
deadlier results. Puller called down artillery fire into the
ravine. The Japanese swarmed out of the open end of the
ravine directly into the sights of Marine rifles and machine
guns. The Japanese ran back and sought refuge in the ravine. More artillery fire drove them quickly out once
more. The action continued until the Marines began to
run low on ammunition. With this, Puller called his troops
off and withdrew, leaving over seven hundred dead Japanese behind.

Meanwhile, the other attackers managed to trap a small
detachment of the enemy between them near the mouth of
the Matanikau. The Japanese attempted to flee eastward.
Sixty of them perished in hand-to-hand fighting with the
Raiders. Others died trying to cross the river.

Unfortunately, even though the operation was a success
the Marines were forced to abandon some of the hard-
earned territory. Vandergrift's intelligence people estimated it was just a matter of time before another strong
Japanese effort to take Henderson Field. For weeks the Tokyo Express had been landing men and supplies on the
island. There could only be one reason for the buildup:
another major offensive. But Vandergrift was not about to

concede all of the captured territory. For too many weeks the Marines had been confined to the perimeter on Lunga Point while Vandergrift waited for the opportunity to extend his lines. Now, with his command reinforced by the Seventh Marines and the leading elements of the Army's Americal division on their way up from the South Pacific, the Marines pulled back only as far as the east bank of the Matanikau. There a strong defensive line was formed. Lack of adequate manpower prevented the line from being anchored to the Lunga line. However, the Matanikau perimeter was linked to Lunga by a series of outposts.

The action was indeed heating up. The next few weeks would make the difference between victory and defeat. Both sides continued to pour in reinforcements. General Hyakutake himself arrived on Guadalcanal to take personal command. Imperial Headquarters fed a steady stream of reinforcements to staging areas at Rabaul and the Shortlands. From there they were ferried down the Slot by the Tokyo Express.

One of the formations dispatched to Guadalcanal was the vaunted Sendai division, veterans of campaigns in China, Manchuria and Java. Hyakutake gave the Sendai's commander, General Maruyama, responsibility for coordination of the offensive and the recapture of Henderson Field. Maruyama was a haughty man who was openly contemptuous of his predecessor's failure.

Maruyama arrived on Guadalcanal radiating confidence. His battle plan called for another dual attack. A force under Major General Sumuyoshi was to attack across the mouth of the Matanikau in conjunction with an assault against that line from the south by another force under Colonel Oka. The latter was to cross the river upstream and coordinate his efforts with Sumuyoshi. At the same time, Maruyama's main body consisting of the bulk of the Sendai division and another force under the hapless Kawaguchi would attack the Marine positions south of Henderson Field near Bloody Ridge. To accomplish this the Sendai would have to make a forced march through the jungle but Maruyama did not consider this a problem for his superbly trained troops. The general ordered his advance formations to hack out a trail through the undergrowth and called it the Maruyama Trail. Thus Maruyama was determined to repeat two mistakes of his predecessors from the start, i.e., a long, forced march through the jungle by a large body of troops, and reliance on a complicated plan of battle requiring precise timing and coordination. A third mistake was destined to be repeated during the battle itself.

Never in his wildest imagination did Maruyama anticipate the difficulties of moving so many troops through thirty-five miles of thick, tangled jungle. Pelted daily by heavy rains the Japanese formation struggled along the slippery trail. The muddy track was soon littered with shells, heavy machine guns, mortars and other heavy equipment discarded by the exhausted troops. Almost all of the artillery was abandoned and left to rust since moving them overland proved far too difficult, even for the Sendai. Maruyama soon found himself behind schedule. Originally, he intended to attack on the night of October 23 in concert with Oka's and Sumuyoshi's attack at Matanikau. But the Sendai were strung out for miles along the trail and as the time for the scheduled attack rolled around, the Japanese troops were still five miles short of their objective. Accordingly, Maruyama radioed headquarters announcing his intention to postpone the attack but the word was never passed to Sumuyoshi.

Just after dark on the twenty-third, Sumuyoshi's troops began massing for the attack. Just then American artillery and mortars opened up on the assembly area on the west bank of the river. Sumuyoshi's troops were blasted. Nine Japanese tanks moved out of the jungle and attempted to cross a sandbar. Only one made it. Eight of the tanks were destroyed by artillery fire immediately. The surviving tank managed to reach the Marine lines before it was finished off from the rear. Then the artillery opened up on the assembly area once again. It was a massacre. Morning revealed 650 dead Japanese troops in front of the American lines.

By the evening of the twenty-fifth Maruyama's troops were in position south of Henderson Field. The Marine line was a few yards east of Bloody Ridge. Chesty Puller's men waited in the rain for the attack they knew was coming. On the Marines' left was a battalion of the 164th Infantry that had just arrived on the island and was immediately rushed into the line.

The torrential downpour ceased for a few hours and allowed Maruyama time to organize the attack. At 2300, just as the attack was ready to jump off, the rains came again. Nevertheless, a few thousand troops swarmed out of the jungle shouting "Banzai" and "Marine, you die," so many that "the sodden ground shook beneath their feet."[7]

The first wave got hung up on the barbed wire as the Marines poured machine gun, rifle, mortar, artillery and canister fire into the advancing ranks. One enemy company opened a gap in the Marine line and broke through. The Japanese horde swarmed toward this gap but Puller's men slammed it shut in their face. Marine machine gunners fired so many rounds that the cooling water in their jackets evaporated. Marines urinated in the jackets to replace the liquid and kept on firing. The slaughter was horrible and the enemy filtered back to their lines.

At 0130 they attacked again. The slopes of the ridge were slick from the rain and the blood of dead Japanese troops but the attackers came on. Holes were punched in the Marine lines and General Geiger, filling in for the absent Vandergrift, committed his reserve and restored the line. The Sendai withdrew into the jungle only to come once more at 0330. This time the 164th Infantry swung into action. Company after company of Japanese were cut down by automatic rifle fire. Artillery shells slammed into the advancing wave. By 0700 it was all over. Over a thousand of Maruyama's crack troops lay dead in front of the Marine lines. But the battle was not over by a longshot.

During the day Japanese planes attacked the Marine positions. Many of them were destroyed by the Cactus Air Force but the air raid hampered Puller's efforts to bring supplies forward. Nevertheless, Geiger did manage to send another battalion of the 164th Infantry into line. At the same time, Puller shortened his line for he knew full well that the Japanese would return.

Late that night Puller's predictions were borne out. The remaining troops of Maruyama's command surged out of the jungle screaming obscenities. Artillery and mortar fire blasted the attackers before they even reached the line. Each charge met with a bloody repulse thanks to the deadly fire of the Americans, particularly that of the 164th Infantry the troops of which at long last were given the opportunity to prove their mettle in action. Maruyama continued to order troops forward into the hail of death. Eventually, the attacks petered out through sheer lack of manpower. By morning Maruyama's attack was smashed. According to Jack Coggins, "The Sendai division was

148

wrecked, with half its officers killed or wounded."[8]

Twenty-five hundred of Japan's finest troops lay dead on the battlefield. Some survivors retreated back along the Maruyama Trail. Others, their spirit broken, made their way east towards Taivu Point. During the retreat many of the wounded perished, bringing the death toll to well over three thousand.

While the Sendai were battering themselves against the American line south of Henderson Field, Colonel Oka finally launched his attack against the southern part of the Matanikau position. This attack should have been made in concert with Sumuyoshi's effort on the twenty-third but just as was true during Kawaguchi's ill-fated offensive, Oka was unable to move his troops into position in time. They came swarming out of the jungle at 2130 and drove the Americans back. There was bitter hand-to-hand fighting as defender wrestled with attacker. Eventually, the Japanese wave receded only to regroup. At 0300 Oka sent another wave against the Marines. Japanese troops occupied abandoned foxholes and turned their guns on the Marines' flank. Marines went along the ridge eliminating each one of these positions with grenades and rifle fire. Around dawn the Japanese began to withdraw. The Marines counterattacked and drove the remnants of Oka's force back into the jungle. The battle was over. Another 650 Japanese had died. Maruyama threw in the towel and ordered all units to disengage.

The one-month period from October 15 to November 15 marked the turning point of the struggle for Guadalcanal. On October 16 Admiral Nimitz decided that Ghormley's defeatist attitude was detrimental to the campaign. Ghormley had been overly cautious and unwilling to risk ships to supply and reinforce Vandergrift's beleaguered troops. He was relieved from his command and replaced by an aggressive fighter, Adm. William "Bull" Halsey.*

Halsey immediately summoned Vandergrift to Noumea so that he might gain first-hand knowledge of what was needed to achieve final victory. The meeting took place during the height of Maruyama's attack. When apprised of Vandergrift's needs, Halsey replied that he would commit everything at his disposal to the campaign on Guadalcanal. But the admiral lacked carriers.

While the battle for the airstrip was in full sway, another of the major naval battles for Guadalcanal took place. On October 25 and 26 during the Battle of Santa Cruz the Navy lost the carrier *Hornet* while the *Enterprise* was badly damaged necessitating extensive repairs. The Japanese cost was damage to two carriers.

Despite the heavy toll of Santa Cruz, the initiative on Guadalcanal appeared to have swung over to the Americans. Vandergrift was anxious to follow up his success and catch the enemy off balance by taking the offensive. On the thirty-first, engineers constructed a bridge across the Matanikau. The next morning Marines and soldiers crossed the river and headed for Point Cruz. At the same time, the 7th Marines and 164th Infantry moved eastward from Lunga towards Koli Point. By November 2, the attackers were dug in along the Nalimbiu River. It took four days' worth of bitter fighting but on the seventh, Koli Point was cleared by the GIs.

The attack in the west was even more successful. Vandergrift's men beat off a heavy enemy attack on the fourth and pushed the Japanese out of Point Cruz. The advance continued against little opposition. On the tenth the 2nd

*See *The Great Admirals of World War II, Vol I: The Americans.*

Marines and 164th Infantry launched an attack toward Kokumbona from Point Cruz. Vandergrift called this attack off the next day when reports were received that the enemy was preparing still another attack against the Lunga perimeter.

On the sixth, the Second Raider Battalion under Col. Evans Carlson made a landing east of Taivu Point and started overland. The Raiders made an epic month-long march through the jungle encountering scattered enemy units retreating toward Mt. Austen. They also managed to destroy a handful of Japanese supply dumps. By the time Carlson's men entered the Lunga perimeter on December 4, they had killed over 450 of the enemy at a cost to themselves of 16 dead and 18 wounded.

Reinforcements for both sides continued to pour into the island. Between the second and eleventh of November, thirty-five hundred men of the Japanese Thirty-eighth Division were safely landed by the Tokyo Express. On the fourth, the Eighth Marines arrived to reinforce Vandergrift. On the twelfth, over six thousand men of Gen. Alexander Patch's Americal division and most of their equipment were safely brought ashore at Lunga Point.

The Japanese were pulling out all the stops. Their plan called for a fleet of cruisers and battleships to sail into Ironbottom Sound and bombard the American positions prior to another major ground attack. A similar force, escorting eleven transports crammed with troops, was to link up with the first force and repeat the bombardment the following night. The ensuing twin battles, occurring on two separate nights between November 12 and 14, marked the turning point in the naval phase of the battle for Guadalcanal.

The First and Second Naval Battles of Guadalcanal cost the Japanese two battleships, three destroyers and extensive damage to a number of cruisers and destroyers. In addition, Henderson's pilots sunk seven of the eleven Japanese transports. Those troops that did manage to land safely lacked weapons. Furthermore, all of their supplies and equipment had been lost at sea. This action broke the back of the proposed Japanese land attack.

The Americans paid dearly for their victory at sea with two cruisers, seven destroyers and the lives of Admirals Callaghan and Scott. But after that, the Japanese navy never again sailed into Ironbottom Sound at will to bombard American positions.

A few days after the naval battle Halsey made a visit to the island. He could readily see that the Marines were in a bad way. Disease had taken a heavier toll than the enemy. Virtually seventy-five percent of the troops suffered from either malaria or another disease. They all suffered from exhaustion. Perhaps the most exhausted of all was Vandergrift. Halsey decided right then that the First Marine Division would have to be replaced by fresh troops lest the stalemate continue.

Halsey told Gen. Alexander Patch, commander of the Americal division, to plan on assuming command of all troops on Guadalcanal as soon as it was feasible.* The admiral promised Patch fresh troops. The Second Marine Division was ordered to Guadalcanal as was Gen. J. Lawton Collins' Twenty-fifth Division which was en route to Hawaii.

In the interim the Tokyo Express continued to run. By now the dominance of American air power made these supply runs precarious at best. The only time Japanese ships could safely approach the island was under cover of darkness. By daylight they had to be far back up the Slot.

*See *The Great Commanders of World War II, Vol. III: The Americans.*

This precluded the use of slow-moving transports. Tanaka seized upon the idea of utilizing high-speed destroyers to drop drums of supplies offshore of the Japanese positions. The troops could then swim out and retrieve the drums. Once the loads were dumped overboard, the destroyers could high-tail it back to the Shortlands. Although the concept rated merit, the strong currents around Guadalcanal prevented many of the drums from being retrieved.

The wily admiral also had one more deadly surprise in store for American naval forces. On the night of November 30, during one of the supply runs, Tanaka's destroyermen ambushed an American force under Adm. Carleton Wright. At the Battle of Tassafaronga, Wright lost the cruiser *Northampton*. Three other cruisers were heavily damaged by torpedoes. Tanaka lost one destroyer (Map 10).

On December ninth, Patch officially relieved Vandergrift. The Marine general had truly earned the high honor bestowed upon him, the Congressional Medal of Honor. For four months he had brilliantly led his men in action. Abandoned by the Navy, without prospect of resupply or reinforcement, Vandergrift's First Marine Division clung precariously to Guadalcanal. The Marines beat back every effort by some of Japan's finest shock troops while enduring almost daily attack by enemy aircraft and nightly attack from Japanese warships. "Red Mike" Edson and two enlisted men also earned the Medal of Honor.

Throughout the month of December a steady flow of fresh troops arrived on Guadalcanal. These troops began to relieve the men of the first Marine Division. The Marines came trudging back from the front lines with weary, sunken, bloodshot eyes, and hollowed cheeks, ravaged by disease. They rested in the rear until late in the month. Then the gallant First Marine Division boarded trans-

THE NAVAL BATTLES FOR GUADALCANAL

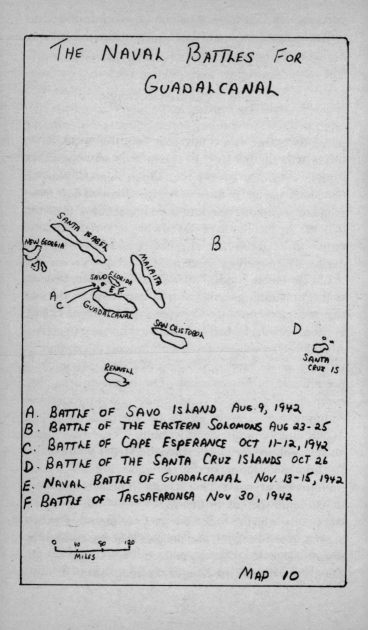

A. BATTLE OF SAVO ISLAND AUG. 9, 1942
B. BATTLE OF THE EASTERN SOLOMONS AUG 23-25
C. BATTLE OF CAPE ESPERANCE OCT 11-12, 1942
D. BATTLE OF THE SANTA CRUZ ISLANDS OCT 26
E. NAVAL BATTLE OF GUADALCANAL Nov. 13-15, 1942
F. BATTLE OF TASSAFARONGA Nov 30, 1942

MAP 10

ports and left Guadalcanal behind for good. In the cemetery at Lunga Point one of them had scrawled this epitaph:

> And when he gets to Heaven
> To St. Peter he will tell
> One more Marine reporting sir
> I've served my time in hell.[9]

There were now, besides Vandergrift's spent force, three fresh divisions on the island: the Americal, the Twenty-fifth Army and the Second Marine. A corps headquarters, the XIV, was established with Patch as commander. Patch began making plans for an all-out offensive in January designed to throw out the Japanese once and for all. In the meantime he launched a small-scale attack against Japanese-held positions on Mt. Austen.

On December 12, General Collins preceded his division to the island and was immediately impressed by the tall, thin general whom he considered full of nervous energy and drive. He later recalled:

> As we entered his underground C.P., located in direct prolongation of the runway of Henderson Field, an air-raid alert sounded. Sandy said, "Don't let that disturb you. Happens all the time," and nonchalantly proceeded with his briefing.[10]

Halsey's orders to Patch were simple and to the point. Eliminate all Japanese forces!

Mt. Austen was the highest point in the low mountain range at the center of the island. Defenders of the mountain could observe all movement on the island and report it to their own headquarters. The Japanese recognized the vital importance of this position relatively early in the game and had built a strong defensive system of fortified bunkers on the slopes. Elimination of this strong point was Patch's first objective.

On December 16 Patch ordered the 132nd Infantry regiment to capture the Japanese positions on Mt. Austen. The following morning the 132nd began to ascend the slopes of the mountain. Hampered by the jungle terrain and stiff Japanese resistance, they were shortly stopped by a withering fire from the main enemy strong point known as Gifu. The Japanese were experts in the construction of defensive positions and the ones on Mt. Austen were a tribute to their ability. Log-covered bunkers were constructed with dug-in supporting machine gun positions. The entire system was honeycombed with trenches through which the enemy communicated with and reinforced his outposts. The positions were impervious to all but a direct hit with heavy artillery. The Americans attacked Gifu without letup for two weeks. At the end of that time the Japanese positions remained intact and the 132nd had to pause and regroup, having suffered a high rate of casualties.

Meanwhile, on January 1, the Japanese High Command finally yielded to the pleas of their army and naval commanders in the Solomons and agreed to evacuate Gaudalcanal and withdraw up the Slot to New Georgia. Their decision was hastened by the fact that their Twenty-eighth Division had been virtually wiped out when American aircraft intercepted the convoy carrying the division to Guadalcanal and sent most of the transports to the bottom. However, the Japanese High Command elected not to inform their forces on Guadalcanal of the decision until the last possible moment, a few weeks hence. In the interim the defenders of Guadalcanal would fight on, feeling that they were there to stay. Reinforcements would still be fed in until the evacuation was ready to proceed.

On the same day that the Japanese were debating the fate of their garrison on Guadalcanal, the Americans renewed their efforts to take Mt. Austen. This latest effort made some initial headway but the tenacious Japanese defense made it obvious that a quick victory was beyond the ability of the attackers.

The planned offensive for the rest of the island called for the assaulting units to break out of the defensive perimeter around Henderson Field in a two-pronged drive toward the center of the island and toward Cape Esperance at the northern end. There could be no broad front since the jungle terrain prohibited that type of assault. The attackers would be required to move forward in single columns and outflank and cut off enemy pockets of resistance.

Patch's offensive began promptly on January 10 after an intense artillery barrage. Immediately after the last gun ceased firing the attack jumped off. Progress was slow and measured in yards as the Americans were forced to hack their way through the heavy jungle growth. The columns were required to halt frequently to deal with enemy rear guard holding up the advance.

Some of the initial objectives fell quickly but the skilled and determined Japanese resisted every step. Each day's attack was preceded by the usual deadly artillery barrage. Then the assault moved forward. The enemy was encountered everywhere along the jungle tracks and gains were measured in terms of yards instead of miles.

On the fourteenth the Tokyo Express landed six hundred reinforcements at Cape Esperance bolstering the Japanese belief that the island was to be held at all cost. The Americans were forced to fight for each yard. Nevertheless, steady progress was made. After over a week of repeated attacks, however, Patch was forced to sanction a pause to regroup. Meanwhile, the defenders of Mt. Austen continued to cling tenaciously to their positions.

After moving fresh troops to the front Patch ordered the attack to go forward on the twenty-second. At the same time Collins' troops noticed a weakening of the enemy defense on Mt. Austen. A daily artillery and aerial pounding was beginning to take its toll.

Five days before Patch renewed the offensive the Japanese formally received word of the intended evacuation. By that time the Imperial troops were half starved, disease-ridden and exhausted from the constant American attacks on land and in the air.

On January 23, relentless American pressure finally yielded results. A large pocket of Japanese was surrounded by American troops driving through the jungle. The pocket was systematically eliminated by rifle and artillery fire. All but a few of the enemy force were destroyed. That same day the last defenders of Mount Austen perished as Collins' troops overran their positions. Since the Japanese rarely surrendered, the Americans had to kill each enemy soldier before declaring the position secure.

Now the drive for Cape Esperance gathered steam. But the Tokyo Express continued to make his presence felt. As the bulk of the Japanese fell back to the cape their rear guards continued to impede the American advance and progress remained slow. The Americans were unaware of the Japanese decision to evacuate Guadalcanal and the enemy took advantage of this. Therefore, there was little slackening in the ferocity of the defense. In the meantime, another chapter in the naval battle for Guadalcanal was written.

Unaware that the enemy had written off Guadalcanal, the Americans continued to reinforce the island. Convoys reaching the area had to be protected from Japanese attacks and naturally required the presence of escorting warships. During the unloading of one of these convoys the veteran of the Battle of Savo, the U.S.S. *Chicago,* was sunk by Japanese aircraft shortly after the Battle of Rennell Island. The attackers had intended to attack the supply convoy but were diverted by the presence of the *Chicago* and decided to attack that hapless vessel.

As Patch's forces approached the coast, the Tokyo Express began to evacuate the Japanese forces. On the first of February three thousand survivors of General Sano's Thirty-eighth Division, once over eight thousand strong, boarded transports and left Guadalcanal behind. Two nights later it was the turn of the remnants of the once-powerful Sendai division, their ranks now decimated. The Sendai would never again be a significant force in battle. Finally, on the night of February 7, the three-thousand man rear guard, having successfully held off all American attacks, boarded ship and sailed away.

After linking up on the fourth, the two American columns drove for the coast but, unaware of Japanese intentions, proceeded with caution. There had been too many ambushes, too many enemy soldiers lurking behind each tree and fallen log. It was folly to drive headlong against an enemy skilled in defensive use of the jungle and who preferred death to surrender. Patch knew that eventually American superiority would prevail and was therefore unwilling to accept a high butcher's bill. In addition, neither he nor the American naval commanders had any idea that the Japanese intended to abandon the island particularly since that concept was in direct conflict with previous

Japanese strategy.

Although small pockets of abandoned Japanese troops required mopping up, by the middle of February all organized resistance on Guadalcanal had ceased. On the eighth of that month Patch sent the following message to Halsey:

Organized resistance on Guadalcanal has ceased.[11]

Halsey replied:

When I sent a patch to act as tailor for Guadalcanal,
I did not expect him to remove the enemy's pants
and sew it on so quickly. Thanks and congratulations.[12]

Japanese losses on Guadalcanal exceeded twenty-five thousand. Countless more perished en route. Five thousand American Marines, soldiers and sailors died fighting for the small piece of steaming jungle. Another sixteen thousand were wounded or laid low by disease during the bitter six-month struggle. It was a costly but significant victory.

On the positive side, the myth of Japanese invincibility was shattered forever. Even more vital, invaluable jungle fighting experience was gained.

More importantly, Guadalcanal became the springboard from which the campaign against the rest of the Solomons was launched. The Americans turned it into a forward staging area for the conquest of places like New Georgia and Bougainville. Eventually, as the Americans climbed the Solomons chain, Rabaul itself was isolated and abandoned as a naval base by the Japanese. Throughout the campaign Henderson Field was an unsinkable aircraft carrier providing aerial cover for the troops and from

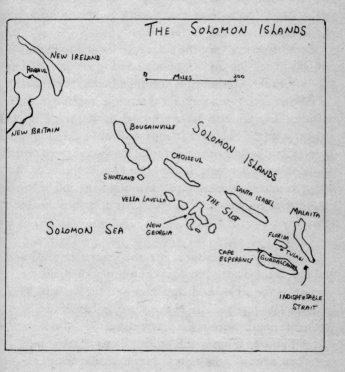

which bombing attacks against Japanese strongpoints were launched. To protect Rabaul the Japanese were forced to strip forces from other theaters thereby allowing the Allied juggernaut to continued unchecked (Map 11).

In those six months of conflict American Marines, sailors and GIs had written a glorious chapter in the annals of American arms. One Japanese general felt that the Japanese army had "bled to death in the jungles of Guadalcanal." He was correct.

Guadalcanal is now the site of the capital of the Solomon Islands. The city of Honiara housing the government sits where the Marine base at Lunga Point sat some ten-odd years ago. Henderson Field is now a bustling modern airport. The Japanese have returned. Under trade agreements with the Solomon Islands government, the former enemy has cut down many of the hardwood trees of the previously thick jungle. Lacking the cover afforded by the treetop foliage, the swamps have dried up and in their place are farmland. Graham Kent has described the scene this way:

> In remote villages there are still reminders of the war; most village schools have an empty shell case for use as the school bell, Japanese swords are used as digging implements; helmets make bowls. Some names remain from the war years . . . Red Beach, Ironbottom Sound, and others; they are reminders of the time when a remote South Pacific Island became a bloody center of a war.[13]

Chapter Four

Tarawa and Makin

On July 20, 1943, the Joint Chiefs of Staff directed Admiral Nimitz to begin making plans for the capture of the Gilbert Islands. The operation was given the code name, Galvanic. The primary purpose of Galvanic was to provide the Americans with bases for the forthcoming and more difficult operation against the Marshalls as well as ensuring the safety of Samoa and the communication line between Hawaii and the South and Southwest Pacific.

The commander of the Fifth Amphibious Corps (VAC) for the Gilbert Operation, Maj. Gen. Holland Smith, stated in his postwar book, *Coral and Brass*, that "Tarawa was a mistake!"[1] But was it?

Over one thousand Americans died there and more than two thousand were wounded during the capture of an island no larger than New York City's Central Park. Opinion still varies but these authors agree with those who feel that the capture of Tarawa was indeed a necessity. The official Army history states:

In the minds of most American military planners and strategists the cost of the capture of the Gilberts was justified both in the terms of the strategic gains realized and the tactical lessons learned.[2]

With the exception of geography enthusiasts, very few people had even heard of Tarawa before November, 1943. What made Tarawa so important was its strategic location. Lying southwest of Pearl Harbor and northeast of New Zealand and Australia, it is directly astride the important lifeline between Hawaii and Australia. As part of the Gilbert Islands, Tarawa Atoll was the main headquarters of the Japanese garrison in addition to being the site of the principal airfield in the island group.

Why Tarawa was selected as a target by the Americans rates examination. In March, 1943, the Joint Chiefs of Staff held a Pacific military conference to deal with strategy in that theater. As in so many prior conferences, differences in strategy between Admiral King and General MacArthur occurred. King was thinking of moving naval forces from Hawaii and the United States across the central Pacific. This plan had been discussed in prewar naval conferences. MacArthur, with a return to the Philippines foremost in his mind, championed the capture of New Guinea and the reduction of the Japanese base at Rabaul, to be followed by a movement northwestward toward the ultimate goal of the Philippine Islands. No definitive plan for a central Pacific operation was agreed upon at the conference but the ground had been broken.

At the Trident Conference two months later in May, King proposed that one of the major objectives of the conference be the development of a master plan for the conduct of the war. On the twenty-first of that month, after tedious days of discussing European strategy, the admiral finally got his chance to review his Pacific strategy. During this session he emphasized the importance of the central Pacific as a potential avenue of approach to Japan.

Although greatly impressed by King's presentation, the British, fearing a dilution of the effort in Europe, refused to allow the admiral carte blanche in the Pacific. Nevertheless, the possibility of a central Pacific drive moved closer to eventual acceptance. As a result, King was confident enough to begin organizing the forces for the offensive.

At the Quadrant Conference that August, King was given approval by the Combined Chiefs for the seizure of the Gilberts, Marshalls and the Marianas. The central Pacific drive was accepted. The first target would be the Gilberts.

Initially, the first objective of the central Pacific drive was to have been the Marshall Islands. In the belief, however, that these islands bristled with defenses and because the Japanese naval base at Truk (believed to be a bastion) was closer to the Marshalls thereby posing a distinct threat, it was proposed that the Gilberts be seized first. The latter appeared to be an easier target and their possession would be of great value to the central Pacific drive.

Under the overall command of the commander-in-chief of the Pacific Fleet, Admiral Nimitz, Operation Galvanic would be directly commanded by Vice Adm. Raymond Spruance whose forces were given the designation, Fifth Fleet. Though considered a "battleship admiral," Spruance's stand-in role at Midway proved without doubt that he was capable of commanding carriers. In addition, Spruance was considered one of the finest thinkers in the Navy. In fact, since Midway, he had been Nimitz's chief of staff. Though he possessed a reserved personality, Spruance was highly respected and would prove repeatedly to be an excellent choice despite the inevitable critics.

For amphibious commander, Spruance requested Rear Adm. Richmond Kelly Turner. Turner had already earned a reputation as an aggressive and hard taskmaster. The amphibious commander had little trouble living up to his nickname, "Terrible Turner." His competence, however, could not be doubted and his role during the Guadalcanal and Central Solomons campaigns bore this out.

For Corps commander, Spruance needed an officer who was an expert on amphibious assaults. Accordingly, he chose Marine Maj. Gen. Holland M. Smith. Nicknamed "Howling Mad" Smith, the Marine general, like Admiral Turner, had a well deserved reputation for gruffness and aggressiveness. Though he had yet to be directly involved in any campaign, Smith had trained both Army and Marine forces in the tactics and techniques of amphibious assaults. Despite his quick temper, Smith's ability was not doubted. The major flaw in his personality was his partisanship for the Marine Corps. That partisanship would later raise ruffles during the Gilberts operation and reach an explosive climax during the Marianas Campaign in the summer of 1944.

Two divisions were selected for Operation Galvanic: the Second Marine Division commanded by Maj. Gen. Julian Smith and the Army's Twenty-seventh Infantry Division, a former New York National Guard unit commanded by Maj. Gen. Ralph Smith. Thus the three leading troop commanders were all named Smith. The Marine division had already bloodied themselves at

Guadalcanal but the Twenty-seventh Division had yet to see combat.

The two targets chosen for the operation were Tarawa and Nauru. During the planning stages for Galvanic, however, Holland Smith and Turner approached Spruance with a proposal to substitute one of the targets for another. The original target, Nauru, they said, should be substituted with Makin. There were a number of logical reasons they used to support their case. Nauru and Tarawa were a distance apart thereby requiring a division of the allotted naval forces who would be required to support separate operations 380 miles apart. Makin, on the other hand, was closer to Tarawa and would allow the fleet to support both operations simultaneously (Map 12).

In addition, Nauru was believed to be heavily defended thus requiring the employment of more troops than Makin. Furthermore, Nauru was devoid of good beaches and did not have an airfield or a lagoon to accommodate large ships. Spruance noted:

Nauru was not needed by us, and we could keep it pounded down. On the other hand, Makin was one hundred miles closer to the Marshalls where we were going and it tied in well from the point of view of fleet coverage with an operation against Tarawa. . . . Makin was an entirely suitable objective, and its capture was well within our capabilities.[3]

Nimitz agreed with the proposal and presented the arguments to King who also gave his consent to the substitution of Makin for Nauru. Apamama was also added

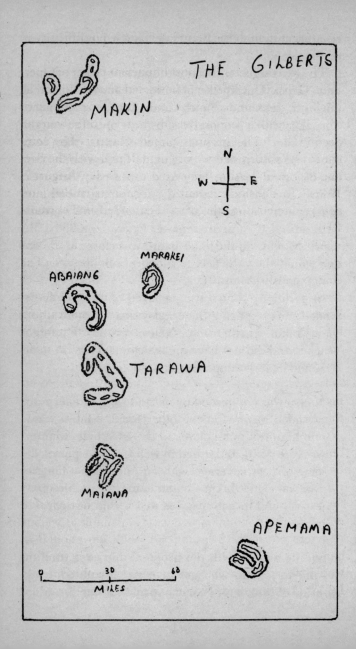

as a target though the planners foresaw no difficulty in taking the atoll.

Tarawa was by far the most important target of Operation Galvanic. Little Betio possessed an airfield and all intelligence estimates pointed to a large Japanese garrison. The task of seizing Betio was given to the veteran Second Marines. This division had proven itself in combat in the steamy jungles of Guadalcanal with the Second Regiment having landed there on D-day, August 7, 1942. The division's remaining regiments landed later and remained until the campaign ended in February, 1943.

After leaving Guadalcanal, the division went to New Zealand for a period of rest and rehabilitation. The change of climate was welcome to the Marines since many of them suffered from scores of jungle ailments. While revitalizing itself, the division also began training for its next objective whatever and wherever that might be. The training consisted of numerous types of maneuvers, chief of which was the amphibious assault.

In August, 1943, Julian Smith and his operations officer, Lt. Col. David Shoup, received the official word that Betio Island on Tarawa Atoll would be the next target. The Marine officers quickly realized that amphibious tactics would have to be honed to a fine edge if the assault was to be successful. Shoup, seeing that the islet was surrounded by reefs, immediately put in a request for amphibious boats capable of traversing the reefs. He was informed that none were readily available as yet but that some were forthcoming, although not enough to handle all the assault waves. Consequently, training would have to be in the non-tractored assault craft, the LCVP (Landing Craft, Vehicle and Personnel).

Betio is a flat island, its highest point a mere ten feet above sea level. Approximately two-and-a-half miles long and six hundred yards across at its widest point, it had been likened to a bird because of its distinct shape. Intelligence reports indicated that it was bristling with defenses (Map 13).

The first problem facing Julian Smith's troops was the traversing of the reef. Amphibious tractors (LVT or Amtracs) could solve this problem. As already indicated, however, these were in short supply and only enough to handle the first waves would be available. The followup waves of attackers would have to rely on LCVPs. These boats drew about three-and-a-half feet of water. Thus a primary concern was, would the water on D-day be more than three-and-a-half feet deep?

Optimistically the American planners accepted the estimate that there would be at least five feet of water above the reefs. Nevertheless, there was always the possibility of a low tide no more than two feet high. There was also the remote possibility of a "dodging tide," a tide with an eccentric course that could not be predicted. The planners tended to discount the latter and believed that there would be sufficient water depth on D-day, scheduled for November 20. One New Zealander, Major Holland, however, said that there was a danger that the invasion tide might experience a neap period characterized by irregular flows. There might be, he stated, only three feet of water.

Based on available information, therefore, Julian Smith felt that there was a fifty-fifty chance that the landing craft would be able to traverse the reefs and prepared his troops for the worst eventuality.

On October 2, Julian Smith and his staff flew to Pearl

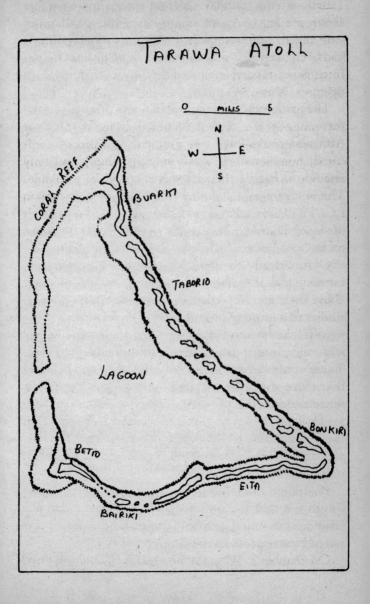

Harbor to present their plans for the capture of Betio. Hydrographic and reef conditions, they pointed out, determined where on Betio the assault troops would land. The reef on the ocean side lies six hundred yards from the island and is subjected to heavy swells from the open sea. Aerial reconnaissance showed Betio's defenses to be heaviest on the ocean shore. For these reasons it was proposed to assault Betio from the lagoon side.

While presenting his plans, Julian Smith was handed unwelcome news. He wanted to secure a small island adjacent to Betio so that artillery could be situated there to support the main landing. But Holland Smith stated that this plan would have to be scrapped since transports for a secondary landing could not be spared. Furthermore, speed of conquest was considered a vital necessity. American intelligence estimates anticipated a strong Japanese reaction by air and from under the sea. Thus Betio had to be taken quickly. No time could be spared for secondary assaults.

Julian Smith was disappointed with the news but he was even more appalled when told that one of his regiments would be held in reserve to be used either at Makin or Tarawa, depending on need. The Second Marine commander stated:

> Not only would the Betio assault be made without preliminary artillery support, but it would be made by only two regimental combat teams.[4]

Preliminary intelligence reports indicated that there was over four thousand Japanese at Tarawa in well dug positions. The thought of losing the services of the extra regiment was not very appealing.

For Galvanic, Admiral Spruance's forces were divided into a Northern Attack Force under Rear Admiral Turner and a Southern Attack Force under Rear Adm. Harry Hill. Turner led the Northern Attack Force at Makin because he believed that its proximity to the Marshalls and Truk placed it at the more threatened point.

Makin Atoll's shape is similar to that of Tarawa. The large island of Butaritari was the target of the 165th Regimental Combat Team of the 27th Infantry Division. The planners estimated that some five hundred to eight hundred Japanese inhabited this six-mile-long strip of coral and sand. The planners did not feel that the reef around the island would present the troops with too much difficulty.

Basically, very little was known about the Gilberts. Though they had been a prewar British possession, existing information regarding tides and water levels were for the most part inaccurate. Precise data was needed before committing men to fight. Through aerial photographs, submarine reconnaissance and the interrogation of former residents, the planners went about their task.

Countless photographs were taken of the islands during bombing raids on September 17 and 18, as well as later on in the month and during October. The bulk of the information on the Japanese defenses were gleaned from these photographs. According to Henry Shaw, Jr.:

The aerial camera had its limitations, however, and the combination of vertical and oblique shots answered only some of the many questions that plagued the planners.[5]

Additional information was garnered by the submarine *Nautilus*. For almost three weeks during September the submarine studied tides and currents at the three objectives. It also photographed the targets which, from its vantage point, gave a reasonably good series of panoramic views. Pearl Harbor received this information on October 7.

Meanwhile, a group of sixteen former residents of the Gilberts were brought to Pearl Harbor in order to share their knowledge of the atolls with Admiral Turner's planners. Those familiar with Tarawa were sent to Wellington, New Zealand to confer with the Second Marine Division Staff. The question that continued to haunt the planners of course was the all-important height of the tides across the reefs. Opinion on that point continued to vary. If the tides were too low for the landing boats and they got hung up on the reefs it could spell disaster for the invading troops.

The reef at Betio was anywhere from six hundred to eleven hundred yards from shore. On the north shore there was a long pier stretching all the way to the edge of the reef. It was this point that the planners concentrated their amphibious plans upon. The western and southern beaches were too exposed to heavy swells and irregular currents making logistical support a nightmare. The northern shore, however, would have the atoll's lagoon as a shield for the ships which, logistically speaking, was necessary to facilitate the landing.

The atoll itself measured twenty-two miles long and was shaped like a triangle. Betio was the atoll's westernmost island on its southern end. The entrance to the lagoon lay three-and-a-half miles north of Betio (Map 14).

While the planners were putting the finishing touches on their plans, the assault continued to rehearse. The

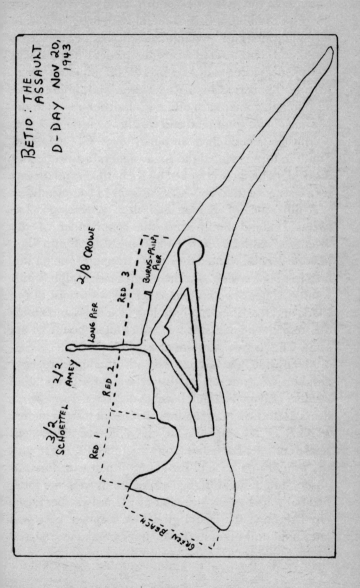

BETIO: THE ASSAULT
D-DAY Nov 20, 1943

2/8 CROWE

3/2 SCHOETTEL

2/2 AMEY

LONG PIER

BURNS-PHILIP PIER

RED 1

RED 2

RED 3

GREEN BEACH

training of the Twenty-seventh Infantry Division was the responsibility of both General Richardson's* Army Headquarters and Holland Smith's VAC. The Army command concentrated on ground tactics while the Marine trainers focused their efforts on amphibious tactics. During this period both Richardson and Smith managed to antagonize each other. Richardson resented the Marine Corps command and rankled over the fact that a Marine general had authority over GIs. Holland Smith in turn resented the Army general's attitude and disliked his being overlooked by Richardson and the latter's insistence that the VAC be dissolved completely.

A difference of opinion had already developed between Holland Smith and the commander of the Twenty-seventh Division, Maj. Gen. Ralph Smith. The Marine general wanted the assault troops to land on Butaritari's lagoon side. On the other hand, Ralph Smith wanted to land two battalions on the west coast of the island and send the other battalion near the island's middle from the lagoon side two hours after the initial assault. The Army's plan was accepted.

Meanwhile, the Twenty-seventh attempted to hold amphibious exercises in the Hawaiian Islands. Bad weather and poor assault beaches detracted from the rehearsals throwing into doubt the value of these sessions.

What of the Japanese in the Gilberts? They had seized control of the islands on December 10, 1941, with the primary purpose of providing Japan with forward observation posts. Originally the islands were not fortified but were instead garrisoned by Coastwatchers scattered through the island group. A seaplane base was later built on Makin from which reconnaissance planes

*Commander-in-chief of Army forces in the Central Pacific.

could scan the vast ocean spaces.

On August 17, 1942, 221 Marines landed on Butari-tari Islands from two American submarines. Led by the indomitable Col. Evans Carlson, the Marines exposed to the Japanese the vulnerability of the Gilberts. Unless they were reinforced immediately, they could easily be captured by the Americans. Almost immediately the Japanese began to dispatch reinforcements to the Gilberts and began to fortify the atolls.

By the end of 1942 the Japanese realized the importance of the Gilberts. If the Empire were going to be held, it must be held from the Gilberts. They designed an ingenious trap. If the Americans attempted to recapture the Gilberts, they would find themselves pinned down by superior defenses.

By holding the attackers at bay long enough, the Japanese felt they could buy time to allow aircraft, submarines and the surface fleet to reach the scene and annihilate the Americans.

Thus the Gilberts became an integral part of Japan's outer defensive perimeter that stretched north to the Aleutians, southward through the Marshalls and Gilberts to the Bismarcks. Strong ground defenses and quick action by the Imperial Fleet would thwart any American attempt to penetrate the outer perimeter.

Betio Island at Tarawa became the focal point of the Japanese defensive plans in the Gilberts. An airfield was constructed there and a series of strong points each mutually supportive of the others was built. The basic Japanese doctrine called for annihilation of the Americans at the beach in the event the attackers gained a foothold. Vigorous counterattacks would be launched to hurl the enemy back into the sea.

Rear Adm. Keiji Shibasaki was in command at Tarawa. He had about three thousand effective troops available and approximately two thousand laborers of dubious quality. The combat troops were Japan's Special Naval Landing Force commonly referred to erroneously by the Americans as Japanese Marines. Nevertheless, they were well trained and tenacious fighters. The laborers, on the other hand, were mainly Koreans and not trained for combat.

On Makin there were about 384 Special Naval Landing Force troops with perhaps 446 laborers. Apamama held 25 Japanese defenders.

Admiral Shibasaki turned Betio into a veritable fortress. All along the shore he placed a series of strong points; pillboxes and gun emplacements were situated so that none had blind side approaches. Many of these were underground or behind thick concrete casings. Others were reinforced with protected layers of coconut logs, coral and sand. Rifle pits, trenches and machine gun nests were numerous. Ringing the island between fifty and one hundred yards off shore were barbed-wire fences, concrete tetrahedrons and other beach obstacles. Around Betio's beaches a log barricade was constructed.

Butaritari was far less fortified. Lieutenant Seizo Ishikawa commanded the forces there. His defenses centered around King's Wharf on the lagoon side. Obstacles were built which crossed the island. In addition the island was dotted by machine gun nests and pillboxes but these were far less than on Betio.

As 1943 waned, Admiral Shibasaki boasted of his defensive strength. He was so confident that Betio was impregnable that he bragged that a million Marines fighting for a hundred years would be unable to take the island. He failed to count on the United States Marines.

As the Marines continued their rehearsals, the commander of the initial assault unit, the Second Regiment, fell ill. To replace him Julian Smith selected Lt. Colonel David Shoup who was given an immediate promotion to colonel.

As the date for Galvanic approached, raids against the targets were stepped up by air forces operating from Canton and Funafute Islands. On November 13 the Seventh Air Force began a systematic attack pattern with the Japanese airfields in both the Gilberts and Marshalls as their primary targets. Rear Adm. Charles Pownall, the commander of Task Force Fifty comprising the carriers, sent his planes to Nauru on November 18 and Jaluit and Mille in the Marshalls on the following day. These attacks were designed to isolate the target area.

On the thirteenth, Task Force Fifty-two (Admiral Hill) left Efate where four days later it rendezvoused with Turner's force moving up from Hawaii.

As the American forces approached their targets many of the Marines were optimistic. They were informed of the heavy pre-landing bombardment by both the carrier planes and the big guns of the battleships, cruisers and destroyers, and felt sure nothing would be left after such an awesome expenditure of explosives. Other Marines, however, were skeptical and knew that the Japanese were fanatical and would find some method to survive the heavy bombardment. Julian Smith commented:

We Marines, all of whom had studied, and in some

cases seen in actual combat the effect of land artillery fire, ships gunfire, and aerial bombardment, found naval officers unduly optimistic as to the results to be obtained from the bombardment.[6]

As the ships approached the Gilberts the troops made ready. Some cleaned their weapons, others read, played cards, wrote letters or prayed. Religious services were well attended. Final instructions were passed down. D-day would be November 20, 1943.

While the assault force was at sea Holland Smith and Kelly Turner embarked for Makin. Convinced that Makin was vulnerable to enemy counterattack, Smith hoped to prod the GIs along to rapid victory. Fortunately for the Americans the Japanese fleet was never a factor since the forces that were destined to sortie from Truk had been severely reduced by a number of battles fought earlier in November near Rabaul and in the Northern Solomons. The wisdom of a two-pronged approach to Japan was beginning to pay dividends.

D-day dawned bright and clear. The early morning hours found the Marines climbing down from their troop transports to their assault vehicles. One hundred of the vehicles were Amtracs, the rest were assault boats. While the men moved into the waiting vessels, the pre-landing bombardment began. First came the carrier planes who strafed and bombed targets on Betio for half an hour. Following the planes the support ships opened up a two-hour-long bombardment concentrated on the coastal defense guns. As the assault waves approached the beaches, the carrier planes returned for a final five-minute strike at beach defenses. Some of the attackers wondered how anything could survive such a pounding.

The bombardment cloaked the target in a thick haze. As the planes dropped their deadly loads, the LVTs made for the lagoon entrance. The first wave was made up of forty-two LVTs. H-hour was scheduled for 0830 but a strong western current delayed the landing for half an hour.

The assault troops headed for three beaches named, respectively, Red 1, Red 2, and Red 3. Red 1 was approximately seven hundred yards long and ran from the northwest tip of the island. Red 2 was six hundred yards long, ending at the coastal pier. The largest beach was Red 3, eight hundred yards long. The long pier was the dominant feature of the landing area and its early capture was essential. First Lt. William D. Hawkins, commander of the Second Scout Sniper Platoon, was given the vital task of securing this target. His forces landed at 0855 and quickly secured the ramp that sloped downward from the pier to the edge of the reef. Japanese fire began to crack near gasoline drums that the defenders had placed at the pier's end. Hawkins waved his men back to their landing boats while Second Lt. Alan Leslie along with four scouts armed with flamethrowers began advancing along the pier toward the shore, systematically destroying anything that might harbor enemy snipers. Fires spread onto the pier itself and soon a large gap formed. Having secured the pier, Hawkins led his men shoreward.

The Americans discovered rather quickly that the Japanese had survived the awesome bombardment. Henry Shaw described it this way:

Awesome as it had been, the preliminary bom-

183

bardment did not knock out all the defenses. The coast defense guns had been silenced, many of the dual purpose anti-aircraft weapons and antiboat guns had been put out of action, but most of the concrete pillboxes and emplacements protected by coconut logs and sand survived both bombs and shells.[7]

Landing on Red Beach 1 was Maj. John Schoettel's Third Battalion, Second Marine Regiment (3/2), Red Beach 2 was the target of the regiment's Second Battalion (2/2) under Lt. Col. Herbert Amey. Major Henry Crowe's Second Battalion of the Eighth Regiment (2/8) headed toward Red Beach 3. In reserve was Maj. Wood B. Kyle's First Battalion of the Second Regiment (1/2).

At 0910 Schoettel's force swarmed ashore on Red 1. I Company quickly pushed over the log wall and began to advance inland. Japanese fire then began to pour into the Marine's ranks and casualties began to mount.

Major Crowe's 2/8 reached Red 3 at 0917. Thanks to the pre-landing bombardment, the Japanese there were temporarily stunned. This allowed two LVTs to advance as far as the airstrip. Of the 552 men who landed in the first three waves, less than 25 became casualties on Red 3.

It was at Red 2 where Lieutenant Colonel Amey's 2/2 landed that casualties were the highest. In one company alone fifty percent of the men went down. Some tractors carrying Marines took direct artillery hits that killed or wounded the occupants. Those who survived were forced to wade ashore under heavy enemy machine gunfire. Casualties mounted at an alarming rate.

Following the first three waves of LVTs came two

waves of LCVPs. When these reached the reef the Marines found to their horror that the water was too shallow to allow the boats to float over. The troops were left with two alternatives: transfer to LVTs if possible, or wade ashore carrying their weapons and equipment.

The heaviest casualties were among those forced to wade ashore. Units became separated as the men scrambled to get to the beach. Few reserve units were able to reach Betio in their normal combat team organization.

On Red 2, Lieutenant Colonel Amey was killed while attempting to wade ashore so Colonel Shoup ordered an observer from the Fourth Marine Division, Lt. Col. Walter Jordan, to assume command of the 2/2.

Getting off the beach and over the wall proved just as deadly as landing. Thanks only to the valor of a few individuals some progress was made. Staff Sgt. William Bordelon survived an enemy shell that destroyed the LVT on which he was riding. Leading the survivors of his unit ashore, Bordelon filled two enemy pillboxes with demolition charges and blew them up. Like a man possessed he advanced toward a third enemy position but was critically wounded. However, that did not prevent the sergeant who denied medical aid and continued to fight. Blood pouring from his wounds, he waded back into the water and selflessly helped the injured. After reaching the beach again, he single-handedly attacked another enemy strong point but this time was cut down by Japanese fire. For his valor, Sergeant Bordelon was posthumously awarded the Congressional Medal of Honor.

Meanwhile, Colonel Shoup had his own particular difficulty getting ashore. Eventually he reached the pier and worked his way along the structure. Around noontime he was finally able to establish his command post on Red 2. Before establishing his CP, Shoup ordered Kyle's 1/2 to move westward from Red 2 and support the embattled forces on Red 1. Enemy fire was so intense that some of Kyle's battalion veered off course and landed on Red 1 while others landed closer to the pier. Landing was an absolute horror with some units suffering up to seventy percent casualties in the effort.

As the day progressed, the number of LVTs began to dwindle. Many of them were destroyed, others were damaged, while some suffered mechanical difficulties. This forced additional assault troops to take the LCVPs to the reef and wade ashore. Five hundred yards from shore and carrying their weapons above their heads, the Marines, under deadly and accurate fire from the concealed enemy, struggled shoreward. Many of the men, in an effort to make themselves as small a target as possible, crouched low in the water. Nevertheless, they remained little more than clay pigeons.

Major Schoettel radioed Shoup that his troops were being held up on the reef on the right flank of Red 1 and were coming under heavy fire in the water. Shoup responded by ordering him to land on Red 2 and work west. That provided Schoettel with little solace for the Japanese had already decimated his unit and reduced the battalion's effectiveness drastically. Schoettel remained on the reef with his men for several hours. If tractored landing vehicles had been available, they could have come right in. Finally, that afternoon, he was ordered to land at any cost and regain control of the battalion. Schoettel and his men waded ashore.

Not only had the heavy Japanese fire caused great

confusion, but lack of communications hampered the American units ashore. Offshore, the blast of the large batteries of the flagship, the battleship *Maryland*, also disrupted communications. On shore, the salt water had ruined much of the vital communications gear. Confusion reigned supreme.

Enemy fire was not the only cause of casualties. Some of the heavily laden Marines stepped into deep holes in the reefs and were dragged under and drowned. Still they continued to wade ashore. The water turned red from the blood of their comrades and yet they continued to come. Bodies and parts of bodies littered the beaches but the Marines fought gallantly on.

The second and third assault waves saw the carnage and knew what to expect. Taking a lesson from the first wave, the assault boats were ordered to the pier. This at least afforded the men some measure of protection, but not enough. Japanese marksmen concentrated their fire on the pier resulting in heavy American casualties.

From his command post on Red 2, Shoup drew a bleak picture of the assault thus far. The 2/8 was in the best shape, holding positions near the airfield. The other battalions, however, barely had a toehold. Despite the poor communications, Shoup was able to piece together a dreary image. Having drawn his conclusion, he sent an officer back to the command ship with a revised attack plan. Shoup proposed to attack south and west in order to unite the beachheads before attempting to seize the eastern end of the island. He was a determined fighter and added this sentence to his message, "You tell the general and the admiral that we are going to stick and fight it out."[8]

Meanwhile, Julian Smith was drawing his own conclusions. One was to ask Holland Smith for the release of the Corps reserve, the Sixth Regimental Combat Team. More troops were obviously needed on Betio. In less than an hour's time, an affirmative answer was forthcoming from Holland Smith and Admiral Turner.

Julian Smith also decided to land the 1/8 at the earliest possible time but because of the communications breakdown was unable to get in touch with Shoup to discuss where this unit should land. The 1/8 waited in their assault craft through the rest of the day and into the night for the order to move shoreward. The men were cramped, hungry, tired and anxious, and many of them became seasick. Poor communications was a plague to the assault. According to Shaw, "Water, shell fragments, bullets, and rough handling played havoc with communications equipment."[9]

Julian Smith urgently needed up-to-date information. To obtain it he sent the assistant division commander, Brig. Gen. Leo Hermle. The latter reached the long pier and despite great difficulties managed to establish sporadic radio contact with Shoup. The colonel informed Hermle of the desperate shortage of ammunition and water. Throughout the night Hermle organized carrying parties to bring the badly needed supplies ashore. During the night he lost contact with Shoup and was forced to send a runner to find out where the colonel wanted the reserves landed. At 0345, Hermle received his answer but then his radio acted up and he was unable to contact General Smith. He went to the lagoon, boarded the destroyer *Ringgold*, and used that ship's radio to inform Smith that Shoup wanted the 1/8 to land near the Long Pier on Red 2. Following that, Hermle was ordered to report to Smith on the *Maryland* where he learned that the evening before he had been ordered to take command of the fighting ashore. The faulty communications resulted in the message going astray thus leaving Shoup in command.

The first day's fighting on Betio had been bloody. The presence of a few tanks helped the situation somewhat but the Japanese menaced the Marines from every angle. There was simply no easy way to approach the mutually supporting enemy positions without coming under fire. One by one, using flamethrowers, satchel charges, and bangalore torpedoes, each strong point was painfully reduced (Map 15).

By nightfall of the first day Shoup was able to state that his forces held a precarious toehold on the island. Although there was no sense of panic, from past experiences the Marines prepared themselves for the inevitable enemy counterattack. The pier was a scene of mass confusion. Men huddled together beneath the structure or close to its sides while supplies were dumped on the pier's end. There they waited for some brave men to attempt to run them onto the beach.

Even after darkness there was no letup in the Japanese machine gunfire. Adding to the Marine's woes was the infiltration of enemy snipers who took advantage of the darkness and moved offshore into damaged landing craft where they were able to fire upon the Americans from improved vantage points.

Incredibly, no counterattack took place the first night. The Marine's precarious toehold could have been easily dislodged by an all-out attack. In fact, after the battle Julian Smith commented, "Admiral Shibasaki lost the battle by failing to counterattack on that first night, for never again would the beachhead be so vul-

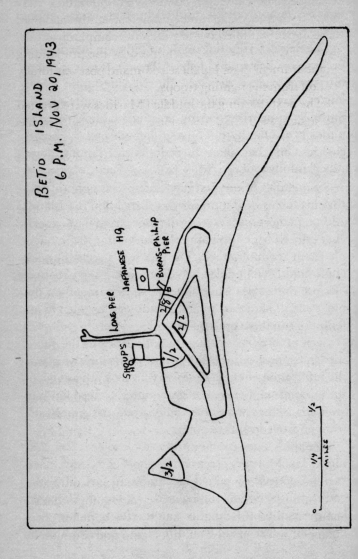

BETIO ISLAND
6 P.M. Nov 20, 1943

LONG PIER

SHOUP'S HQ

JAPANESE HQ

BURNS-PHILIP PIER

1/2

2/2

2/8

B

3/2

0   1/4   1/2
MILES

nerable."[10]

Shibasaki's failure to launch a counterattack may have been due to his own communications breakdown. The Japanese relied heavily on wire communications. Most of this system was chewed up by the pre-landing bombardment. The Japanese command post was totally cut off from the fighting troops.

The next morning the huddled Marines were greeted by a sight of utter devastation. The crowded beaches were littered with LVTs, weapons, supplies, grounded tanks and bodies. Doctors administered to the wounded while bodies covered with ponchoes dotted the Dantesque landscape. Men mingled with others from different units. All shared one thing in common, they had survived the first night on Betio. Could the day be worse?

By dawn the tide had also gone out and looming in front of the men on the assault crafts was the exposed reef. Bloated bodies could be seen floating near or on the reef. The tropical heat quickly decomposed bodies creating a stench fit for the scene:

The unforgettable odor was everywhere. The men on Betio were saturated with it, it clung to their clothing and filled their nostrils and it reached out across the reef and provided an unpleasant fore-taste of the island to the men of the First Battalion, Eighth Marines.[11]

The 1/8 had spent the night huddling in their boats at the line of departure anxiously waiting for orders to land. Along with Major Hays, the battalion commander, was Colonel Hall, the regimental commander.

Hall finally received his orders to land on Red 2. Almost immediately their LCVP grounded on the reef and the slow, deadly wade to the shore began. On shore the survivors of D-day watched the macabre scene of their fellow Marines bracing the deadly Japanese fire. Added to the fire from shore was that of snipers holed up in a destroyed ship's hulk. The snipers opened up on the backs of the Marines.

Even quicker than the previous day, if that was possible, the casualties began to mount. Major Hays reported to Shoup for orders. With only half his battalion ashore, and badly disorganized, his command was in poor shape.

Fortunately for the Americans, Shoup's leadership proved inspired. He overcame the uncertainty of the situation and began to make sense out of chaos. He told Hays that his battalion was to attack westward where Major Ryan's force was isolated. Shoup then went over the rest of his attack plan for D + 1.

The main feature of the plan was a drive across Betio by the 1/2 and 2/2 to gain a foothold on the ocean shore. Before beginning the attack Shoup called in carrier aircraft to soften up the enemy positions south of the airstrip. Unfortunately, bomb fragments and richocheting bullets fell on the Marines and Shoup was forced to call off the bombing attack.

The Japanese raked the airfield with machine gunfire. American casualties mounted at an alarming rate. At 1300, two hundred men leaped from their foxholes and dashed onto the runway. Luckily, the Japanese positions in the interior were not as strong as those along the shore. Despite heavy fire, the attackers' casualties were light. After crossing the airfield the Marines entered the tangled growth and shattered palm trees south of the airfield. But no sooner had they arrived on the south shore than they were struck by a strong enemy counterattack. Heavy casualties were sustained by both sides and soon the American ammunition stocks reached a critical low point. The nagging radio problems prevented the men on the south shore from notifying Shoup of their plight.

At the eastern end, on Red 3, Major Crowe's 2/8 was involved in a bitter struggle. Japanese resistance was extremely heavy, particularly in the vicinity of Betio's rather short second pier, called the Burns-Philip Pier. By dusk of D + 1 the Americans managed to occupy the pier but enemy strong points south of the position prevented further progress (Map 16).

On Red Beach 1, after their precarious landing, Hays' 1/8 moved steadily eastward. With the help of a medium tank, initial progress was relatively good. Unfortunately, one lone tank was simply not enough. Lacking flamethrowers with which to burn out the enemy strong points, the attack ground to a halt. The unit's flamethrowers had been lost during the passage from the reef to the shore. At dark the 1/8 consolidated its position with hopes the next day would bring further success.

The most significant progress was made by Major Ryan on the west end of Betio. There, with the help of accurate naval support, the Marines were able to advance down the island's western coast (Green Beach). After proceeding along the beach, Ryan shifted his forces inland about two hundred yards from the shore. Bypassed Japanese positions were taken care of with flamethrowers and satchel charges.

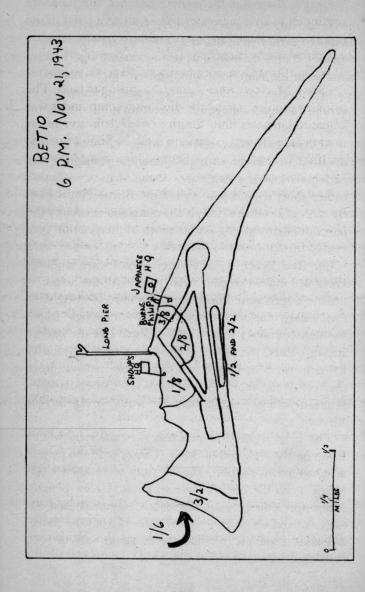

Despite the loss of the western beaches, the Japanese continued to hold the eastern and southern parts of the island. At the same time, many of the northern beaches were still bitterly contested.

While the battle ashore raged, the reserve regiment, the Sixth Marines, were anxiously waiting to land.. The primary problem facing the divisional commander was where to land this unit. Smith needed definitive information as to the best location to send the Sixth Marines. At 1022 Shoup had sent a depressing message stating, "Situation ashore uncertain."[12]

As a result, Smith was determined to land the Sixth at the earliest possible moment. The capture of Green Beach gave him a landing point.

At 1400 the first wave of the 1/6 began landing. The fresh unit quickly established a defensive position in anticipation of the next morning's counterattack.

By nightfall of D + 1, the beachhead extended almost five hundred yards along the lagoon side of Betio on either side of the long pier. On the right the 1/8 held a line running from the beach directly inland to the west taxiway. On the left the 3/8's position stretched from the Burns-Philip Pier southward in an arch to the airfield. Red 2's and Red 3's beachheads had been enlarged while the 1/2 and 2/2 had traversed the island.

By evening, therefore, Shoup was able to send a more optimistic report. Shortly after 1700 he radioed, "Casualties many. Percentage dead not known. Combat efficiency—We are winning."[13]

Shoup continued to control operations from his command post located in the shadow of an enemy bunker. Japanese troops continued to occupy this bunker requiring the posting of guards at each exit. Overall, the fighting that second day was still bitter but by evening Shoup felt more confident.

At 2030 Colonel Edson, the division chief of staff arrived at Shoup's headquarters and assumed overall command. Shoup had done a brilliant job and for his effort was awarded the Congressional Medal of Honor. The award citation stated:

> For conspicuous gallantry and intrepidity at the risk of his life above and beyond the call of duty as commanding officer of all Marine Corps troops in action against enemy Japanese forces on Betio . . . from 20 to 22 November, 1943. Although severely shocked by an exploding enemy shell soon after landing at the pier, and suffering from a serious, painful leg wound . . . Colonel Shoup fearlessly exposed himself. . . . Rallying his hesitant troops by his own inspiring heroism, he gallantly led them across the fringing reefs to charge the heavily fortified island and reinforce our hard-pressed, thinly held lines. . . . By his brilliant leadership, daring tactics and selfless devotion to duty, Colonel Shoup was largely responsible for the final decisive defeat of the enemy.[14]

As soon as Colonel Edson arrived, he immediately began planning the next day's attack with the aid of Shoup. Prior to the attack was the coordination of air support and naval gunfire on Betio's eastern end. The bombardment would work westward to the airstrip. The attack plan called for the 1/6 to pass through the 3/2, strike eastward from their position on Green Beach, and move along the south shore. Meanwhile, the 1/8 would attack westward along the lagoon shore with the objective of eliminating the Japanese pocket on the Red 1 Red 2 boundary. The remaining two battalions of the Eighth Marines were to drive eastward. To add weight to the attack, artillery batteries were ordered to land and take up positions on the neighboring island of Bairiki.

At 0700 on November 22, the 1/8 launched its attack. With the support of three light tanks they poured point-blank fire into the Japanese pillboxes. Even so, the enemy positions refused to yield. Once more the Marines were forced to rely on bangalore torpedoes and satchel charges to reduce the enemy strong points. Although little ground was gained, many stubborn strong points were eliminated. Later in the day, the Japanese attempted a counterattack but this failed. By day's end the enemy on this part of the island were effectively isolated and the Marines dug in for the night.

Major Jones' 1/6 began their attack at 0800 with the objective of clearing the south side of Betio and making contact with the 1/1 and 1/2. Those battalions, it will be remembered, had crossed the island on D11. Once contact was established with those two units, Jones' orders called for him to continue eastward.

Tanks, flamethrowers and satchel charges again became the most valuable weapons during the advance. Resistance proved relatively light and casualties were kept to a minimum. By 1100 Jones had made contact with the 1/2. By that hour, except for the lone enemy pocket between Red 1 and Red 2, western Betio was for all intent and purpose, secure.

In the northern end of the island the 2/8 prepared to launch its assault. The Japanese remained holed up in strong positions near the Burns-Philip Pier. One steel pillbox proved particularly hazardous along with a co-conut log emplacement from which the enemy raked the ranks of the advancing Marines. There was one other strong point: a large bomb-proof shelter somewhat to the south of the steel pillbox which proved a great menace. Each of these strong points were mutually supporting. To attack one, exposed the attack to the others. The entire Second Battalion found itself involved in the effort to reduce these positions.

Mortar shells rained down on the Japanese positions while a medium tank fired its 75mm shells at the steel pillbox. Flamethrowers and demolition teams attacked the bombproof shelter. Finally, after a savage hour of fighting, the Marines managed to gain the top of the structure. At that point, the enemy counterattacked in large numbers. Thanks to the bravery of First Lt. Alexander Bonnyman, who personally drove back the attackers with a flamethrower, the position was held. Bonnyman died in the fight but his action allowed the 2/8 to advance. For his action, the lieutenant was posthumously awarded the Medal of Honor.

The failure of their counterattack caused the Japanese to flee eastward. As they pulled out of their strong points, they were mowed down by American machine gunfire, rifle fire and hand grenades.

Following the elimination of the enemy strongpoints on their front, the 2/8 moved forward to the end of the airfield. There they halted the attack and dug in for the night.

In the interim, the 3/6 had landed on Green Beach late in the morning. By 1700 the battalion, following the route of Jones' battalion, halted approximately six hundred yards behind the 1/6 and remained there in support. Thus, with the exception of the enemy pocket between Red 1 and Red 2, by evening of November 22 the Japanese had been driven back to that portion of the island known as Betio's tail.

Julian Smith, who had established his headquarters ashore during the day, still felt that days of fighting lay ahead. He sent the following report to Admiral Turner:

> Progress slow and extremely costly. . . . Complete occupation will take at least five more days.[15]

During the night of the twenty-second the Japanese played into American hands by staging more counterattacks. At 1930 some fifty enemy soldiers began infiltrating the Marines' lines. These were swiftly eliminated. At 2300 more Japanese left their positions and advanced. The Marines used machine guns, grenades and mortars to beat off this attack. At 0300 and again an hour later, hundreds of Japanese troops charged the American lines. By 0500 it was all over. The counterattacks were smashed and countless Japanese bodies littered the landscape.

On D + 3 the Second Division still faced two major tasks: the elimination of the Japanese pocket between Red 1 and Red 2, and the elimination of resistance on Betio's tail. The 3/2 and 1/8 were given the job of reducing the pocket between the beaches while the Sixth Marines struck for the tail. The 3/6 battalion commander, Major McLeod, commented on the drive into the tail:

> At no time was there any determined defensive. I did not use artillery at all and called for naval gunfire for only about five minutes which was all the support used by me. We used flamethrowers and

could have used more. Medium tanks were excellent. My light tanks didn't fire a shot.[16]

Shortly after 1300 the 3/6 reached the eastern tip of Betio thus securing the island. The final push had cost the Marines 9 lives and 25 wounded. In turn, they managed to kill 475 of the enemy while capturing 14. The Japanese were simply too tired, thirsty and disorganized to put up a coordinated defense. Though they were not lacking in spirit and physical courage, exhaustion took its toll and their supplies had simply run out. That afternoon also saw the elimination of the enemy pocket between Red 1 and Red 2.

Of the 4,836 Japanese troops and Korean laborers who had defended Betio, only 146 were taken prisoner. Of these, only 17 were Japanese. On the American side, 51 Marine officers were killed, 853 enlisted men, 2 naval officers and 28 sailors for a total of 934 American dead. 92 Marines later died of their wounds bring the total to 1,026. A total of 2,292 Marines and naval personnel were wounded; 88 men were officially listed as missing. The entire cost to the Americans of capturing Betio was 3,406 casualties.

Betio itself was a shambles. The ferocity of the battle which had been fought at such close quarters was by far the worst yet encountered by the Americans. The smell on the island was suffocating. The scene was apocalyptic.

When word of the excessive casualties hit the newspapers in America, Admiral Nimitz came in for a great deal of criticism. He was flooded with letters, some of them blaming him personally for the death of loved ones. Questions as to Tarawa's value were hotly debated. Was the attack worth the cost? Perhaps a review of the simultaneous fighting on Makin and Apanama will answer these questions.

In the early morning hours of November 20, 6,472 assault troops of the 165th Regimental Combat Team (RCT) began boarding their LCVPs. While the troops settled into their landing barges, carrier planes struck targets on Butaritari Island. At the same time the naval support ships began their pre-landing bombardment.

The Japanese commander elected to forfeit the beaches, choosing to defend the area around King's Wharf where he had constructed tank traps and barricades on each flank. It was fortunate indeed for the Americans that the enemy did not contest the beaches because, just as at Betio, the LVTs landed with little trouble but the LVCPs were unable to cross the reef. Once more the attackers were forced to wade ashore. If the Japanese had been waiting on the beaches it would have been a bloodbath.

Around 0830 the attackers landed and easily secured the western end of Butaritari in just under two hours. When the First Battalion began to advance toward the western tank trap however, heavy Japanese resistance was encountered. While the battalion slugged it out with the enemy, Gen. Ralph Smith sent the Second Battalion to land on the island's lagoon beach. For most of the first day the men of the Second Battalion battled a determined enemy intent on preventing the landing.

As night settled over the battlefield, the stalled First Battalion dug in from the western tank trap. During the night the inexperienced GIs were infiltrated by the Japanese. Trigger-happy American troops shot at anything that moved. This caused Holland Smith's temper to

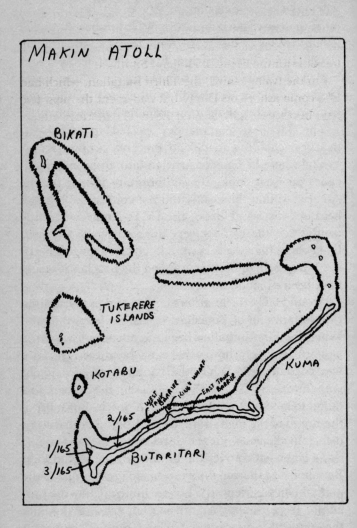

rise.

The Americans spent the next day in an effort to reduce the enemy strong points. Again, as at Betio, they found that the flamethrower and the satchel charge were the most valuable weapons. Progress was slow, much too slow for the liking of Holland Smith.

On the twenty-third, the Third Battalion, which had also come ashore on D-day but had spent the next two days in reserve, spearheaded the main American attack. After crossing the eastern tank trap, the battalion moved steadily forward against the Japanese positions. At nightfall the Japanese again infiltrated the American lines and attacked in small groups but to no avail. By the evening of the twenty-third, Ralph Smith signalled Admiral Turner that the island was captured.

To eliminate Makin the Americans suffered 218 casualties, 66 of whom were killed. The enemy lost 445 dead. It was the Navy that incurred the greatest loss of life at Makin. The Japanese submarine I-175 torpedoed the escort carrier *Liscome Bay*. A total of 644 of the carrier's crew were lost.

The loss of the *Liscome Bay* was proof positive that amphibious assaults had to be swift thereby allowing the fleet freedom to roam. The naval aviators ranted against Spruance for retaining the carriers in support of land targets. Holland Smith, however, placed the blame elsewhere: on the Twenty-seventh Infantry Division. He later stated that the capture of Makin was "infuriating slow."[17] Considering the size of the atoll, the nature of the enemy's defenses, and the great superiority of force enjoyed by the attackers, the capture of the target should have been accomplished much faster. Smith was not finished with his castigation of the hapless Twenty-seventh Division. This was merely the beginning of a storm that would later burst in all its fury at Saipan.

The third target in the Gilberts was Apamana. A reconnaissance force landed there on November 21 and found only a handful of Japanese. By the time the island was secure, two Marines were dead and two more wounded. In all, twenty-five Japanese were killed on Apamana, eighteen by their own hands. Believing that suicide was more honorable than surrender, they killed themselves.

Operation Galvanic was over. To the Second Marine Division the experience at Tarawa was a horrible nightmare. On December 4, Julian Smith turned command of Tarawa over to the Navy and the Second Marines sailed to their new base, Camp Tarawa in Hawaii. The History of the Second Marine Division gives a vivid portrait of the trip to Hawaii:

> The transports reeked of the awful smell of the island, of disinfectant and of blood. There were no fresh clothes for unwounded Marines, and almost everyone had lost his gear in the shuffle of battle. Every day there were funerals aboard the transports, and flag-covered bodies slipping into the silent seas.[18]

On December 6, 1943 *Time* Magazine phrased the battle in these terms:

> Last week some two or three thousand U.S. Marines, most of them now dead or wounded, gave the nation a name to stand beside those of Concord Bridge, the Bonhomme Richard, the Al-

amo, Little Big Horn, and Belleau Wood. The name was Tarawa.

How important were the Gilberts? Never one to mince words, Holland Smith stated bluntly that Tarawa was a mistake. In fact the Gilberts, he went on, should have been bypassed completely. After the war the volatile Marine general published his memoirs, *Coral and Brass*. In the book Smith vented his anger, giving his reasons why the Gilberts should have been left alone. Many critics have taken exception to Smith's theories and have explicitly demonstrated why the capture of the Gilberts was critical. The official Army history states that "in the minds of most American military planners and strategists the cost of the capture of the Gilberts was justified both in the terms of the strategic gains realized and the tactical lessons learned."[19]

Operation Galvanic marked the beginning of a major effort against Japan. The capture of airfield sights in the Gilberts brought the Marshalls (which were considered the more important and more dangerous objective) within effective range of land-based aircraft.

Unquestionably, additional and more accurate photographic coverage was needed for the next invasion. The need for tractored landing craft was made painfully clear during the campaign. Underwater demolition teams were also a requirement for future operations. If these had been available at Betio they could have destroyed the underwater obstacles and cleared a path for the LCVPs. Improved methods of transporting supplies across invasion beaches had to be developed also. Thanks to the difficulties at Tarawa, better techniques were found. The Americans also learned the painful lesson that radios had to be waterproofed. Improvements in naval gunfire techniques were also learned at Betio. The latter would be of great value in the invasion of the Marshalls. Unquestionably a few hours of pre-landing bombardment was insufficient. A great volume of shelling was necessary in addition to a higher degree of accuracy.

The need to capture lightly defended islands within range of the major objective was also emphasized. Additional artillery support was considered vital to overall success.

Jeter A. Isely and Philip A. Crowl in their book on the theory and practice of amphibious doctrine state that "Betio became the textbook for future amphibious landings and assaults. Lessons learned were widely disseminated."[20]

In retrospect, the capture of Tarawa was indeed necessary. Granted, the casualties were high but few victories come cheap. The lessons learned at Tarawa had to be learned somewhere. If not at Betio then they would have been learned in the Marshalls where the cost might have been even higher. Amphibious warfare knowledge is learned only from experience and the Gilberts provided the Americans with that vital knowledge. A French naval historian has placed the importance of Tarawa in proper perspective:

Tarawa was the staging base to the Fiji and Samoan Islands, and although the need for its capture was not too apparent in November, 1943, its possession by the United States was the final link in the denial of the South Pacific to Japan.[21]

And what of the Second Marine Division? No finer tribute is needed other than the one contained in Admiral Spruance's action report:

> The part that will be longest remembered in American History was the magnificent courage and tenacity of the Marines in carrying on their assault . . . after suffering staggering losses. Nothing in the record of the Marine Corps can exceed the heroism displayed at Tarawa by the officers and men of the Second Marine Division and by the naval units that accompanied them in their landing.[22]

Chapter Five

The Marianas:
Saipan, Tinian, Guam

After three long years of one disaster piled upon another, 1942 found the momentum of World War II firmly in the grasp of the Allies never to be relinquished. The previous May the mighty carrier force of the Imperial Japanese Navy was devastated at Midway. In August the Americans went on the offensive by invading Guadalcanal in the Solomons. November witnessed the defeat of the seemingly invincible Field Marshal Rommel followed by a successful Anglo-American invasion of North Africa (Operation Torch). In December the powerful German Sixth Army thrust its neck into a fatal noose at Stalingrad. With the pendulum swinging in their direction it was time for the Allies to begin serious planning for the ultimate defeat of the Axis.

On January 14, 1943 the Combined Chiefs of Staff began a round of meetings at Casablanca. Foremost on the agenda was strategy for the pursuit of the war during the coming year. The American Joint Chiefs, led by Gen. George Marshall, insisted on a cross-channel invasion of Europe later in the year. The British on the other hand, recognized that the invasion would be impossible that year and pressed for further action in the Mediterranean. This was totally unacceptable to Marshall and Adm. Ernest King. As a result, Marshall and King demanded that a heavier emphasis be placed on the war in the Pacific. Instead of the eighty-five to fifteen ratio of resources, the American chiefs argued for a seventy to thirty ration between Europe and the Pacific.

Eventually a compromise was reached. The Americans agreed to the invasion of Sicily in exchange for a heavier emphasis on the war against Japan.

> The upshot of the discussion on the Pacific-Far East operations at Casablanca was a series of limited and contingent agreements. The United States was to conduct a two-way advance in the Pacific. Plans and preparation were to be made for the recapture of Burma in 1943, but final decision on the operation was to be postponed until the Summer of 1943. Increased aid to China in the way of air forces and transports would be provided by the United States. The delegates agreed that the Pacific-Far East operations for 1943 were to be aimed at maintaining pressure on Japan, holding the initiative, and attaining positions of readiness for a full-scale offensive against Japan immediately upon the defeat of Germany.[1]

The central Pacific strategy was the brainchild of Admirals Nimitz and King. Both felt that a two-pronged offensive was essential to final victory. General MacArthur, on the other hand, disagreed and championed a single thrust aimed at the recapture of the Philippines.

At the Trident Conference in May, King pointed out that a central Pacific drive with the final objective of the Marianas Islands would allow the Americans to strike from there to the Philippines, China or even Japan itself. In addition, the capture of the Marianas would sever the line of communications between Japan and her bases in the Carolines and cut off the flow of vital natural resources from the Dutch East Indies.

During the Quadrant Conference a few months later the British chiefs gave their final blessing to King's central Pacific strategy. The Americans would seize the Gilberts, Marshalls, Carolines, Palaus and finally the Marianas.

The Gilberts were successfully invaded in November, 1943. In February and March of the following year the Marshalls fell to Nimitz's Central Pacific Force. By that time King's eyes were firmly riveted on the Marianas. In the interim, however, Nimitz had developed a change of heart.

General MacArthur sent his chief of staff, General Sutherland to Pearl Harbor for a meeting with Nimitz. Sutherland did a masterful job of salesmanship and convinced Nimitz that the attack on the Marianas was a mistake. Instead the Americans should concentrate on the recapture of the Philippines. This area could then be used as a staging area for an invasion of China. Although Nimitz bought the argument, convincing Ernie King was another matter. When Nimitz suggested that the Marianas operation be cancelled King exploded. He told Nimitz in no uncertain terms to stick to the original plan.

In March Nimitz and Sutherland appeared before the Joint Chiefs in Washington. King was still unhappy over Nimitz's change of opinion. And by this time, King had an ally.

General Henry "Hap" Arnold of the Army Air Forces

was enthused over the prospect of securing air bases that brought the Japanese homeland within range of his B-29 bombers. Accordingly he cast his lot with King and the Central Pacific Drive was reprieved. Despite all of MacArthur's arguments King's theories won the day.

Once more King and Nimitz found themselves at loggerheads. Nimitz wanted to capture the heavily fortified Japanese on Truk in the central Carolines. King wanted no part of Truk. He felt that the seizure of the Marianas would effectively isolate Truk and neutralize its effectiveness. Nimitz was bluntly ordered to forget it.

Once the subject of the next objective was settled once and for all, Nimitz began planning in earnest for the operation, code named "Forager." At the same time he started to assemble his team of subordinates. The overall commander would be his old friend and former chief of staff, Adm. Raymond Spruance. Already he had proven himself at Midway, the Gilberts and the Marshalls while commanding the Fifth Fleet.

To command the amphibious phase of Forager, Nimitz stuck with the newly promoted vice-admiral, Richmond Kelly Turner, the battle-tested amphibious expert whom *Time* Magazine called a "mean son of a bitch."[2] Turner cut his teeth in amphibious operations at Guadalcanal. From there he proved his mettle in the Marshalls and Gilberts. By late 1943 he had no equal insofar as commanding amphibious operations was concerned.

For ground commander Nimitz selected Gen. Holland M. "Howlin' Mad" Smith of the Marine Corps. This appointment caused immediate controversy since the designated assault forces comprised not only three Marine divisions but a pair of Army divisions as well.

The Army generals objected vehemently to being placed under a Marine general, but to no avail. Not only had Smith trained the Marines in amphibious attacks but he was a proven leader in battle as well.

The island of Saipan would be the first objective in the seizure of the Marianas. Saipan rated the highest priority because the Air Force was eager to begin construction of airfields large enough to accommodate B-29s. Once the island was secured construction could begin immediately while the assault forces turned their attention to the islands of Tinian and Guam.

The American plan called for two Marine divisions, the Second and the Fourth to invade Saipan. The Twenty-seventh Army Division was designated for reserve. The Marines were to drive overland from the invasion beaches, cut the island in two, then swing around and force the enemy into the northern part of the island where they could be eliminated. Once this was accomplished the attackers would regroup and jump to the nearby island of Tinian. Admiral Turner felt that Saipan could be captured in a week. But he seriously underestimated the strength of the Japanese garrison on Saipan and he knew very little of the brutal terrain.

Meanwhile, if all went well on Saipan, three days after the landings the Third Marine Division would invade Guam with the Seventy-seventh Army division in reserve. The entire American plan for the invasion of the Marianas was incredibly ambitious in light of the strong Japanese defenses.

The man in whose hand rested the defense of Saipan was Lt. Gen. Yoshitsugo Saito. The general's main claim to fame was not his brilliance on the battlefield but his knowledge of horses. Prior to being sent to Saipan

Saito was in charge of securing horses for the Japanese army. He was considered one of the keenest judges of horseflesh in the empire. During the battle for Saipan, however, Saito proved more than equal to the task.

Saito's force was part of the overall command of Gen. Hideyoshi Obata's area. But Obata's headquarters was on the island of Palau placing him a long way from the scene of the action. Therefore, although technically in charge of the defense of Saipan, Obata played a relatively minor role in the battle.

The most famous defender of Saipan was Adm. Chiuchi Nagumo. The legendary commander of the Pearl Harbor attack had fallen into disfavor after the battle of Midway.* With his mentor, Admiral Yamamoto dead, Nagumo found himself relegated to the backwater of the war. In addition, since the defense of the Marianas was primarily the army's responsibility, Nagumo too played but a minor part in the campaign. His command consisted of a few aircraft and a handful of patrol boats.

At the beginning of 1944 the Japanese began to realize the strategic importance of the Marianas. Troops were withdrawn from China and dispatched to Saipan. Unfortunately for the Japanese, marauding American submarines prevented many of these troops from reaching their destination. In February, a troop transport with over four thousand troops was sunk. Some survivors eventually managed to reach Saipan but all of their equipment was lost. In June, five more troop-carrying ships managed to reach Saipan but once more all of their equipment had been lost at sea. Nevertheless, by the time of the American attack there were over thirty

*See *The Great Commanders of World War II, Volume IV: The Japanese*

thousand Japanese troops on Saipan. The American planners estimated that there were less than fifteen thousand which accounted for their ambitious schedule.

Getting supplies through to Saipan was as hazardous as sending troops. The American submarines had the supply routes pretty much to themselves. A supply ship that managed to make the perilous journey was the exception rather than the rule.

Despite the lack of equipment and supplies General Saito managed to make skillful use of what was available. He was determined to stop the invasion on the beaches. The general was well aware that once the Americans were established their superiority in supplies and men would win the day. Accordingly, Saito positioned his artillery and mortars where they could pour the maximum amount of fire onto the landing areas.

Besides the strong positions on the anticipated landing beaches, Saito set his troops to constructing strong defenses in the interior. Every advantage was taken of Saipan's natural terrain. Avenues of advance were protected by hidden sniper positions. In addition to those already existing, caves were carved into the rocky hills. These caves were connected by a series of tunnels that in some cases ran clear through the mountains. Saito preferred to wait for his enemy in well constructed, heavily fortified positions. Unlike his fellow commanders on many of the Pacific islands, Saito had no intention of wasting his manpower in wasteful banzai attacks.

Despite King's directive to ignore Truk, the threat from this powerful naval base continued to gnaw at Nimitz. He could not rest until he was absolutely certain that the Japanese naval forces at Truk posed no problem. A series of raids were carried out against the island in the first months of 1944. Then, on April 29, the carriers of Task Force 58 began a two-day attack against the base. Truk was subjected to repeated bombings and strafing runs. When Task Force 58 withdrew, Truk had been blasted into oblivion. Never again was this great bastion of the Pacific a factor in the war. Nimitz could now rest easy and concentrate on Saipan.

Shortly after 0500 on the morning of June 15 the assaulting forces began climbing over the sides of their transports and dropping into their assault craft. To the north of the actual landing areas the assault craft began making a run toward the island. Turner hoped to deceive the enemy into thinking that the invasion was further north. Although the feinting forces did come under some fire from Saipan Saito refused to swallow the bait. He had guessed right and did not move his forces to meet the threat.

Offshore, the naval support ships opened up on Japanese positions on Saipan. At 0700 the bombardment ceased abruptly. Then, sweeping low over the circling assault craft came waves of planes from the escort carriers. The planes strafed enemy positions near the beaches and dropped bombs on suspected strong points. After the planes finished their attack the ships opened up once more.

The Second Marine Division under Gen. Thomas Watson comprised the northern half of the assault force. The Sixth and Eighth Regiments would land on four beaches, Red 2 and 3 and Green 1 and 2. The Second Regiment, which had participated in the feint earlier that morning, would follow the two assaulting regiments later in the day.

South of Afetna Point Gen. Harry Schmidt's Fourth

Division was scheduled to land on beaches Blue 1 and 2 and Yellow 1, 2 and 3. The assault force itself was the Twenty-third and Twenty-fifth regiments with the Twenty-fourth slated to follow. Once ashore the attacking units would move inland on an outward axis designed to link up the two divisions behind the enemy forces on Afetna Point. The gap between the regiments as they moved outward would be filled by the followup regiments.

At 0812 the order went out for the hovering landing craft to commence the assault. As the waves of small boats headed for the beaches another wave of planes from the carriers escorted them in and softened up the enemy positions with another load of high explosives.

Despite the intense pre-landing bombardment, as soon as the assault craft drew within range they came under heavy fire from concealed Japanese artillery. Unlike the Marshalls where the Japanese allowed the Marines to land before attempting to destroy them, General Saito intended to inflict as many casualties as possible on the attackers before they even landed.

Half an hour after setting off, the first wave of Marines landed on beach Red 2. On the Second Division's front, strong currents resulted in the bulk of the forces landing in Red 2 and 3 and Green 1. There the confused and bunched up formations found themselves excellent targets for the Japanese gunners. In the first half hour American casualties were enormous (Map 18).

Probably the most dangerous place on Saipan to be was on the landing beaches. Out of desperation more than anything else the Second Division began to move inland. The enemy fought back with a few weak counterattacks that were beaten off easily but the murderous

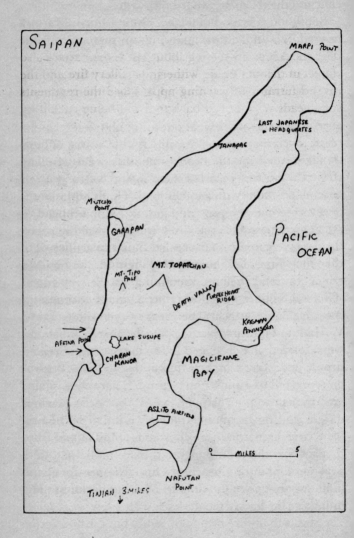

SAIPAN

MARPI POINT

LAST JAPANESE
HEADQUARTERS

TANAPAG

MUTCHO
POINT

GARAPAN

PACIFIC
OCEAN

MT. TIPO
PALE

MT. TOPATCHAU

DEATH VALLEY
PURPLE HEART
RIDGE

KAGMAN
PENINSULA

AFETNA POINT

LAKE SUSUPE

CHARAN
KANOA

MAGICIENNE
BAY

ASLITO AIRFIELD

0   MILES   5

NAFUTAN
POINT

TINIAN 3 MILES

artillery fire continued to take its toll. By early after-noon Watson's casualty rate was almost thirty-five per-cent and the attack began to bog down.

South of Afetna Point the Twenty-third Marines headed inland without pausing to regroup on the beaches. After progressing about a mile their attack also stalled in the face of the withering artillery fire and the rugged terrain. As evening approached the regiments spearheads were pulled back to avoid being cut off by enemy counterattacks.

Of all the landing forces that day the fiercest opposi-tion was encountered by the Twenty-fifth Marines. The concentrated artillery fire plastered the landing beaches with deadly accuracy. At 0930 Japanese infantry coun-terattacked and threatened to destroy the beachhead it-self. Only the intercession of a company of tanks saved the day. Nevertheless, on this beach too casualties were extremely high. Like the Second Division, the Fourth's casualty rate approached thirty-five percent.

At the landing points the beaches were strewn with American corpses and burning landing craft. Wounded, awaiting evacuation to the ships offshore, were not immune to the deadly barrage. Many survived the advance only to perish while receiving aid at the wa-ter's edge. Other stretcher cases were wounded again, sometimes two or even three times. When the Marines dug in for the night they were only halfway to the first day's objectives, the line of hills and ridges inland from the beaches.

General Saito did not plan to ease the pressure on the battle-weary Marines with the onset of darkness. His orders for the first night were:

Each unit will consolidate strategically important points and will carry out counterattacks with reserve forces and tanks against the enemy landing units and will demolish the enemy during the night at the water's edge.[3]

First to feel the brunt of Saito's orders were the Sixth Marines on the extreme left flank of the American front. Around 0200 a strong enemy force backed by tanks hit the Marines. Since their artillery had not yet landed the Americans were forced to beat off the attack with machine gun and rifle fire. In this effort they were aided by starshells fired by the battleship *California* which illuminated the battlefield. Hard pressed, the Marines held their ground. They allowed the Japanese tanks to pass over their foxholes before emerging and destroying the tanks from the rear. Although the attack eventually failed some of the enemy managed to infiltrate the American lines. Two further attacks were hurled against the Sixth Marines that night but these lacked the strength of their predecessor and were dealt with in good fashion. Morning found the Marines mopping up the infiltrators. Over seven hundred dead Japanese were counted on the Sixth Marines' front.

The Sixth Regiment was not alone in its ordeal that first night on Saipan. The Twenty-fifth Marines received a shock around 0330 when a group of civilians approached their lines supposedly bent on surrender. When they were in range Japanese troops in the rear of the civilians opened up on the American positions. Fortunately, some of the Fourth Division's artillery had managed to come ashore during the day. Fire from these guns was called down on the enemy formation, civilians notwithstanding. The attack petered out.

By attacking the flanks of the American assault forces the Japanese missed a golden opportunity. A yawning gap loomed between the Eighth and Twenty-third Marines since the two divisions had been unable to link up before nightfall. Except for a sporadic effort, however, this area was largely ignored during the night's counterattacks. Had Saito consolidated his forces and driven them into this gap he most likely would have split the entire American front in half. Then he could have attacked the flanks of both sides simultaneously or held one in place while the other was destroyed.

While the Marines clung to Saipan by their fingernails, Holland Smith began to alter his plans. The reserve units of both Marine divisions were committed to the fight. Smith also decided to commit the Twenty-seventh Army Division, albeit reluctantly. In the Marine general's eyes the Twenty-seventh had performed poorly at Makin and Smith had little confidence in this unit's fighting ability and its leadership. Nevertheless, reinforcements were urgently needed on Saipan so the Twenty-seventh was committed. At the same time, plans for the attack on Guam three days hence were scrapped in case the designated assault units might also be needed on Saipan. Guam would have to wait. Kelly Turner and Spruance endorsed Smith's plan.

The morning of the sixteenth found the entire American line on the move with the exception of the Sixth Marines who were occupied by their mopping-up effort from the previous night. Later in the day the Eighth and Twenty-third Marines linked up at the town of Charan Kanoa thus cutting the base of Afetna Point. However, during the night most of the Japanese on the point had pulled out so the Marines held an empty bag. Nevertheless, communication between the two divisions was established and the Americans held a continuous line.

On the Fourth Division front the Twenty-fifth regiment managed to penetrate to within half a mile of Aslito airfield before the attack bogged down. The advance was called off around 1700 and once more the Marines dug in for the night to await the inevitable attack.

During the day, even though the entire American line had moved forward and fresh units were committed to the battle, the casualties continued to mount at a dramatic rate. The enemy artillery situated in the hills continued to pound the American positions. Well dug in Japanese strong points had to be eliminated one by one.

That night the heaviest Japanese attack fell once more on the Sixth Marines in the north. Shortly after dark the Marines began hearing engines behind the Japanese lines. This could only mean the presence of tanks. The regimental commander called for the handful of Sherman tanks that had landed during the day. Fortunately, heavy artillery had also managed to get ashore during the day. This too was poised to await the Japanese attack.

At 0330 the Japanese began to move forward. A company of 40 tanks formed the spearhead of the attack. Colonel Jones of the First Battalion called for starshells from the battleships offshore. The illuminated battlefield revealed Japanese troops clinging to the sides of tanks like a swarm of ants. Marine small arms fire poured into the hitchhiking enemy troops. Then the Shermans went tank hunting.

Many of the enemy tanks were quickly set on fire by

the marauding Shermans. Some Japanese tanks managed to penetrate the Marine lines only to be destroyed from the rear by bazooka-firing riflemen. Twenty-four of Saito's forty tanks were destroyed in the attack. The rest retreated to the safety of the hills. The Marines spent the rest of the night mopping up pockets of infiltrators. Daylight found three hundred more Japanese dead around the Sixth Marines' lines. In two nights the regiment had killed over a thousand Japanese, but not without cost. Casualties were high and the Sixth Marines were severely understrength.

Despite the night's activity, at 0700 on the seventeenth the Sixth, Eighth and Second Marines began their attack. The Eighth Regiment found the going more difficult than their neighbors who were attacking a void left by the retreating Japanese. The Eighth found itself bogged down in a swamp. This made it virtually impossible to bring their heavy equipment forward. The Marines were harassed every step of the way by hidden enemy snipers as they threaded their way through the swamp.

The next two units in line, the Twenty-third and Twenty-fourth Marines made good progress in the face of stiff enemy resistance. Casualties continued to mount but the two units moved steadily forward.

The most significant event of the day occurred on the extreme southern flank. By the morning of the seventeenth the leading element of the 27th Infantry Division, the 165th Infantry, was ashore and moving into line. The Army troops were ordered to capture Aslito airfield. They attacked up the ridge in front of the airfield late in the afternoon but were unsuccessful. The Army was not used to incurring the high casualties that the Marines by this time considered second nature. Unwilling to make another attempt, the commander of the 165th found what he considered ideal nighttime positions and dug in for the night.

Meanwhile, on the left flank of the 165th, the 25th Marines attacked and managed to cut off the airfield from reinforcements from the north. The left flank of the 165th was thus secure. In the face of the Marine advance the Japanese abandoned the airfield. Despite the urgings of the Marine commanders, the 165th refused to attack again that day. It was an ominous foretaste of what lay ahead.

After dark, Saito abandoned the lower third of the island and pulled his troops back to a defensive line running across the island north of the American positions. The only Japanese troops remaining in that portion of the island were a handful of troops defending Nafutan Point.

That night Holland Smith moved his headquarters ashore. In the wake of the 105th Infantry, Gen. Ralph Smith, commander of the 27th Division, also moved his headquarters. Ralph Smith immediately sent word to his officers that henceforth both the 105th and 165th would be under his direct operational control instead of that of the Marines. The first seeds of friction were thus sowed.

In contrast to the two previous nights, the dark hours of the seventeenth were relatively quiet, with two exceptions. An attack was made against the juncture of the Sixth and Eighth Marines. The assault managed to sever communications between the two regiments and the line was forced back. Communications were quickly restored and the attack was eventually beaten off.

But General Saito's bag of tricks still contained some surprises. Around 0430 approximately thirty barges crammed with amphibious troops set out from Tanapag Harbor intent on landing behind the American lines. The flotilla was discovered by American ships patrolling offshore. Over half of the Japanese barges were sunk in the ensuing action with heavy loss of life. The balance beat a hasty retreat back to Tanapag Harbor.

By now Saito was becoming a frustrated man. Every tactic he tried ended in failure. The Americans had not been prevented from landing and establishing a toehold on Saipan nor was he able to destroy them on the beaches. His amphibious attack turned into a disaster. On top of this came the news that no reinforcements would be forthcoming from Guam and Tinian. The only remaining hope lay with Admiral Ozawa's Imperial Fleet that was out hunting for Spruance.

Holland Smith's orders for the morning of the eighteenth called for the Fourth and Twenty-seventh Divisions to strike for the far side of the island. The Twenty-seventh secured Aslito airfield within three hours against relatively light opposition. All three regiments of the Fourth Division also met little opposition all along their front. By late afternoon, both divisions had reached their objectives. In the north, except for some straightening of the lines, the Second Division remained relatively stationary and acted as a flank guard for the Fourth. With Saipan cut in two, Holland Smith was free to wheel his three divisions around and attack northward.

Thus far American casualties had been extremely high. During the first two days of the battle the Marines had been subjected to an incessant mortar and artillery barrage. As explosion after explosion rocked the American lines human bodies were put to their severest test. Some men cracked under the strain of seeing their comrades blown away. Because of the threat of enemy counterattacks, sleep was a luxury. During the advance, each Japanese position had to be dealt with individually. The well dug in Japanese would not surrender. Nevertheless, for the most part, the bravery of the Marines withstood every test. But the toughest was yet to come.

Meanwhile, by the seventeenth, Spruance was aware that the Japanese fleet was at sea. He consolidated his four carrier task groups and moved away from Saipan to deal with the threat.* Spruance felt that the Japanese would attempt to maneuver around his flank and position themselves between the Fifth Fleet and the landing beaches. To protect against this eventuality he ordered Turner's amphibious force to move away from the beachhead and out of harm's way. Consequently, the flow of supplies and reinforcements to the battered forces on Saipan ceased. Holland Smith would have to make do for the time being.

Before wheeling his units around for the attack north Holland Smith wanted to ensure that his rear was totally secure. His orders to Ralph Smith directed the Twenty-seventh Division to secure the lower end of the island, particularly the pocket of enemy troops holding out on Nafutan Point.

Japanese forces on Nafutan Point numbered just over a thousand. These were made up of coastal artillery units and the remnants of the units that had been driven out of Aslito airfield. However, although relatively few in number, without hope for reinforcement, and with

*See *The Great Commanders of World War II, Volume IV: The Japanese*

their backs to the sea, the Japanese on Nafutan Point were prepared to sell their lives dearly.

Holland Smith felt that the Army was capable of securing Nafutan Point. While the 2nd and 4th Divisions consolidated their positions and moved forward to the jumping off point for the next phase of the battle Holland Smith ordered Ralph Smith to leave one battalion of the 105th Infantry to deal with the situation on Nafutan Point. The balance of the Army units would move into reserve behind the Marine line. Ralph Smith objected. He requested that the entire 105th Regiment be committed to the reduction of the salient on Nafutan Point. Although he concurred, Holland Smith placed one more black mark in his book alongside Ralph Smith's name. The 27th's poor performance at Makin was still fresh in Holland Smith's memory.

By nightfall of the twentieth the Marines were in position. The Battle of the Philippine Sea was history and the overwhelming American victory killed forever any hope General Saito entertained for reinforcements. The general knew this and was even more determined to make the Americans pay dearly for every inch of ground. Saito had built a formidable defensive line that stretched the width of Saipan. His troops took full advantage of the caves and valleys in the northern half of the island. Thus far, American casualties were over six thousand.

The Americans spent June 21 bringing up supplies from the beaches and moving into position. Holland Smith ordered Ralph Smith to move his two remaining regiments into a position from where they could support either of the Marine divisions quickly depending on where they were needed. Ralph Smith complied but when the 105th Infantry relieved the 165th at Nafutan Point he failed to order it to attack the enemy salient. Instead, the 105th was directed to hold its position.

On the twenty-second the American attack moved out. The Second Division's objective was Mount Tipo Pale. Although the Marines made steady progress up the mountain they found their descent of the other side barred by a large concentration of Japanese troops. In addition, the mountain was honeycombed with ravines interconnected by tunnels through the hill. Forced to concentrate on the elimination of the enemy troops in these ravines the Marines attack ground to a halt.

Further west, the Fourth Division also encountered stiff opposition. The advance here was measured in feet instead of miles and by the end of the day, the division was only halfway to the first day's objectives.

From the outset of the operation the Americans had seriously underestimated the strength of the Japanese on Saipan. The Navy planners estimated that the island's garrison numbered a little over ten thousand. Even taking into consideration the losses incurred so far, however, General Saito still had at least fifteen thousand troops still facing the Americans on June 22.

Because of the heavy resistance encountered on the twenty-second, Holland Smith decided to commit the Twenty-seventh Division the next day. Ralph Smith's division was ordered to move into the center of the line between the two Marine divisions and attack Mount Topatchau in conjunction with the Marine attacks on either flank.

The American attack on the twenty-third yielded virtually no ground at all. Both Marine divisions stalled in the face of stiff resistance and the Japanese positions dominating their flanks. The Army's attack was a disaster. The 106th Infantry failed to move forward on time and did not attack until 11:30. This in turn held up the attack of the 8th Marines on the left. When the 106th did finally move forward it was stopped in its tracks by strong enemy resistance in an area known as Hell's Pocket. At the same time, the 165th Infantry division did manage to secure a few high points but their attack resulted in heavy casualties from trying to eliminate the well dug in Japanese. The high point was dubbed Purple Heart Ridge.

By the end of the day Holland Smith was thoroughly disgusted with the 27th Division's performance. Not only had the main attack failed to achieve its objective but the 105th Infantry's attack on Nafutan Point was making little progress. The Marine general sent an Army officer, Gen. Sanderford Jarman, to have a talk with Ralph Smith.

Jarman told Ralph Smith that Holland Smith was greatly displeased with the Twenty-seventh's performance thus far. To Jarman's surprise, Ralph Smith concurred and promised to prod his officers. He said:

> On June 24 the Twenty-seventh Division was going to move and he personally was going to make sure that it went forward. If the division failed to move, then he, Maj. Gen. Ralph Smith, should be removed from command.[4]

Jarman relayed this to Holland Smith. The latter responded with a message to Ralph Smith stating that the Twenty-seventh Division's failure had held up the attack of both Marine divisions.

The next day the Second Marines captured the outskirts of the town of Garapan. The Eighth Marines moved around the base of Mount Topatchau and advanced through a thick forest.

In the center of the line the Army's attack failed once more to achieve its objectives. The 106th Infantry attacked into an area known as Death Valley. The area was dominated by enemy positions on Purple Heart Ridge on the right and Mount Topatchau on the left. In Death Valley the 106th's attack bogged down. The 165th Infantry did manage to gain the eastern side of Purple Heart Ridge but otherwise Ralph Smith's attack was a failure.

Again Holland Smith railed at the failure of the Army's attack. At nightfall on the twenty-fourth he went to Admiral Turner's flagship, *Rocky Mount*, and told the admiral that the Twenty-seventh Division had held up the entire attack for two days. Smith stated that he had not intended that the Army troops spearhead the attack but that they were only intended to protect the internal flanks of both Marine divisions. The Twenty-seventh failed to accomplish this.

Holland Smith held no personal animosity toward Ralph Smith. The Marine felt that the real fault lay in the fact that the Twenty-seventh Division was a New York National Guard unit.

Employer noncommissioned officers in the Twenty-seventh were sometimes commanded, if that is the word, by employee officers; there was sometimes a gentlemanly reluctance on the part of officers to offend their messmates through harsh criticisms or rigorous measures; in the eyes of many, especially the ambitious, there were reputations — New York reputations — to be made or broken; and behind all there was Albany, where the State Adjutant General's office allocated peacetime plums.[5]

Holland Smith was a firm advocate of breaking up National Guard units and amalgamating them with the ranks of regular Army troops but there was little he could do about it. Instead, he recommended that Ralph Smith be relieved of command since it was felt that he lacked the leadership ability necessary to inspire the Twenty-seventh to a better performance.

After stating his case to Kelly Turner, both officers went to Admiral Spruance's flagship, the cruiser *Indianapolis*. Turner shared Smith's appraisal of the situation and confronted Spruance with it. The Fifth Fleet commander pondered the consequences. The relief of an Army general in combat by a Marine general would reverberate throughout the Pacific. All three men were painfully aware of this. Nevertheless, Spruance quickly gave his consent. Ralph Smith would be replaced by General Jarman, the officer slated to be garrison commander of Saipan.

Back at his headquarters Holland Smith drafted the necessary orders and handed them to Jarman. Of the action, Smith recalled:

Relieving Ralph Smith was one of the most disagreeable tasks I have ever been forced to perform. Personally, I always regarded Ralph Smith as a likable and professionaly knowledgeable man. However, there are times in battle when the responsibility of the commander to his country and to his troops requires hard measures. Smith's division was not fighting as it should, and its failure to perform was endangering American lives. As Napoleon has said, "There are no bad regiments, only bad colonels," and the basic remedy for the defective performance of the Twenty-seventh Division was to find a leader who could make it toe the mark.[6]

Spruance was right regarding the repercussions. General Robert Richardson, commander of all Army troops in Nimitz's command, was incensed. He immediately appointed Ralph Smith to command the Ninety-eighth Division. Richardson was infuriated that Holland Smith and Spruance had taken it upon themselves to select a new commander for the Twenty-seventh Division. He considered it his sole prerogative to make such an appointment and exercised his option a few days later. Major Gen. George Griner, who was Ralph Smith's predecessor with the Ninety-eighth Division, arrived on Saipan on June 28 and replaced Jarman. The latter resumed his former command.

After the fall of Saipan Richardson arrived on the island to express his views in person. Holland Smith was under orders from Spruance to hold his tongue in spite of what Richardson might say. A loyal subordinate, Smith did not reply when Richardson stated that the Marines were ignorant in the ways of land warfare. He called them a bunch of "ridge runners." What both Smith and Spruance failed to reckon with though was the reaction of "Terrible Turner." When Richardson attempted to reiterate his statements in front of Kelly Turner, all hell broke loose:

When Richardson presented himself aboard Turner's flagship, the latter gave him the rough side of a very rough tongue. Turner reminded Richardson of a few things I was too speechless to say. To my official report of this entire episode Kelly Turner added a scorcher of his own in which he reported Richardson for "unwarranted assumption of command authority" and "irregular interference" with me in the performance of my duties.[7]

Richardson left Saipan and convened an Army Board of Inquiry. The board completely exonerated Ralph Smith. This was hardly surprising in view of the fact that the board was made up entirely of high-ranking Army officers. Blame for the poor performance of the 27th Division was placed on the shoulders of the commander of the 106th Infantry and the commander of the troops that had failed to capture Nafutan Point quickly. At the same time, the board said that Holland Smith's harsh action had been tactless.

To emphasize his lack of personal motives in sacking Ralph Smith, in his memoirs Holland Smith stated:

To do Ralph Smith credit, I must say that his testimony was the most fair-minded of the lot. He repeatedly warned his inquisitors that he had few if any records and was forced to rely on memory, and, despite repeated openings offered him in Richardson's Star Chamber, he never once launched into a diatribe or a sob story. Adversity, I think, became him well.[8]

Even with the change of command, the 27th Division's performance failed to improve significantly. On the twenty-fifth, the 165th Infantry finally did secure the rest of Purple Heart Ridge but then its attack stalled. The 106th attacked into Death Valley but the Japanese there resisted with such ferocity that the Americans were forced to withdraw to their original position.

The Marines fared a little better that day in spite of the Army troops. The Second Marines continued to make headway at Garapan while the Eighth Marines battled their way up the slopes of Mount Topatchau. Heavy defensive fire forced the latter off the slopes. After dark, however, under cover of heavy mortar fire, the Marines attacked again and gained the heights. There they settled down, dug in and beat off a strong counterattack. On the right side of the American line the Kagman Peninsula was secured by the Fourth Division.

The success of the Americans on the twenty-fifth sealed the fate of Saito's forces. Besides those killed, hundreds of troops had been cut off and surrounded in small pockets. Only four thousand troops remained in contact with General Saito.

The isolated Japanese pockets posed a real problem to the Americans. The Marines were forced to blunt their spearheads and assign units to mop up the holdouts. There were simply too many Japanese in the rear to ignore.

June 26 brought a resumption of the attack and still another failure by the 27th Division. The 106th was repulsed again in Hell's Pocket. Exasperated, General Jarman relieved the regiment's commander and replaced him with his own chief of staff. The action was long overdue. Further south, the 105th Infantry continued to struggle in their effort to capture Nafutan Point.

Shortly after midnight on the twenty-seventh the remaining Japanese troops in Nafutan attempted to break out and link up with Saito's main force. A fierce attack breached the American lines and the Japanese surged forward. But when they reached their destination, instead of finding Saito's main body, the Japanese found the Twenty-fifth Marines. The desperate Japanese attacked the Marines and were bloodily repulsed. With all hope gone the survivors committed suicide.

Morning brought a resumption of the American attack northward and finally, success by the 27th Division. One battalion of the 106th Infantry bypassed Hell's Pocket by taking the ridge overlooking the Japanese positions. The remaining two battalions moved into Death Valley and began to eliminate the enemy positions systematically one by one. Flamethrowers were used against some of the hollowed-out caves. Others were dynamited shut sealing the defenders inside.

General Jarman did not remain to share in the division's success. On June 28 General Griner arrived and assumed command. Griner was just the tonic the Army troops needed. He provided the aggressive leadership that had been lacking thus far.

Under his inspired command the Twenty-seventh proved it was worthy of sharing the battlefield with the Marines. On the twenty-ninth the Twenty-seventh accomplished what it had been trying to do for over a week. Death Valley, Hell's Pocket and Purple Heart Ridge were secured.

Once the obstacle in the center of the line was finally overcome, the entire American line surged forward.

During the next few days the Japanese were steadily compressed into a small pocket on the northern part of Saipan.

Meanwhile, Holland Smith had shifted his units. The 2nd Marine Division attacked across the front of the 27th Division. General Griner's division was then entrusted with the left flank of the American line, their attack spearheaded by the rested 105th Infantry. On July 6 the 105th's attack was brought to a halt in front of a narrow canyon dunning diagonally across the path of advance. Throughout the day and far into the night the 105th attacked the enemy position with a zeal heretofore lacking. On the second day the Americans heard small arms fire and explosions coming from the Japanese lines. When they advanced cautiously into the valley the Americans found over one hundred Japanese dead by their own hands. The men of the 105th dubbed the scene Harakiri Gulch.

The previous day Saito's surviving forces had been forced into a small pocket by the Marines. General Saito knew that the position was hopeless but he was unwilling to surrender.

Capitulation meant a loss of face. The general therefore decided to launch a counterattack in an attempt to take as many American lives as possible. "Whether we attack or whether we stay where we are there is only death,"[9] he said and asked his troops to adopt the motto: Seven lives for each one of theirs.

After a celebration during which the Japanese troops worked themselves into a frenzy while consuming the balance of their supplies, General Saito went off into seclusion and took his own life. His subordinate, General Suzuki was left to lead the final charge. By that time the noble Admiral Nagumo had also perished by his own hand.

At 0400 on July 7 the Japanese, four-thousand strong, attacked their tormentors. The drunken, screaming horde hit the 105th Infantry head on. Many of the Japanese were armed with only swords, others were reduced to carrying clubs and sticks since weapons were in short supply. Those that did possess rifles had only a few rounds of ammunition apiece. The howling mob plowed directly into a gap between two battalions. The American defenders were quickly overrun. Individual groups of soldiers manned machine guns and poured fire into the ranks of the advancing enemy but the tide swarmed over them and continued to surge forward. On the heights above the hapless 105th the 23rd Marines lobbed mortar shells into the enemy ranks with little effect.

Once they passed the 105th, the Japanese fanned out. The 10th and 27th Marines were the next to feel the fury of the attack. American artillerymen fired point blank into the enemy swarm before they too were overrun and forced to abandon their guns. General Griner ordered the 106th Infantry to move up and support the beleaguered defenders.

Inevitably, the Japanese horde became strung out. The American reserve units and those that had managed to stand their ground eventually slowed the momentum of the Japanese attack. Then the 106th Infantry moved in and began mopping up pockets of resistance. The next morning forty-three hundred dead Japanese were counted along the route of the attack.

The counterattack was the last Japanese gasp. The American soldiers and Marines went over to the attack and pushed the remaining enemy toward the edge of the island. On July 9 the Americans approached the north coast. There they were greeted with a sight that would be indelibly stamped on their minds forever. Hundreds of Japanese soldiers and sailors hurled themselves off the high cliffs onto the rocks below. They were accompanied by the Japanese population of the island. As the Americans looked on in horror mothers pushed their children over the edge before taking their own lives. Old men and women, believing the Japanese propaganda joined in the massive suicide. There was little the American troops could do.

At 1800 that evening Admiral Turner informed Spruance that Saipan was finally secure. A few small pockets of Japanese holding out in caves remained to be eliminated but for all intents and purposes the battle was over. For the Americans it had been a costly victory. Over seventeen thousand casualties, including four thousand dead, was the cost. Enormous casualties, even for the Marines.

The Japanese cost was over twenty-four thousand lives. But this figure did not include those that had jumped into the sea or were sealed forever in dynamited caves.

Saipan's fall also had far-reaching political consequences. Faced with the breaching of the inner Japanese defensive ring, Prime Minister Tojo resigned. Saipan was the beginning of the end and the Japanese knew it.

With Saipan secured the Americans once more turned their attention to Tinian. Originally Tinian was scheduled to be invaded a few weeks after the invasion of Saipan since the American planners thought that

Saipan could be taken after a brief fight. The skill and determination of Saipan's defenders had allowed the Tinian garrison a reprieve.

There were a number of reasons for the Americans to invade Tinian. Foremost among these was its proximity to Saipan. Less than three miles separated the northern tip of Tinian from Agingan Point on Saipan. Left alone the Japanese on Tinian could harass the American occupation forces on Saipan via amphibious attacks across the narrow strait separating the two islands. In addition, the Japanese had built four excellent airfields on Tinian. Aerial attacks against American positions on Saipan could be easily launched once the Fifth Fleet left the area.

The Japanese defenders of Tinian numbered in excess of nine thousand under Col. Keishi Ogata. However, less than half of them were considered front line troops. The balance were naval units and support personnel.

The selection of a suitable landing site posed a vexing problem for the Americans. Admiral Harry Hill was chosen to command the amphibious operation. The proximity of Saipan made landings on the northeast corner of Tinian the most direct route. Unfortunately, that corner of Tinian contained but two narrow beaches backed by high cliffs. An amphibious attack against a fortified position of this nature would be mass suicide. In addition, the restricted landing areas were not suitable for moving large quantities of troops and supplies ashore in a short period.

Colonel Ogata was well aware of the perils of an attack across the strait separating the two islands and felt that the Americans would never consider undertaking such a hazardous operation. Instead, with their vast resources the Americans would seek out a more suitable landing point. The best landing beaches were at Tinian Town on the southwest coast of the island and near Asiga Bay. These two areas were the most obvious points for an invasion. Asiga Bay seemed the most logical because it was closer to Saipan but Tinian Town possessed the better beaches. So it was in those two places that Ogata concentrated his main defenses.

But Colonel Ogata underestimated Admiral Hill. The American commander sent a small detachment of Marines and underwater demolition experts to explore beaches White 1 and 2 on the northern coast. Under cover of darkness this force landed and explored the area in question. A second force surveyed Asiga Bay further south on the same side of the island.

The findings of the two parties were added to the rest of Hill's intelligence. Aerial reconnaissance revealed that Ogata's concentration of force around Tinian Town and Asiga Bay was growing with each passing day. In addition, Hill knew that those Japanese positions on Tinian closest to Saipan had been subjected to a constant artillery barrage for a number of weeks. It was an easy matter for American gunners to fire across the strait at anything that even resembled an enemy position. No matter how many options Hill explored his mind kept returning to one factor: casualties. Therefore, in spite of the difficulty of bringing supplies ashore, the admiral decided to make the assault on beaches White 1 and 2.

Hill prepared an elaborate deception plan for the Tinian garrison. For over two weeks Tinian Town and Japanese positions near Asiga Bay were subjected to a heavy aerial bombardment. Battleships and cruisers

242

added the weight of their guns to the bombardment. Scant attention was given to the area around the White beaches. The intensive bombardment served to firm up Ogata's convictions regarding the actual invasion point.

On the morning of July 24, seven transports escorted by the battleships *Colorado* and *Tennessee* appeared off Tinian Town. The heavy ships began a steady pounding of the beach area. At the same time the Second and Eighth Marines began boarding landing craft in full view but out of range of the defenders. The assault boats mingled about then tied up on the side of the transports that was out of sight of land. Then the Marines climbed down the other side of the transports into waiting landing craft again. To the Japanese on shore it appeared as if the Americans were sending an endless stream of troops to attack them.

Ogata ordered his heavy artillery to open up on the American ships. The *Colorado* ventured too close to shore and was hit over twenty times as was the destroyer *Norman Scott*. Around 0730 the Marines boarded their transports one final time and headed out to sea. Colonel Ogata sent a message to Tokyo announcing that his brave troops had repelled a strong invasion attempt with heavy loss of life to the enemy. Radio Tokyo jubilantly broadcast the news to the nation.

Meanwhile, while Ogata celebrated, on the White beaches the Twenty-fourth and Twenty-fifth Marines moved ashore against light opposition. So confident was Ogata that he had nothing to fear from this quarter that the area was defended by only one company of troops. The Marines had come from Saipan by landing craft. The relatively short distance between the two islands precluded the need for transports. By the time Ogata realized that the landings at the White beaches were more than a feint it was too late to do anything about it. The Marines were ashore in force.

After moving inland for a few miles the Marines dug in to secure the landing area. It was a wise decision. That night the inevitable counterattack came as Ogata, who by now realized his error, repositioned his units in an effort to hurl the Americans back into the sea.

Counterattacks struck three separate sections of the American lines. The Marines used starshells to light up the battlefield. In some areas the fighting was fierce and the situation was desperate for a while. But the Marine line held. In the morning over twelve hundred dead Japanese were counted in front of the Marine positions.

The Americans were simply too strong for the Japanese defenders. From the beachhead two Marine divisions struck out across the island and cut it in two. The two divisions then advanced in opposite directions across the width of the island. Heavy rains arrived on July 28 and hampered the advance but the Marines made steady progress. Each day it was the same story: advance, dig in for the night and prepare to beat off the Japanese attack. With these counterattacks the defenders of Tinian played right into American hands. Each attack met with a bloody repulse until the Japanese had exhausted their manpower. The final charge came on the night of August first. Like its predecessors this attack failed to achieve anything but more Japanese deaths.

American casualties on Tinian totalled just over two thousand killed and wounded. Japanese losses were four times as great. One significant factor the Americans noticed on Tinian was the capture of more enemy prisoners. Nevertheless, a vast majority of the defenders still preferred death to surrender. Their fanaticism resulted in the loss of more American lives. On Tinian also, the civilian population, for the most part, refused to join the Japanese troops in sacrificing their lives. Apparently the population of Tinian did not believe Japanese propaganda about the fate that would befall them should they fall into American hands.

With two of the three objectives in the Marianas secured, American attention turned to Guam. This island would prove a tough nut to crack. The Japanese garrison there was nineteen thousand strong. However, the defenders were a hodgepodge of formations. Most of the Japanese reinforcements for the Marianas had been split between Saipan, Tinian and Guam. Those on Saipan and Tinian were now gone.

The American planners relied heavily on the experiences of Saipan and Tinian. Fifty-six thousand Marine and Army troops would be committed to the battle. The landing beaches selected were on the west coast of the island on either side of Orote Point, at Agat Bay and Asan Point. For over a month American air attacks pounded targets on Guam. Two weeks prior to the invasion the island was subjected to an around-the-clock bombardment from sea and air. It was the heaviest pre-invasion bombardment thus far in the war.

In spite of the heavy bombardment the Japanese positions were hardly dented. Their guns were well concealed and dug into the rocks. On July 21 when the invasion began, the defenders were waiting.

At both landing points the story was the same. The attackers found themselves under heavy artillery and mortar fire. The Americans incurred heavy casualties.

As at Saipan, the beaches were littered with dead, wounded and burning amphibious vehicles. In spite of the heavy fire, however, the Marines moved steadily inland and the buildup continued. As night fell the barrage subsided and the Marines dug in to face the inevitable.

Throughout the war in the Pacific the Japanese failed to learn from their mistakes. Banzai charges against well dug in American positions were rarely successful. Nevertheless, the Japanese commanders continued this wasteful expenditure of manpower. The first night on Guam was no exception. The Japanese Thirty-eighth Regiment was virtually wiped out attempting to overrun the Fourth Marines. All along the line the tactic was repeated. The Japanese attacked, killed a few Marines, and suffered enormous casualties in turn.

July 22 was no different than similar days on Saipan and Tinian. The Marines moved inland step by step, destroying enemy positions every yard of the way. At night they dug in and beat off yet another costly enemy attack.

By the morning of the twenty-third the best of the defenders were dead, sacrificed in futile banzai charges. Others, electing to hold their ground, were overrun and killed by the advancing Marines.

On the night of the twenty-fifth the Japanese launched their heaviest counterattack. An American hospital was overrun and the wounded and medical personnel killed. Despite their exhaustion from four days of fighting the Marines clung to their positions and killed over three thousand of the enemy. Many senior Japanese officers perished in the attack. The defenders had shot their bolt.

It took the Americans two more weeks to secure Guam. The prolonged defense was not due so much to the enemy as it was to the terrain. The Japanese utilized the jungles and swamps brilliantly. Snipers and small pockets of defenders harassed the Marines and infantrymen every step of the way. The advance bypassed thousands of the enemy but, lacking supplies and scattered, the Japanese could offer only a token, albeit deadly, resistance:

In twenty-one days of battle the Marines, who bore the assault in the beginning, had 7,000 killed and wounded. The Army suffered about 1,000 casualties. The Americans counted 11,000 Japanese bodies, but many more were sealed in caves. The propaganda campaign of later months did bring some Japanese out of hiding; by the end of the war, 1,250 Japanese had surrendered, most of them starving. But finally the Americans counted 18,500 Japanese dead on Guam, which meant that another 8,000 soldiers and sailors had starved or been killed after the island was lost.[10]

The Marianas campaign was the last great campaign of the central Pacific drive. Okinawa and Iwo Jima still lay ahead but never again was such an ambitious operation undertaken by Nimitz's command.

Even before Saipan was declared secure, American Seabees began work on the construction of runways. From the air bases in the Marianas the B-29 bombing offensive against the Japanese homeland moved from strategic planning to reality. The Japanese were absolutely correct in their assessment that the Marianas were the bulwark of the empire's inner defensive ring. Accordingly, they had little choice but to make the Americans pay dearly for every square inch of ground. The casualty figures on both sides bear grim testimony to their success. Despite their best efforts, however, the Marianas campaign marked the beginning of the end of the Japanese Empire.

Chapter Six

Iwo Jima

On February 19, 1945, the United States Marines crashed ashore on the island of Iwo Jima thus initiating the bloodiest battle in Marine Corps history. One book has likened the battle to "throwing human flesh against reinforced concrete."[1] The Japanese commander had vowed to hold onto Iwo Jima at all cost. In order to fulfill that vow he turned the island into a veritable fortress. It was this fortress that three Marine divisions were ordered to assault that day in February. Before the battle was over, 27 marines would earn Congressional Medals of Honor, but 6,281 of their comrades would lie dead. An additional 21,865 would become casualties. Admiral Nimitz later commented, "Among the Americans who served on Iwo Island, uncommon valor was a common virtue." This "supreme test" cost the Marine Corps dearly. From this battle has come the corps symbol immortalized in bronze: the raising of the American flag on Mount Suribachi. Although the battle was marked by ferocity it was not lacking in bravery. The scars of this battle would never leave its participants, the horror left an indelible mark. The dead did not die in vain, however, for this crucial island economized the war effort for America and in the long run saved more lives than were lost taking it.

The autumn of 1944 found the Americans firmly entrenched in the Marianas with General MacArthur poised to make his historic return to the Philippines. In less than one year's time, Nimitz's central Pacific forces had travelled over three thousand miles from Tarawa in the Gilberts, through the Marshalls to Saipan, Tinian and Guam in the Marianas. In September of that year, Nimitz's forces assaulted Peleliu in the Palaus in support of MacArthur's invasion of the Philippines. Also that fall, the Army Air Force began its devastating bombing campaign against Japan from the recently occupied Marianas. Delivering the deadly loads were the world's largest bombers, the great silver giant, the B-29 Superfortress.

For the Japanese, 1944 witnessed the virtual end of their mighty Imperial Navy. In the battles of the Philippine Sea in June and the Battle of Leyte Gulf in October, this once-proud navy was all but obliterated. The Japanese had very little left to oppose the American Navy.

In January, 1945, the Americans were on Luzon in the Philippines, effectively dividing Japan from its southern empire and all its vital natural resources. Japan was truly reaping the whirlwind.

The Japanese homeland was approximately 1500 miles from the nearest American bases in the Marianas. Halfway between Japan and these islands lay the island of Iwo Jima. From the entrance of Tokyo Bay southward for 750 miles stretches a chain of islands known as the Nanpo Shoto. Three major groups comprise the Nanpo Shoto: the Izut Shoto, the Bonin Islands, and the Volcano Islands. Iwo Jima is located among the latter group approximately 670 miles south of Tokyo and 700 miles north of the Marianas, about equal distance between the two.

The English translation for Iwo Jima is Sulphur Island, so named because of the extensive sulphur deposits found throughout the island. It is shaped like a pork chop, measuring less than five miles long and two-and-a-half miles across in the north, narrowing to one half mile in the south. At its southern extremity is the island's highest point, an extinct volcano rising 546 feet named Mount Suribachi. The northern half of the island is rocky and hilly and rises over 300 feet above sea level. This area features many cliffs, canyons and caves, excellent terrain for conducting a protracted defense. Between Mt. Suribachi and the northern plateau is a large layer of volcanic ash. There is very little about Iwo Jima to make it attractive. This is probably the reason it had been left untouched by the Europeans during the land grab of the previous few centuries.

It was the Japanese who first showed an interest in the stark island. Following the historic visit by Commodore Perry in 1853, the Japanese sent their colonists to the island chain. By 1861 they had laid claim to the Bonin and Volcano Islands thus placing Iwo Jima under direct Japanese jurisdiction.

By 1943 there were eleven hundred Japanese civilians on the island employed in a number of occupations ranging from sugar refining to sulphur mining. The northern part of the island housed the civilians in five small settlements. But Iwo was not a pleasant island to live on. Fresh water was nonexistent. It had to be either collected in concrete cisterns from rain or supplied from the main islands by tanker. Adding to the population's discomfort was the constant odor of sulphur vapors, similar to the smell of rotten eggs. In addition, vegetation is sparse with a few twisted trees and some coarse grass found in the northern end. An American chaplain described the island, "After God got through making the world, he must've took all the dirty ash and rubble left and made Iwo Jima."[2] So why did this desolate island achieve such strategic importance to warrant such attention?

Up until the time of the American conquest of the Marshalls, Iwo Jima was lightly fortified. With the likelihood of an American advance to the Marianas, however, the Japanese re-evaluated their position in the Volcano-Bonin Islands. In March, 1944, the Thirty-first Army was activated for the purpose of garrisoning the island and continuing work on another airfield. Two airfields had already been completed. Command of the Thirty-first Army was given to Gen. Hideyoshi Obata.

As the Americans approached the Marianas, the Japanese increased their troop strength on Iwo Jima. With the troops came reinforcements of heavy artillery. Slowly but surely Iwo was formed into a bastion. After the successful American campaign in the Marianas during the summer of 1944, the Japanese realized that their home islands could be subjected to bombardment from these islands. Thus Iwo Jima, halfway between Japan and the Marianas, increased in importance. For the Japanese, Iwo acted as a block with which to hinder both the American advance and their air effort. To the Americans, Iwo's central position was also vital for, in their hands, it could serve to enhance their bombing offensive against the Japanese cities.

The Japanese realized that if Iwo Jima were going to

be held, it would have to be reinforced heavily. In late May, 1944, even before the American attack on the Marianas, Prime Minister Hideki Tojo summoned Lt. Gen. Tadamichi Kuribayashi and gave him an Imperial mandate to defend Iwo Jima to the last.

Kuribayashi was a member of an honorable Samurai family. At fifty-four years of age he already had a distinguished military career behind him. In the 1920s he spent two years as military attache in the United States. In a letter to his wife during that period he expressed his opinion of America:

> The United States is the last country in the world that Japan should fight. Its industrial potentiality is huge and fabulous, and the people are energetic and versatile. One must never underestimate the American fighting ability.[3]

After working his way through many varied assignments, both on staff and in the field, Kuribayashi was well suited for the vital command on Iwo Jima. With the eyes of his country upon him, he sensed his awesome responsibility. Therefore, he was determined to make Iwo Jima into an invincible fortress. Upon his arrival on Sulphur Island on June 8, 1944, he immediately went to work. Kuribayashi was on Iwo only a few days when American Carrier Task Groups 58.1 and 58.4 under Adm. J. "Jocko" Clark raided the island. The resulting loss of many of their aircraft was a bitter pill for the Japanese to digest. Saburo Sakai in his book *Samurai* gave his reaction to the loss:

> The loss of forty planes and pilots in a single action staggered me. Equally disturbing was the sight of

our inexperienced pilots falling in flames, one after the other, as the Hellcats blasted their outmoded Zeros from the sky.[4]

Additional attacks took place during the next month as American carrier planes struck repeatedly in order to prevent the Japanese planes from interfering with the Marianas operation. Early in July, American ships moved close enough to shell Japanese positions on Iwo.

Kuribayashi, who had personally experienced the air strikes and naval bombardment, was more than ever determined to fortify the island against an attempted invasion. Realistically, he knew that without air and sea domination, the result of an invasion was a foregone conclusion. The best he could hope for was a long campaign with the resultant spilling of American blood.

One of Kuribayashi's first acts was to order the evacuation of all civilians. That accomplished, he began to prepare his overall plan for the defense of the island. The original plan drafted by his predecessor was faithful to the belief that an invasion must be stopped on the beach. As a result, Kuribayashi found most of his heavy artillery and numerous pillboxes situated to rake the beaches. He quickly changed all that. In light of American air and naval supremacy, it would be futile to defend the island at the water's edge. Instead, he ordered the artillery, mortars and rockets to Mt. Suribachi and the plateau north of the airfields.

In order to ensure a prolonged defense, Kuribayashi then began construction of an extensive system of tunnels and caves. Recent experience had demonstrated that surface weapons and installations could be easily destroyed by naval gunfire. Mining engineers arrived from Japan and drew up elaborate blueprints noting places where underground fortifications and tunnels could be placed.

While the engineers worked to honeycomb the island, reinforcements flowed into Iwo Jima: infantry, artillery units, and anti-tank companies. By the end of 1944, despite the deadly work of the American Air Force and the numerous sinkings of Japanese supply ships by U.S. submarines, Kuribayashi could boast of 361 artillery pieces of varying size and a large defense force of more than twenty thousand troops including a regiment commanded by the dashing 1932 Olympic gold medal winner for horsemanship, Lt. Col. Baron Takeichi Nishi.

To say that the Japanese fortifications were formidable would be an understatement. So skillfully did the engineers construct the pillboxes that they blended right into the stark landscape. Made of four-foot-thick walls, they were built so that many were connected by underground tunnels that allowed the defenders mobility despite having to defend fixed positions. A great many of the fortifications were so far underground that they were all but immune from air or naval bombardment. The official Marine Corps history commented on the caves:

> Positions constructed underground ranged in size from small caves for a few men to several underground chambers capable of holding three hundred or four hundred men. In order to prevent personnel from becoming trapped in any one excavation, the subterranean installations were provided with multiple entrances and exits, as well as stairways and interconnecting passageways.[5]

257

Kuribayashi himself had his headquarters on the northern part of the island just south of Kitano Point. It was seventy-five feet underground and resembled a vast subterranean chamber. Because of the intricacy of the cave system he could communicate instantly with every defense sector.

While turning the island into an impregnable fortress, the general formulated his battle plan. Anticipating a lengthy pre-landing bombardment, he ordered his artillery to remain silent so as not to disclose their location to the enemy. He also directed his forces not to fire on the invaders until they advanced approximately five hundred yards inland at which point the artillery would decimate them. Then, after inflicting heavy casualties, the artillery would be moved further north. Kuribayashi's plan called for a flexible or elastic defense designed to inflict maximum damage to the enemy for as long as humanly possible.

By early February, 1945, the Japanese force had risen to twenty-three thousand men, each one determined to do his duty for the emperor. Many of the defenders wore white headbands similar to those worn by the kamikaze pilots. Their determination to stop the Americans was so strong that each vowed to die fighting. Each one took what was called the "Courageous Battle Vow":

Each man will make it his duty to kill ten of the enemy before dying. Until we are destroyed to the last man, we shall harass the enemy by guerrilla tactics.[6]

To the Americans Iwo Jima was the focus of intense interest following the conquest of the Marianas. In mid-

July Admirals King and Nimitz reviewed the Joint Chiefs' decision to place four B-29 groups in the Marianas. The desirability of establishing fighter escort bases in the Bonins was also discussed. Other more pressing concerns diverted attention from the Bonins but plans for their capture continued to be discussed along with the possibility of setting up more B-29 bases in the Marianas.

When the long-range bombing offensive against Japan became a reality in the fall of 1944, Iwo Jima quickly assumed major strategic importance. Of all the Bonin and Volcano Islands, only Iwo had terrain suitable for construction of airfields capable of handling the Superfortresses and house a sufficient number of fighters to escort the huge bombers to their target.

Originally, Admiral King advocated the invasion of Formosa*, but most of the Allied planners were cool to this plan. Gradually, therefore, after taking all things into account, the needs of the Army Air Force predominated. By autumn, an operation designed to seize Iwo Jima was approved.

Although still desiring an attack on Formosa, King reluctantly agreed on Iwo Jima and set the target date for Operation Detachment for January 20, 1945. Delays in the Philippines campaign eventually caused the Iwo attack to be postponed until February 19. The basic purpose of this operation was to turn the island into a springboard from which an attack on Japan's home islands could be launched. In addition, the island was to serve as an emergency base for the bombers and an airstrip for the fighters escorting the B-29s to Japan.

*See *The Great Admirals of World War II, Volume I: The Americans*, Chapter 1.

The task of seizing Iwo Jima was given to Adm. Raymond Spruance, commander of the Fifth Fleet. Admiral Richmond Kelly Turner was designated amphibious commander, commander of the expeditionary troops was Gen. Holland M. Smith and to head the Fifth Amphibious Corps (VAC), Maj. Gen. Harry Schmidt was tabbed. The designated assault troops were the Third, Fourth and Fifth Marine Divisions.

The Third Division was commanded by Maj. Gen. Graves B. Erskine. It had seen action in the jungles of Bougainville, the Solomons, and had fought at Guam. The Fourth Division, commanded by Maj. Gen. Clifton B. Cates had been at Roi-Namur at Kwajalein in the Marshalls and had participated in the difficult battle on Saipan and the less difficult attack on Tinian in the Marianas. Major Gen. Keller E. Rockey's Fifth Marine Division was newly organized but its ranks were filled with combat-hardened veterans of Guadalcanal and Tarawa. After the battle General Rockey made this comment on his division:

> From its earliest days to the hours of its disbandment, I found the Fifth to possess and maintain a high standard of military performance and an esprit exceptionally fine. And when the Fifth Division entered combat, it acted from the first hour like a unit of veterans. It fought that first tough fight with the utmost vigor, courage and intelligence.[7]

These, then, were the warriors chosen to face the Marine Corps' hardest test.

The VAC commander, General Schmidt, issued his

first operational plan for Detachment on October 19, 1944. Modifications would follow before the final plans were accepted. When Spruance assumed command of the Fifth Fleet on January 26, 1945, the accepted plan called for the Fourth and Fifth Divisions to land first with the Third remaining on board ship to act as corps reserve.

The landing was to take place on Iwo's southeastern beaches with the Fourth Division on the right and the Fifth on the left. The attack plan called for the forces to exploit the beachhead as rapidly as possible while advancing in a northeasterly direction. One regiment of the Fifth Marines was assigned the task of capturing Mt. Suribachi. After the southern portion of the island was secured, the two divisions would wheel north. At this point the Third Division would land to reinforce the drive.

The Marine planners made two serious miscalculations. First of all they numbered the Japanese garrison at only fourteen thousand. Secondly, they assumed that the enemy would contest the landing:

The enemy may be prepared to attempt small local counterattacks prior to the establishment of our beachhead in order to annihilate our forces at the beach. His doctrine specifies that the enemy must not gain a foothold on shore and that in order to combat this all troops must be prepared to attack with the mission of splitting our forces and destroying them by local counterattacks.[8]

The planners were wrong. General Kuribayashi had learned from prior Japanese failures and was not about to make the same mistake.

The American invasion fleet was made up of over eight hundred vessels with an assault force numbering 70,647. Additional auxiliary personnel and naval forces increased the number of men involved in the Iwo Jima attack to 250,000.

As the American force approached its objective, General Kuribayashi and his garrison had done all that was possible under the circumstances. Now all they could do was wait with anticipation for a duel to the death against the invaders.

Experience had taught the American command that extensive preliminary air and naval bombardment was essential to soften up the target before the assault troops made their landing. Since August Iwo had become a regular target for the air forces. The attacks were carried out by the Seventh Air Force using B-24 bombers based in the Marianas. On December 8, the bombing began on a continuous basis right up until mid-February. Day and night the island was subjected to the heaviest pre-invasion bombardment of any target in the Pacific.

In evaluating the effectiveness of the bombing, it was realized that numerous strong points remained despite the constant weight of bombs. Even the airfields remained operational:

At no time were all of Iwo's strips rendered inoperational and no single strip was out of service for a whole day.[9]

In an effort to clear a path for the assault troops, between February 1 and 16 the Seventh Air Force conducted no less than 283 daylight and 233 night attacks. Over six hundred tons of bombs and eleven hundred drums of napalm were dropped during the daylight attacks alone. Yet the results proved disappointing because the bombers had to fly at high altitudes and were therefore unable to concentrate on specific targets. Thus, the pre-landing naval bombardment took on increased importance.

The length of this bombardment became a matter of dispute between the Navy and Marine commands. Holland Smith, relying on his experience in the Gilberts, Marshalls and Marianas, was acutely aware how much damage enemy guns left intact could do to assault troops:

> My own study of early air photographs indicated that a situation of incredible nature existed on the island. It was plain that Iwo Jima had fortifications the like and extent of which we had never encountered. . . . My opinion was that far more naval gunfire was needed on an island five times the size of Tarawa, with many more times the number of defenses.[10]

The Marine planners, and Smith in particular, requested that ten days of intense naval bombardment precede the attack.

In the meantime, acting independently, Admiral Turner had ordered a study of naval gunfire requirements for the forthcoming invasion. The results of this study contrasted sharply with that of the Marines. Turner believed that tactical surprise was absolutely vital and feared the loss of this by a premature naval bombardment. The loss of the element of surprise, he said, would allow enemy aircraft from the Japanese homeland to hinder the operation. He therefore concluded that three days of bombardment would be adequate. At the same time he ordered a subsidiary attack by carrier aircraft to be made against air bases in Japan. This would reduce the threat of air strikes from that quarter.

When Gen. Harry Schmidt, commander of the VAC, received Turner's plan he ordered an alternate study that would demonstrate the absolute necessity for a ten-day bombardment. Despite this study, Turner remained adamant. Schmidt was not to be undone and continued to press for more than three days even if it was only one more. Holland Smith endorsed Schmidt's request and stated that four days of pre-invasion bombardment was an absolute minimum. He predicted dire consequences if the enemy strong points were not eliminated.

Turner's resolve finally weakened but he said that he would need the approval of Spruance. The latter rejected the request, insisting that the onset of the surface bombardment had to coincide with the initial carrier attack on the Tokyo area scheduled for February 16. Spruance felt that the weeks of aerial bombardment were more than equal to the extra days desired by the assault forces. The Marines would have to live and die with that decision.

In the early morning hours of February 16, just as the carriers of Admiral Mitscher's TF 58 were launching their planes against targets in Japan, the naval bombardment of Iwo Jima commenced in all its fury. The island was divided into sectors with each battleship or cruiser assigned to a particular area (Map 19).

During the next three days the warships pounded the

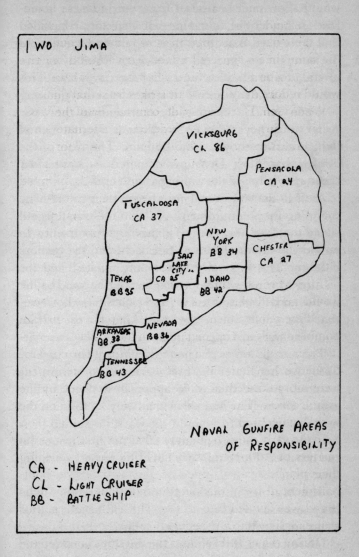

IWO JIMA

VICKSBURG
CA 86

PENSACOLA
CA 24

TUSCALOOSA
CA 37

NEW YORK
BB 34

CHESTER
CA 27

SALT LAKE CITY
CA 25

IDAHO
BB 42

TEXAS
BB 35

ARKANSAS
BB 33

NEVADA
BB 36

TENNESSEE
BB 43

NAVAL GUNFIRE AREAS
OF RESPONSIBILITY

CA - HEAVY CRUISER
CL - LIGHT CRUISER
BB - BATTLE SHIP

targets while underwater demolition teams cleared the way to the assault beaches. On the eve of D-day, a morose Holland Smith found himself deeply apprehensive. Still convinced that three days of bombardment were not enough, he expected a bloodbath. Would his dire predictions prove accurate or had the naval bombardment been able to eliminate the Japanese strong points?

It was Monday morning, the nineteenth of February. A light mist hovered over Iwo Jima as the first sign of light began to show on the horizon. The men of the Fourth and Fifth Divisions prepared to leave their transports to board the waiting assault craft.

At 0640 the large naval guns began their pre H-hour softening-up bombardment. At 0800 the warships fell silent to allow the carrier planes an opportunity to pound the slopes of Mount Suribachi and the landing beaches. The sight of the swooping planes filled the waiting Marines with hope that very little would be left on Iwo. The veterans knew from experience, however, that that would not be the case. After almost half an hour, the warships opened up again.

The assault forces reached their line of departure by 0730. An hour later the first wave started toward the beaches. As the first wave approached their landing points, the rockets and shells that were landing on the beaches halted abruptly and the warships shifted their fire inland. At approximately 0900 the first troops hit the beaches. Three minutes later, the second wave followed.

The Marines immediately found themselves ankle-deep in sand and volcanic ash. The soft terrain caused them to stumble forward and reduced their upward climb to a crawl. To their amazement, they encountered very little opposition. Had the days of bombardment eliminated the enemy? They were falling right into Kuribayashi's trap. He was more than willing to yield the beaches in order to annihilate them in the interior later on.

As the numbers of attackers increased, the Japanese began to open up. Their fire was devastating and quickly dissipated American optimism. Airfield Number 1 was one of the preliminary D-day objectives. When the assault troops moved toward the airfield, the Japanese defenders hit them with everything they had. From concealed pillboxes the Japanese raked the Marines with machine guns and lobbed hundreds of mortar shells.

The Twenty-eighth Regiment of the Fifth Division had the assignment of traversing the island at its narrow neck along the base of Mt. Suribachi. As the Twenty-eighth moved inland, heavy mortar and artillery fire enveloped the beaches making the reorganization of companies all but impossible. Nevertheless, the buildup continued and the Marines continued their bloody step-by-step advance.

The bravery of the Marines was incredible. By noon the island was cut and the advance toward Suribachi had begun, but movement was painfully slow.

At the beaches the situation was chaotic. The Fifth Division's official history records:

At the water's edge amtracs, LCMs and LCVPs were hit, burned, beached and capsized, and otherwise mangled. The loose, black volcanic cinders slid past the churning tires of wheeled vehicles, mixing them axle deep; the steep terraces blocked egress from the beach and extensive mine-fields took a heavy toll. Debris piled up every-where. . . . Wounded men were arriving on the beach by the dozen, where they were not much better off than they had been at the front. There was no cover to protect them and supplies of plasma and dressings ran low. The first two boats bringing in badly needed litters were blown out of the water. Casualties were being hit a second time as they lay helpless, under blankets, awaiting evacuation to ships.[11]

While the Twenty-eighth moved to isolate Mt. Sur-ibachi, the Twenty-seventh Regiment headed toward the southern sector of Airfield Number 1 and the west-ern beaches. The Twenty-sixth Regiment landed later in the day and quickly took up positions near the south-ern end of the airfield. The end of D-day found the men of the Fifth Division huddled in foxholes on Iwo's bleak landscape.

While the Fifth Marines sliced the island in the south, the Fourth Division landed on the beaches to the north. The initial landing was easy but as the troops moved inland they encountered stiff resistance. By nightfall, the Fourth Division had managed to occupy the edge of the airfield and an area known as the Quarry. The battle for the Quarry was particularly brutal, marked by heavy loss of American lives. Lieutenant Colonel Chambers, commander of the Third Battalion, Twenty-fifth Regiment, earned a Congressional Medal of Honor for his aggressive leadership in taking the Quarry.

As darkness approached, the Japanese continued to

rain death on the attackers. The Marines were forced to halt their attack and dig in short of their D-day objective. The Americans prepared for the usual counterattack. It never came.

Bunched in foxholes along the perimeter, the Marines took turns on watch, fighting to stay awake, waiting, waiting for the crazy banzai. . . . Still the rush didn't come.[12]

Kuribayashi was sticking to his plan of not wasting lives in suicidal counterattacks.

During the first day of Iwo Jima, 2,420 Marines became casualties. 566 of these were fatalities. But this was only the beginning.

The first night on Iwo Jima was a nightmare:

About the beach in the morning lay the dead. They died with the greatest possible violence. Nowhere in the Pacific were seen such badly mangled bodies. Many were cut squarely in half. Legs and arms lay fifty feet away from any body. All through the bitter night, the Japs rained heavy mortar and rockets and artillery on the entire area between the beach and the airfield.[13]

As morning of the second day dawned, the weather was cold and damp with a light rain falling. With the exception of the twenty-eighth Regiment, the Marines prepared to move to capture the airfields and the remaining portion of the island. Colonel Harry Liversedge's Twenty-eighth Regiment had the awesome task of taking Mt. Suribachi, "Hotrocks" to the Marines.

In support of the Twenty-eighth, carrier planes blasted Suribachi with rockets, napalm and bombs while the larger support ships fired their huge projectiles onto the slopes. By 0830 the Marines were ready to move out. The Second Battalion was on the left, the Third on the right; the First Battalion remained in reserve. Suribachi became a symbol to the attackers, dominating the scene:

> On this day and increasingly as days went by, Suribachi seemed to take on a life of its own, to be watching these men, looming over them, pressing down upon them. When they moved, they moved in its shadows, under its eye.[14]

By noon the Marine had managed to advance only seventy-five yards. The enemy's strong points had incredibly survived the massive shelling. From their camouflaged pillboxes the defenders rained death on the Marines. It was obvious that the elimination of these positions would have to be accomplished by the troops themselves with demolitions and flamethrowers. One pillbox after another was systematically reduced by this painstaking method. By nightfall, the Twenty-eighth had advanced another two hundred yards. Once more they sought protection in foxholes and again the expected counterattack failed to materialize.

One participant in the attack on Suribachi summed up the horror of the Japanese shelling:

> The very worst I can remember our taking. The Jap mortarmen seemed to be playing checkers and

270

using us as their squares. I still can't understand how any of us got through.[15]

On D + 2 the Twenty-eighth Marines continued their deadly ascent. The weather remained damp. Like the previous day, preliminary attacks were carried out by carrier planes that dropped their deadly loads on the mountain slopes just in front of the Marine positions. At 8:25 the attack order was passed down the line.

Once more the fighting was intense and casualties mounted at an alarming rate. From concealed positions the unseen enemy fired their deadly tracers. Each Japanese positions had to be taken one at a time. Flamethrowers, grenades and demolition charges were the best weapons in this strange war against an unseen enemy. Valor was commonplace among the attackers. By nightfall, the Twenty-eighth had managed to form a semicircle around the north face of the mountain. That night the Marines again huddled in their foxholes awaiting the morning and the continuation of the attack. After three days of fighting, the casualty count stood at 4,574.

Once darkness descended, the Japanese kamikazes hit the American carriers lying off the beaches. The carrier *Bismarck Sea* was sunk, the *Saratoga* severely mauled and the *Lunga Point* damaged to a lesser degree.

On the morning of the fourth day the Twenty-eighth continued its grueling drive to the summit. The attack was a repeat of the previous day's except that the weather deteriorated even more as the island was hit by a heavy, soaking rain. By nightfall, the Marines had reached their final positions prior to climbing the summit.

Friday the twenty-third dawned bright and clear. Colonel Liversedge ordered the regiment to attack. During the night the trapped Japanese had attempted to evacuate the mountain and assume positions in the island's northern defenses. A number of them actually made it, but most died in the attempt. This left Suribachi's summit defended by a handful of stragglers. Thus, when the Marines began their final climb at 0800 they reached the crater in forty minutes without encountering much enemy resistance.

With a detachment of forty men, Lt. Harold G. Schrier occupied the crest of the crater of the volcano. There the men found a twenty-foot length of pipe to which they attached an American flag.

From a boat off Iwo's beach, Secretary of the Navy James Forrestal, who was present on this operation as an observer, and General Smith viewed the spectacular sight of the flag raising on Suribachi. Forrestal looked at Smith and commented, "This means a Marine Corps for the next five hundred years."[16]

Marines from all over the island cheered. Some wept openly at the moving sight. Horns from the support ships blew, whistles wailed and bells rang. The Japanese, however, were not about to remain silent for the moment of U.S. exultation. Two of them rushed from a cave near the summit and threw grenades at the Marines. Both were hastily sent to join their ancestors.

The commander of the Second Battalion, Lt. Col. Chandler Johnson wanted the flag for a souvenir so he sent one of his men to fetch another from one of the LSTs. The Marine returned with a flag much larger than the first. As he ran back up the slope, an Associated Press photographer, Joe Rosenthal, followed him up the mountain hoping for a unique picture. Lieutenant Schrier wanted the new flag raised at the moment the original one was lowered. Another length of pipe was found to which to the new flag was attached. Rosenthal photographed the new flag raising. Little did he know at the time that his picture of the flag raising would become the most famous picture of World War II and would, after the war, become the symbol of the Marine Corps and be immortalized in a large bronze statue near Arlington National Cemetery. Six Marines participated in the flag raising ceremony: Pfc. Ira Hayes, Pfc. Franklin Sousley, Sgt. Michael Strank, Navy Pharmacist's Mate Second Class John Bradley, Pfc. Rene Gagnon, and Cpl. Harlon Block.

As spectacular as the flag raising was, most of Iwo Jima remained in Japanese hands. The worst was yet to come. No sooner was the second flag raised than the forces on Suribachi had to seal up one cave after another all along the mountain's slope. The task was extremely dangerous and time consuming.

To Kuribayashi, the loss of Mt. Suribachi in a few days was a bitter blow. He had hoped that his forces could hold out for at least two weeks. With the mountain in American hands, Kuribayashi knew he could expect the American offensive northward to gain momentum.

Meanwhile, as the epic battle for Suribachi went on, the remaining Marines on Iwo were attacking northward toward the main Japanese defenses (Map 20).

At 0830 on D + 1, following the usual preliminary naval bombardment, the Twenty-sixth and Twenty-seventh Regiments attacked with the objective of reaching the D-1 line (See map 20). The Japanese hit the attack-

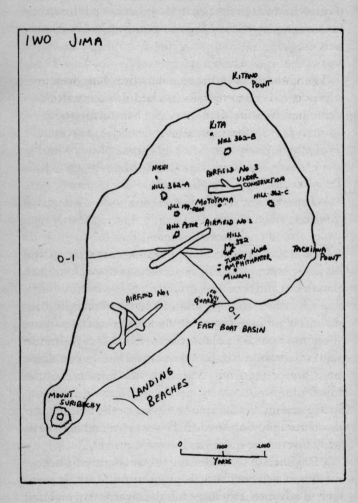

IWO JIMA

KITANO
POINT

KITA
HILL 362-B

NISHI
HILL 362-A
AIRFIELD No 3
UNDER
CONSTRUCTION
MOTOYAMA
HILL 362-C
HILL 199-OBOE
HILL PETER   AIRFIELD No 2
HILL
382
TURKEY KNOB
AMPHITHEATER
MINAMI

O-1   TACHIIWA
POINT

AIRFIELD No 1
QUARRY
O-1
EAST BOAT BASIN

MOUNT
SURIBACHI
LANDING
BEACHES

0   1000   2000
YARDS

ers with a withering mortar and artillery fire. A Regimental Combat Team from the Twenty-seventh with the First Battalion of the Twenty-sixth moved to the open terrain west of the first airfield. Japanese pillboxes and land mines slowed the Marine advance. Carl Proehl has written:

> There was no cover from enemy fire. Japs deep in reinforced concrete pillboxes laid down interlocking bands of fire that cut whole companies to ribbons. Camouflage hid all the enemy installations. The high ground on every side was honeycombed with layer after layer of Jap emplacements, blockhouses, dugouts and observation posts. . . . Whenever the Marines made a move, the Japs watched every step.[17]

After an all day fight, the Twenty-seventh had gained but eight hundred yards. In the center of the American line, the Regimental Combat Team of the Twenty-third, along with the Second Battalion of the Twenty-fourth, advanced on the airfield. The Japanese mortar and artillery fire was so heavy that it stopped the Marines in their tracks. A little progress was made when some tanks joined the unit. Thanks to the presence of the tanks, the Twenty-third reached the airfield by noon. Strong enemy resistance, however, prevented the advance from moving beyond the northern end of the airfield. The forward units dug in for the night.

A Regimental Combat Team of the Twenty-fifth Regiment was also held to little progress on D + 1. It managed to advance only three hundred yards. By nightfall it too had to consolidate its line.

Night provided no respite for the weary Marines as mortar and artillery fire continued to harass them. To add to their woes, the Japanese launched two counterattacks which the Americans managed to stop but only with great loss of life.

On D + 2 the fierce fighting continued with gains registered in yards. The most significant gains were made whenever the Marines had tanks to support their attacks.

The terrain north of the first airfield was exceptionally rugged. Japanese resistance was most severe here. The intricate web of minefields and pillboxes was especially deadly. Again it was up to the flamethrowers to burn out the hidden enemy. The valor of some exceptional Marine sometimes meant the difference between advancing or not. As the Twenty-five RCT (Regimental Combat Team) approached the ravines in front of the second airfield, one such Marine, Sgt. Ross F. Gray, single-handedly destroyed numerous enemy positions, disarmed a Japanese minefield, and killed scores of Japanese. Thanks to his action, the Twenty-five RCT was able to advance three hundred yards along its front. For his heroic action during combat, Gray received the Medal of Honor.

Fanatical Japanese resistance was the rule on Iwo Jima. Everywhere the Marines turned they experienced this fanaticism. In three days time the Fourth Division's combat efficiency was reduced to sixty-eight percent. The heavy casualties caused the corps commander to consider landing the reserve force, the Third Marine Division.

On the evening of the twenty-third, the commanders of the Fourth and Fifth Divisions met to plan their next move, Airfield Number 2.

After preparatory fire from the air, sea and their own artillery, the attack was launched by the Twenty-one RCT in the center of the line at 0930 on the twenty-fourth. More than eight hundred pillboxes ringed the second airfield and each one fired its deadly tracers into the Marine ranks. One by one the Marines were forced to reduce each pillbox. They did so almost oblivious to the high cost of life. With impunity they continued to fight while their ranks were steadily depleted. While reinforcements came into the line, the Marines fought on:

> They resorted to bayonets, picks, shovels, and anything they could use to kill Japanese when their rifles and machine guns became clogged by the volcanic ash.[18]

One particular strong point on the southeastern edge of Airfield Number 2 was known as Charlie-Dog Ridge. There the Japanese had built their most formidable defenses. It was left to the Twenty-fourth to destroy them. The Marines were hit with everything the Japanese had to offer: anti-tank guns, machine gunfire, mortars and rifle fire. Shell for shell the Marines answered back at the ridge. Then they made their move into the foreboding land filled with:

> dangling ledges, and caves carved by nature as well as the Japanese. Fissures of steam spewed from cracks in the ground, and evil-smelling sulphur fumes vied with the repulsive odor of decomposing bodies. Everywhere were Japanese defenses, grottoes, bunkers, blockhouses, pill-

boxes, deep caves, anti-tank ditches and walls, minefields and a profusion of flat-trajectory anti-tank guns, dual purpose, automatic anti-aircraft weapons, and small arms, all backed by lethal mortars and rockets firing from reverse slopes. At a loss of words to describe this devil's playground, correspondents and officers writing their action reports sometimes recalled a Goya sketch or Dore's illustrations for Dante's *Inferno*.[19]

It was on this day that General Erskine's Third Division came ashore. By the end of D + 5 there were three entire Marine divisions on Iwo Jima. Thus far casualties were extremely high with 1,605 dead, 5,496 wounded and 657 evacuated for combat fatigue. Iwo Jima was exacting a heavy butcher's bill. Nevertheless, despite their heavy losses, the Marines made progress, slowly but surely.

Each night on Iwo contained various problems for the Marines as they huddled in their foxholes. With their heads to the ground they could hear the sound of troops moving beneath them. One never knew if the sound heard in the dark was friendly or an enemy who had infiltrated the line by passing under the American positions via one of the numerous caves honeycombing the island. Many a Marine longed for the light of day while dreading it just the same, for with light would come the inevitable order to advance against a stone wall of resistance.

The recently landed Third Division was given the task of capturing the high portion of the Motoyama Plateau by attacking through Motoyama Village toward the incomplete Airfield Number 3. At 9:30 on the twenty-fifth, the division began its attack with the other two divisions on either flank. As usual carrier planes and warships contributed a pre-assault bombardment. Characteristic of the fighting on Iwo Jima, the Japanese immediately poured a deadly fire into the Marines. The savage fighting in this area added to the high casualty rate.

Even while the fighting went on, Iwo Jima was being turned into a major American base. Seabees quickly began repairing Airfield Number 1 and the strip was soon ready for use by fighter planes. Admiral Turner's amphibians worked tirelessly to bring in needed stores to the beleaguered Marines in spite of wretched landing conditions. The medics did a monumental job of evacuating the wounded while grave registration units continued their grim task of identifying and burying the dead.

On the twenty-sixth and again on the twenty-seventh the fighting netted the Americans very little ground. The Marines were moving into Kuribayashi's main defenses. If Iwo was going to hold, the Japanese would have to do it here.

Once more individual heroism cleared the path. Private Wilson Watson of the Second Battalion, Ninth Regiment, single-handedly killed sixty Japanese and destroyed a major pillbox. His action allowed the battalion to penetrate deeper into the defensive position known as Hill 199 Oboe. Watson was awarded the Medal of Honor for his heroic action. On the evening of the twenty-seventh, the Marines finally captured Hill 199 and another Japanese position called Hill Peter.

Before the battle, the VAC commander, General Schmidt, predicted that the battle would be over by February 29, D + 9. By that date, however, the Marines were still bogged down with much of Iwo Jima still in Japanese hands.

By nightfall of the twenty-eighth, the twenty-first Marines of the Third Division had finally taken Motoyama Village and the high ground overlooking the incompleted airfield. But the cost was high.

Meanwhile, the Fifth Division ran into rugged resistance on the island's western side. One particular strong point was Hill 362-B. For days the Japanese had rained death on the Marines from this elevated point and, on March 2, the Marines moved to take it. After a savage day of fighting, the position fell. The next day found the Marines advancing to their next obstacle.

March 4 was a memorable day on Iwo Jima. A B-29 bomber was forced to make an emergency landing on the island after developing a gas valve problem. Without the airfield the plane probably would have crashed since it could not have made it as far as the Marianas. To many Marines the heavy cost now seemed to have a purpose after all.

In the interim the high casualties on Iwo Jima were causing a stir in American newspapers. Just as at Tarawa the ire of the press was directed at Admiral Nimitz. One woman wrote to the Navy Department saying:

> Please for God's sake stop sending our finest youth to be murdered on places like Iwo Jima. It is too much for boys to stand, too much for mothers and homes to take. It is driving some mothers crazy. Why can't objectives be accomplished in some other way? It is almost inhuman and awful. . . . Stop. Stop.[20]

The *San Francisco Examiner* published an editorial chastising the Marine Corps on the front page of their February 27 edition. In the article MacArthur, who usually had low casualty rates during his battles, was compared to the Marine operations. Nimitz had to absorb the criticism.

After fourteen straight days of savage combat, orders were received to cease fighting on March 5. The day was to be used for rest and reorganization. Even the Japanese seemed to welcome the respite though the artillery on both sides fired throughout the day.

All were tired and listless, their key personnel were largely casualties, and it was little short of miraculous that they could advance at all. Some gained comfort and a much-needed lift from a powerful drink called "Suribachi Screamer," sick bay alcohol and fruit juice.[21]

On the sixth the offensive resumed. Again a heavy barrage pounded the Japanese positions. A total of 22,500 shells ranging from 75mm to 175mm were fired by the Americans. Despite the intense barrage, the Marines found that thousands of Japanese survived and were ready and willing to die fighting. After an entire day of struggle the Americans hadn't advanced beyond their line of departure.

The following day, the Third Division's commander, General Erskine, altered the usual attack strategy by ordering an attack without the preparatory barrage. In this way he hoped to catch the enemy offguard. The trick actually worked for a while until the Japanese woke up to the ruse and put up a stiff resistance. By late afternoon, however, the tough obstacle, Hill 362-C was captured. But the Third was soon hit by fierce counterattacks from Baron Nishi's tank regiment. Nishi held his troops in a strong point known to the Marines as Cushman's Pocket. Nishi's men held that position tenaciously until March 16 when the Marines finally took it after heavy loss of life.

On March ninth, elements of the Third Division reached the northeastern beaches of Iwo Jima. Though the event was not as dramatic as the flag raising on Suribachi it was far more significant, for the island was now split in two. To convince General Erskine that the sea had been reached, a canteen full of sea water was sent to him with a note stating: For inspection, not consumption. Erskine was overjoyed.

With the exception of Cushman's Pocket, by the evening of March 10 the Third Division was able to declare their zone of action secure. The cost during the division's drive up the center of the island was 3,563 casualties of which 827 were killed.

On D + 18 the Army Air Force's Fifteenth Fighter Group began to support the Marines from Iwo Jima's own bases thus allowing the carriers to return to their base at Ulithi in preparation for the invasion of Okinawa scheduled for April 1.

While the Third Division inched its way through the formidable defenses of the island's middle, the Fifth Division struggled along the ridges and ravines on the western side of Iwo. Ferocity characterized the advance. A great deal of the division's advance was dependent on the Third's success in the center.

Strong points blocked the Fifth's way. One such strong point was Hill 362-A. For two days the battle for this hill raged. On March 1 the Twenty-eighth Regiment, conquerors of Mt. Suribachi, relieved the Twenty-seventh Regiment. The Twenty-eighth managed to make it to the crest of the hill but when they arrived there the Japanese raked them with machine gunfire from Nishi Ridge, the next ridge further north. As some companies cleared Hill 362-A of snipers, the rest of the regiment maneuvered around the hill toward Nishi Ridge. Heavy Japanese fire quickly halted the advance. At evening the Marines dug in for the night.

As the Fifth moved further north, their zone of action was enlarged thanks to Iwo's shape. General Rockey was forced to commit the Twenty-sixth Regiment to fight to the right of the Twenty-eighth.

All throughout the day of March 2 the Twenty-eighth inched closer to Nishi Ridge amid heavy Japanese opposition. On Saturday, March 3, the Fifth Division had its most memorable day next to the flag raising on Suribachi. Five of its men earned Congressional Medals of Honor for acts of bravery thereby setting a record for the most Medals of Honor earned by any single division in one day.

Three of the medals were earned by the Twenty-sixth Regiment as this unit assisted the Third Division in its drive on Hill 362-B. The other two were earned by the Twenty-eighth Marines during their assault on Nishi Ridge. The latter fight was particularly brutal. Just as the Marines reached the crest of the hill it went up in a sudden blinding flash. The entire hill shuddered. Men were thrown into the air; those further away were stunned by the concussion. Dozens of Marines were buried in the crater while their comrades worked frantically to dig them out. Battle-hardened veterans vomited

283

at the sight of their charred friends, others walked away weeping at the sight. Forty-three Marines were killed in the blast but by nightfall the ridge was completely in the hands of the Twenty-eighth.

There were few gains made on the fourth but the casualties were still heavy. The Marines spent the fifth resting in preparation for a resumption of the advance the next day.

On the morning of the sixth the Marines launched the most intensive artillery barrage yet seen against Japanese positions on Iwo Jima. Still, when the barrage was ended the Japanese resisted just as if it had never occurred.

On March 7 the Twenty-seventh Marines were ordered to advance northeast. Again the story was the same: fierce, fanatical resistance.

Valor was common on Iwo Jima such as that evidenced by the former all-American football player from Baylor University, Lt. Jack Lummus, served as an inspiration to his platoon. On March 8 Lummus rallied his men during an attack against a Japanese strong point. An enemy grenade suddenly blew up directly in front of him but, wounded only slightly, Lummus continued to lead his men forward. A second grenade shattered his shoulder but he continued to urge his men forward. Then Lummus stepped on a mine. The explosion blew his legs off, leaving only two bloody stumps. Still alive, standing on the stumps, the lieutenant ordered his platoon forward. Jack Lummus died later in the day at a divisional field hospital, but his act of heroism spurred his men forward in the face of deadly opposition. It was men such as Lummus who made victory possible on this island of death.

On the ninth, the Twenty-eighth Regiment was able to advance a mere forty yards. The Twenty-sixth and Twenty-eighth Regiments' gains were equally small.

The next day the Fifth Division secured a line from the west coast to the ridges overlooking the east coast. The Japanese were squeezed into the area around Kitano Point, Iwo Jima's northern tip. During the division's drive, 4,292 casualties were incurred of which 1,093 were killed. The deadly toll continued to mount.

While the Third Division drove up the island's center with the Fifth on its left, the Fourth Division under General Cates was assigned the right side of the advance. Strong points like Hill 382, the Amphitheatre, Turkey Knob and the village of Minami fell within the division's area. Needless to say the story was the same as it was for the other two divisions. Ferocity, savagery and heavy casualties marked every step of the way. The Marines lumped the enemy strong points together and gave them an appropriate name, the "meat grinder."

Hill 382 was 250 yards northeast of the second airfield. Typically the Japanese had turned the hill into a veritable fortress:

> The hill was built to house artillery and anti-tank guns. Each gun emplacement was further protected by ten or more mutually supporting machine gun emplacements, and the slopes and approaches to the hill were honeycombed with caves and tunnels much like other similar areas on the island.[22]

Located six hundred yards south of the hill was Turkey Knob. Southwest of this was a low depression shaped like a bowl which was aptly dubbed the Amphitheatre. This area comprised Kuribayashi's major defensive position.

The Fourth Division began its attack on these position on February 25. The Marines were peppered with murderous machine gunfire, mortars and artillery every inch of the way. Having gained no ground on the twenty-fifth, the Marines dug in for the night. The next day they managed to advance one hundred yards before machine gunfire and mortars halted the advance just short of Turkey Knob and the Amphitheatre. The fight for Hill 382 was equally brutal. Once more the heroics of individuals spurred others on. Private first class Douglas Jacobsen acted like a man possessed. He picked up a bazooka dropped earlier by a comrade, stormed and destroyed sixteen Japanese strong points and killed seventy-five Japanese in the progress. Jacobsen too earned the Medal of Honor.

The Japanese continued to cling to the top of the hill and on February 27 the fighting developed into hand-to-hand combat with the defenders vowing to hold onto the hill and the attackers swearing to capture it. Despite all American efforts the Japanese held onto the summit.

To the south of Hill 382 the battle for Turkey Knob and the Amphitheatre continued unabated. February 28 saw a repeat of warfare of the day before. By late afternoon the Marines had blasted the enemy positions with everything available. Planes dropped napalm while artillery units pounded them with tons of shells. Still the Japanese remained entrenched in their positions.

By nightfall on the twenty-eighth the Marines felt that some progress had been made. The Japanese on

Hill 382 were outflanked and the Marines were in positions to outflank the enemy in the Amphitheatre. This would allow them to continue the drive up the east coast. But the Japanese remained entrenched in these positions. They had to be eliminated.

On March 1 the battle for Hill 382 continued. Having blasted the hilltop with everything imaginable, the Marines inched forward a yard at a time. At evening the defenders still clung to Hill 382. The Marines called off the attack until the next day.

Little progress was also made around the Amphitheatre and Turkey Knob. By nightfall the Fourth Division was reduced to fifty-five percent combat efficiency and the Japanese retained control of the "meat grinder." On March 2 the "meat grinder" received its newest victims. In a frenzy of activity the Marines attacked Hill 382. By mid-afternoon they had reached the summit but Japanese diehards led counterattacks from their intricate network of underground passageways. Each cave had to be located and sealed up individually. Because of the time-consuming job of mopping up Hill 382, the Fourth Division could not claim its capture until March 3.

The battle for Turkey Knob did not go well. All through the third and fourth the fight continued. On the fourth both this position and the Amphitheatre were completely surrounded thus cutting the Japanese off completely. The "meat grinder" was finally eliminated but the division had suffered 2,880 casualties in the process.

On the fifth, the Fourth Division enjoyed a well deserved day of rest. The time was spent preparing for a resumption of the offensive.

On March 6, following a heavy preliminary barrage,

the Twenty-third Regiment jumped off at 0900 and advanced 350 yards. Two other regiments, the Twenty-fourth and Twenty-fifth, also swung into action. The former managed a meager 250 yards while the latter occupied itself in mopping up bypassed enemy positions. Casualties continued to mount steadily, however, reducing the Fourth Division's combat efficiency to forty percent. The night of March sixth brought another round of horror to the exhausted division as Japanese fanatics infiltrated the American positions.

The slow and bloody advance continued on the seventh and eighth but the enemy's night infiltrations stepped up also. This presented a particular nightmare to the weary Marine who had spent all day in combat. One particular attack on the night of the eighth, was led by Captain Inouye who charged with over 1000 troops. The next morning 984 Japanese bodies were counted. American casualties were 90 dead and 257 wounded.

On the ninth the attack resumed and managed to make some small gains. Thanks to Captain Inouye's counterattack, many would-be defenders that might have slowed down the Marine advance lay dead on the field. The official Marine Corps monograph said of the attack. "It was now evident that the Japanese counterattack had marked the turning point in the battle."[23]

The next day the Twenty-third Regiment reached the coast near Tachii Wa Point. At the same time the Twenty-fifth eliminated the Turkey Knob salient. The Fourth Marines had accomplished its task but at heavy cost. Between February 25 and March 10 the division suffered 4,075 casualties of which 847 were killed. It was estimated that the enemy had suffered more than 18,000 casualties thus far.

The Japanese were now bottled up in Kitano Point. General Kuribayashi's forces occupied an area less than one square mile, but within that area were over fifteen hundred men eager to do their duty for emperor and country.

Since Kitano Point was within its zone the Fifth Division was given the lion's share of finishing the job. The Third Division still had one final enemy force left to reduce in the area southwest of Hill 362-C known as Cushman's Pocket. For the next two days the Ninth Regiment pounded away at the solidly entrenched Japanese in the pocket. Using the slow but proven method of demolitions and flamethrowers, the Marines began the painstaking task of reducing one strong point after another. Cushman's Pocket was finally overrun on March 16. Once this task was completed, the Third Division was ordered to relieve elements of the Fifth Division in the latter's struggle to reduce Kuribayashi's remaining stronghold.

The remaining Japanese strong point stretched from Kitano Point southward through Kita Village to the northwest coast of Iwo. Southwest of Kitano Point was Kuribayashi's final defensive position known to the Marines as the Gorge or Death Valley.

The Fifth Division began its attack on March 11. The Gorge was approximately seven hundred yards long, from two hundred to five hundred yards wide, and honeycombed with caves. Besides the caves, the Gorge contained blind canyons and large piles of rocks that made excellent hiding places for well placed machine guns.

Meanwhile, on March fourteenth, the flag that had been flying on Mt. Suribachi since D + 4 was lowered and at 0930 an official flag-raising ceremony took place at VAC headquarters. It was a brief ceremony with dignitaries from both the fleet and the landing force in attendance. After the ceremony, Gen. "Howlin' Mad" Smith left Iwo Jima with his staff for Pearl Harbor. For this fighting Marine the war was over.

The battle for the Gorge and Kitano Point continued in all its fury. Throughout the fifteenth and sixteenth the Marines painstakingly reduced one cave after another. By 1800 on March 16 the island was considered secure with only small enemy elements remaining in the area west of Kitano Point and in the Gorge.

By the seventeenth Kuribayashi knew that he could hold out for only a day or two more. He ordered the regimental flag burned and then sent a final message to Imperial General Headquarters informing them that Iwo Jima would soon be completely in American hands. In his message the general apologized profusely for not preventing the enemy from taking the island. He also included a poem.

> My body shall not decay in the field
> unless we are avenged.
> I will be born seven more times again
> to take up arms against the foe.
> My only concern is
> Our country in the future
> When weeds cover here.[24]

Kuribayashi went on to say that he would personally lead the final attack.

Following the transmission of his final message the general moved his headquarters from the Gorge to a cave on Kitano Point. For the next week the Marines continued to fight in the Gorge. It was finally subdued on March 25.

On March 26, a force of three hundred Japanese appeared out of nowhere and attacked some U.S. Army garrison units that had recently arrived on Iwo Jima to serve as occupation forces. The battle quickly deteriorated into a confusing melee as GI and Marine fought side by side against a fanatical enemy. The Japanese were slaughtered in this, the final attack. General Kuribayashi's body was never found but it is believed that at some point on March 27, he committed hara-kiri. His body was then secretly buried.

The battle for Iwo Jima was finally over and the Marines prepared to leave the island. The Fourth Division had already left for Hawaii on March 19. The Fifth followed on March 26 while the Third Division, minus the Ninth Regiment, sailed the next day. The Ninth Regiment remained on Iwo until April 12.

By the time the Marines left Iwo Jima behind it was estimated that about three hundred Japanese still remained alive. In reality, there were at least three thousand. Little by little they were discovered and either killed or captured. The last two survivors surrendered in 1951. More than twenty thousand Japanese lay dead.

Iwo Jima was turned into an advanced American base with roads, houses, piers and of course runways large enough to accommodate the B-29s. The cost, however, was high in human life. To capture this strategic position 6,821 men lost their lives, 21,865 more were considered casualties. Nevertheless, the cost was worth it. By the time the war ended a total of 24,761 airmen were rescued. 2,251 B-29s made emergency landings on the island. The number of lives spared by the ability of fighter planes to use Iwo Jima as an advanced airfield and provide coverage for the B-29s cannot be calculated. Without Iwo Jima, what would the airmen's fate have been?

> Located about midway between Guam and Japan, Iwo broke the long stretch, both going and coming. If you had engine trouble, you held out for Iwo. If you were shot up over Japan and had wounded aboard, you held out for Iwo. Formations assembled over Iwo, and gassed up at Iwo for extra long missions. If you needed fighter escort, it usually came from Iwo.[25]

Iwo was always there to fall back on.

Iwo Jima, however, had been murderous to take. Kuribayashi had truly developed the island into a fortress. In essence the Marines' mighty endeavor at Iwo Jima proved that no matter how formidable the defense, or fanatical the defenders, the combined might of the Navy and Marine Corps could take it, the cost notwithstanding.

Some have asked if toxic gas should have been used against the entrenched Japanese on Iwo Jima. A little-known fact is that this alternative was explored. Preliminary studies were conducted on how this could be accomplished. A moral debate ensued with the president himself putting the squash on any consideration of using this lethal weapon. He said:

> It has been and is the policy of this government to do everything in its power to outlaw the use of

chemicals in warfare. Such use is unhuman and contrary to what modern civilization should stand for.[26]

If, however, the use of lethal gas is inhuman and contrary to what modern civilization stands for, in which category does one place flamethrowers, napalm, or even the atomic bomb? Roosevelt's edict condemned the capture of Iwo Jima to be achieved by conventional methods. The moral of that decision is still debated to this day.

Iwo Jima represented the largest Marine operation during World War II. As demonstrated, victory was costly. In fact, it was one of the few operations where American casualties exceeded those of the Japanese. The reasons the Marines were able to prevail against a firmly entrenched enemy can be found in the detailed and meticulous planning and the superb support they received. This is not meant to discount their courage. The logistical support was superior, the medical care the finest in the Pacific, and the coordination of naval gunfire, close air support and artillery support was a decisive factor. It has been recorded that:

Without supplies and medical care the assault would have ground to a halt, and without close air, naval gunfire, and artillery support, there would have been no neutralization to permit the tank-infantry demolition teams to advance.[27]

Controversy still continues as to how many days of pre-landing bombardment were actually required. The Navy still contends that three days was enough.

There is no reason to believe that ten or even thirty days of naval and air pounding would have had much effect on the defenses than the bombardment that was delivered. The defenses were such, by and large, that the only way they could be taken out was the way they were taken out, by Marine Corps infantry and demolitions. . . . Aerial bombardment and naval gunfire simply could not reach underground into the maze of caves and tunnels. Yet these had to be cleared or sealed shut before the island could be secured as an air base on the Bonins road to Tokyo.[28]

Yet Maj. Gen. Harry Schmidt, the Fifth Amphibious Corps commander said that with additional time available for "pre D-day firing, naval guns might have accomplished much in this area to facilitate its capture."[29]

Nevertheless, the Navy stands by its case and goes so far as to add a logistical reason for insisting on three days. Heavy ammunition replenishment at sea had not as yet been service tested and with the bombarding ships being far from a supply base and unable to carry enough ammunition for a prolonged bombardment, three days were all that was possible. It is hard, though, to explain the cold facts of logistics to a Marine who had just seen his buddy torn to pieces by enemy artillery that might have been eliminated by a longer bombardment. The controversy remains unsettled.

Iwo Jima was truly the Marine Corps' "Supreme Test." Marine losses were so high that the average battalion that landed with 36 officers and 885 enlisted men, ended the battle with only 16 officers and 300 enlisted men despite the addition of replacements. By the conclusion of the fighting a large percentage of replacements lacked the combat training and experience of the men they replaced. Yet they fought gallantly. The Marine Corps must be commended for their firm resolve. They saw the objective and conquered it despite the terrible cost and difficulty. Although 27 combatants earned Medals of Honor there were many more who deserved the honor. These men had brought the United States closer to victory and the honor of helping to end the war must be shared by both the living and the dead.

Chapter Seven

Okinawa

On April 1, 1945, the United States Tenth Army crashed ashore on the island of Okinawa initiating a campaign that would last eighty-two days and cost the Americans almost fifty thousand casualties. The ferocity of the fighting never abated and, as was customary with the Japanese, once defeat was in sight, the more determined they became to sacrifice their own lives for Japan and the emperor. The story of the Okinawan campaign is epic in proportion, for more ships were used, more troops put ashore, more medical supplies transported, and more naval guns fired against shore targets than in any previous battle in the Pacific.

Okinawa is the major island in the Ryukyu chain. Knowledge of the island was scanty until it was chosen as a target. The selection of Okinawa stemmed from decisions reached at the Cairo Conference of November, 1943 when Churchill and Roosevelt established a Pacific timetable. Because of its proximity to Japan, Okinawa was an ideal terminus for the two-pronged assault against Japan, one across the central Pacific and the other from the southwest Pacific. Admiral King argued for the need to assault Formosa, "Operation Causeway," at Cairo.

For the Formosan operation, Admiral Nimitz placed Admiral Spruance, commander of the Fifth Fleet, in complete charge. Vice Adm. Richmond Kelly Turner was designated commander of the amphibious assault and Lt. Gen. Simon Bolivar Buckner was appointed to command the expeditionary troops.

As 1944 progressed, doubt was raised by some of the Pacific commanders as to the need or practicality of invading Formosa. Alternatives were sought. King, however, remained adamant. He wanted Formosa since it was closer to both Japan and China than Luzon, the target General MacArthur was pressing for. King said that Formosa would eliminate the need to invade Luzon completely.

MacArthur was dead set against King's proposal. His promise to return to the Philippines had to be fulfilled. He stated that it was the moral obligation of the United States to liberate the Filipinos who had suffered under Japanese brutality. The general did not wish to see his theater reduced to a secondary role as it surely would if the Philippines were bypassed. In addition, he added, any assault of Formosa would require land-based air protection from Luzon. The latter, then, was a vital prerequisite.

King went to Pearl Harbor in mid-July, 1944 for a meeting with Nimitz. After some preliminary discussions he and Nimitz flew to Saipan for a close-up view of that battle-ravaged island. All the while King continued to argue for Formosa. On Saipan they met with Spruance and Turner and found both of them cool to the Formosan plan. Both felt that Luzon should be attacked first. In addition to creating air bases, they argued, Luzon would provide an excellent anchorage for future operations. King asked Spruance what operations he suggested. The Fifth Fleet commander quickly answered, Iwo Jima and Okinawa. Although King could see the wisdom of attacking those two objectives, he was not dissuaded from Formosa.

Later in the month Roosevelt himself arrived at Pearl Harbor to discuss the divergent strategies. MacArthur flew up from the southwest Pacific to argue for his Philippine plan. King did not participate in the meetings, leaving Nimitz to argue for the Formosan plan. MacArthur's arguments won out, the Philippines would not be bypassed. Where did that leave Formosa?

In September King met with Nimitz again in San Francisco. During this meeting King was finally convinced to abandon his Formosan plans once and for all. Nimitz used the argument that there were simply not enough Army troops available for an invasion of that island. There would, however, be enough for an invasion of Okinawa and enough Marines available for an attack on Iwo Jima. On October 2, 1944, King yielded. The Joint Chiefs quickly ordered MacArthur to seize Luzon after Leyte while Nimitz was given the green light to attack Iwo Jima in January and Okinawa in March, 1945.

Delays in freeing the fleet from supporting MacArthur's attack on Leyte caused the invasion of Iwo Jima and Okinawa to be postponed until February 19 and April 1, respectively. Thus, the invasion of Okinawa, "Operation Iceberg," became a reality.

Okinawa's importance to both the Americans and Japanese lay in its strategic location. For the Americans, the capture of the island would provide them with an excellent base from which to stage the final assault on

Japan itself. Kyushu, Japan's southernmost island was a mere 350 miles from Okinawa. Being a rather large island, Okinawa possessed many air bases from which the Air Force could support both the invasion of Japan's main islands and the continued bombing offensive against its cities and strategical sites. Okinawa also contained two fleet anchorages large enough to support the Pacific Fleet.

Okinawa itself is sixty miles long and eighteen miles across at its widest point. The northern part of the island is heavily wooded and mountainous. Most of the population lives south of the Ishikawa Isthmus. From the isthmus to Naha the terrain features steep cliffs, deep ravines and rolling hills. The southernmost part of Okinawa is hilly and contains a five-hundred-foot-high plateau (Map 21).

The island's coastline ranges from rocky shoreline in the north to raised beaches and sea cliffs in the south. Very few areas of the shoreline were suitable for large-scale amphibious operations. On the east coast the largest beaches were on the Nakagusuku Wan while on the west coast the most suitable invasion beaches lay between Zampa Misaki and the Oroku Peninsula.

The area around Naha was the most heavily populated sector. A road network existed along the coast and some good roads were found in the Naha area but in the rest of the island there were very few roads. Those that did exist in the interior were no more than dirt tracks and trails that turned into quagmires during heavy rains.

Okinawa's climate is tropical with periodic rainfall the heaviest of which falls from July through November. The natives were culturally closer to China than Japan

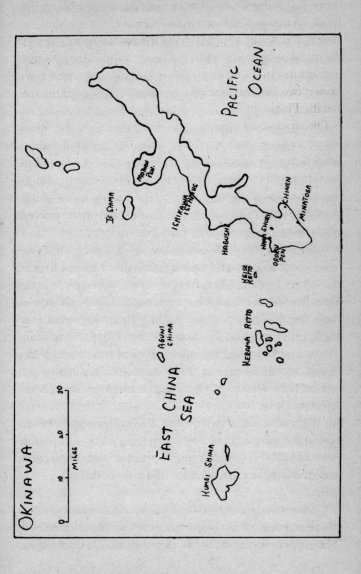

OKINAWA

PACIFIC OCEAN

EAST CHINA SEA

Pacific Ocean

Ie Shima

Motobu Pen.

Ishikawa Isthmus

Hagushi

Naha Shuri
Oroku Pen.

Chimen
Minatoga

Keise Retto

Kerama Retto

Aguni Shima

Kumei Shima

MILES
0   10   20   30

but over the years the Okinawans diffused both Chinese and Japanese cultural traits and developed a cultural pattern unique to themselves.

Okinawa was a backwash of the war until April, 1944 when the Japanese Thirty-second Army was activated there with the responsibility of defending the Ryukyus. After one American victory after another, Imperial General Headquarters realized that Japan's interior defenses needed strengthening.

In August, 1944, Lt. Gen. Mitsuri Ushijima was appointed commander of the Thirty-second Army. As his chief of staff he chose Maj. Gen. Isamu Cho, one of Japan's most competent officers. Both of these men were saddled with the awesome task of preparing to prevent the inevitable invasion of Japan's doorstop.

Ushijima was well known for his integrity, character and competence, and was a man who inspired loyalty. Cho had a reputation for aggressiveness and exactitude. He drove himself and his men hard. Ushijima needed men for his garrison but finding them was extremely difficult since most combat-effective troops were being dispatched to the Philippines at that time. Gradually, however, through late 1944 and into 1945 a steady stream of troops began arriving on Okinawa from Manchuria.

With the situation in the Philippines rapidly approaching the critical point Imperial Headquarters diverted all remaining reinforcements and desperately needed supplies to Okinawa. Because of this the:

Thirty-second Army thus possessed a heavier concentration of artillery under a single command than had been available to any other Japanese organization in the Pacific at any time.

In addition to this impressive force of artillery, by the time the Americans landed, Ushijima could boast of more than one hundred thousand troops made up of sixty-seven thousand regular army troops, nine thousand naval personnel and about twenty-four thousand native Okinawans who had established a homeguard called the Buertai.

Ushijima followed the battles raging on Japan's island possessions with intense interest. He saw that from the pattern of Allied assault operations, no longer could the Japanese hope to stop the invaders at the beaches. Naval gunfire was just too powerful and would knock out most shore defenses with ease. Defensive positions established in the interior were the only way to stop the invaders. With this in mind Ushijima laid down his plans:

> In situations where island garrisons cannot expect reinforcements of troops from rear echelons, but must carry on the battle themselves from start to finish, they should exhaust every means for securing a favorable outcome, disrupting the enemy's plans by inflicting maximum losses on him, and even when the situation is hopeless, holding out in strong positions for as long as possible. [2]

The general's staff devised a battle slogan to help raise the morale of the troops:

> One Plane for One Warship
> One Boat for One Ship

One Man for Ten of the Enemy
Or One Tank[3]

Ushjima cautioned his troops against opening fire prematurely. General Cho was a long-time advocate of defense in depth and took it upon himself to order the construction of strong underground and cave fortifications. Okinawa's topography was ideally suited for this and Cho took advantage of it to make each gun position mutually supportive with others. Utilizing what nature gave and modifying it somewhat, the Japanese effectively made Okinawa into an impregnable fortress. There was not one defensive trap untried; reverse as well as forward slopes of hills were fortified, cave mouths bristled with artillery, mortars and automatic weapons were situated everywhere. The natural caves and tombs of Okinawa fit right in with the defensive plans. With little modification, they were transformed into mini-fortresses. Many of the caves were connected by tunnels which allowed the static Japanese defenders mobility. Okinawa was eventually turned into a stronger fortress than Iwo Jima.

From his command post in Shuri, Ushijima oversaw the mammoth preparations. Obviously, because of the sheer size of the island and the number of men available, the general was limited as to where he could position his strongest defenses. He realized that he would have to concede much of Okinawa in order to concentrate his main strength in one sector. The primary defensive sector he developed ran along a line north of Naha, Ynabaru and Shuri. Any landings north of that line would be unopposed, south of that would be another matter.

The main defensive area was the Shuri area where nature had provided the Japanese with numerous natural barriers. Ushijima expected the American landing to take place on Okinawa's southeastern beaches off Minatoga. Because of this, he positioned the bulk of his artillery in that sector and along the Chinen Peninsula (Map 22).

Believing that the Americans were least likely to land across the Hagushi beaches on the island's western sector, Ushijima left only one regiment to guard that area with orders to fight a delaying action only and, after destroying the Yontan and Kadena airfields, then withdraw to the Shuri line. If the Americans landed off Minatoga, then they would be struck hard before reaching the Shuri line.

At Shuri, the Japanese had shrewdly and industriously constructed a stronghold centered inside a series of ever-diminishing concentric rings, each of which bristled with well dug in, expertly sited weapons. [4]

No matter what beaches the Americans landed on, the Japanese planned to fight a delaying action with the intent of luring the invaders into the death trap at Shuri.

The area north of the Ishikawa Isthmus was assigned to troops under the command of Col. Takehiko Udo. His job was to defend the Motobu Peninsula and Ie Shima. Udo's orders were to destroy the airstrip on the island of Ie Shima before it fell into enemy hands. All its aviation material was to be transferred to Okinawa. Udo's forces, however, were totally inadequate for the task and little hope was given for his force.

Ushijima was a realist who knew that his own forces

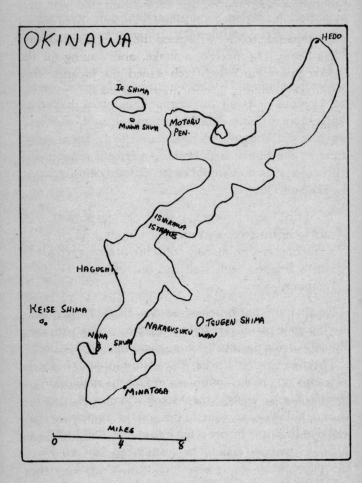

OKINAWA

HEDO

IE SHIMA

MINNA SHIMA

MOTOBU PEN.

ISHIKAWA ISTHMUS

HAGUSHI

KEISE SHIMA

NAHA   SHURI

NAKAGUSUKU WAN   O TSUGEN SHIMA

MINATOGA

MILES

0   4   8

were insufficient to stop the Americans but, like his counterpart on Iwo Jima, General Kuribayashi, was not lacking in spirit. The general was painfully aware of the awesome responsibility facing him and was prepared to meet it for the sake of his country. In his diary one Japanese soldier expressed the general's dilemma: "It's like a frog meeting a snake, and waiting for the snake to eat him."[5] As March waned, the Japanese frog waited expectantly for the American snake.

Meanwhile, the American commanders prepared for the assault on Japan's doorstop. On October 25, 1944, Nimitz's headquarters published and distributed the Joint Staff Study on "Operation Iceberg." According to the study, the campaign was to be conducted in three phases, the first being the capture of southern Okinawa and the small islands adjacent to it. In coordination with this would be the transformation of the island into a massive staging area for operations against the home islands. In Phase II, Ie Shima, with its vital airfield, and the remainder of Okinawa were to be seized. Phase III called for the capture of the remaining Ryukyu Islands.

"Iceberg" saw one of the largest armadas in the history of warfare assembled. The Tenth Army under General Buckner consisted of 182 thousand assault troops divided into two corps, the III Marine Amphibious Corps and the XXIV Army Corps. The Fifth Fleet by now contained forty aircraft carriers, eighteen battleships, two hundred destroyers and countless numbers of various other ships. 548 thousand Army, Navy and Marine Corps personnel were involved in he assault.

The fast carrier force, Task Force 58, was commanded by the very capable Vice Adm. Marc Mitscher. Attached to the American fleet was a British carrier group, Task Force 57. Both carrier groups were scheduled to conduct pre-landing air strikes against Japanese airfields in hopes of neutralizing the enemy air capability. The Army Air Force, from bases in China and the Pacific, was slated to bomb Japanese bases.

Admiral Turner, who was culminating a career as an amphibious commander from the dark days at Guadalcanal, through the Gilberts and Marshalls to the Marianas and Iwo Jima, played an integral part in the Okinawan assault. Never before had he been called on to support such large numbers as here.

The assault forces themselves were divided into a northern and a southern attack force. The northern one, Task Force 53, under Rear Adm. Lawrence Reifsnider had the responsibility for landing the III Amphibious Corps commanded by Marine Maj. Gen. Roy Geiger. The Marine force comprised the First and Sixth Marine Divisions. The southern attack force under Rear Adm. John Hall, Jr. contained Maj. Gen. John Hodge's XXIV Corps made up of the Seventh and Ninety-sixth Infantry Divisions. In addition to these two, there were three other attack groups, a western island attack group, a demonstration group, and the floating reserve group. Attached to the Tenth Army was the Tactical Air Force, Tenth Army, which had the vital task of providing land-based air support for the troops once its squadrons were established ashore.

Turner estimated that the enemy air force would strike back in force against the American invasion. At the same time he feared an enemy submarine and surface fleet attack. Because of this, in conjunction with the Tenth Army planners, Turner drew up "Plan Fox" calling for an assault landing on Okinawa's west coast at beaches both north and south of Hagushi. This would allow for the early occupation of the Kadena and Yontan airfields and allow the air forces to begin supporting the ground forces shortly after the invasion. Turner also called for a pre L-day* landing on Keise Shima where artillery could be set up to support the actual amphibious operation.

Turner also asked that in addition to Keise Shima, Kerama Retto be captured prior to L-day. The latter, Turner said, was large enough to provide a protected anchorage where the supporting naval elements could be refueled and resupplied. For the admiral, the protection afforded by Kerama Retto was essential to the logistical support operation. The task of taking Kerama Retto was given to the veteran Seventy-seventh Infantry Division. The division had received its baptism of fire on Guam and was bloodied at Leyte. This was to be its third combat operation.

The American assault plans called for the III Amphibious Corps to land on the left of the XXIV Corps. The dividing line would be the Bishi Gawa River. Once ashore, the Marine divisions would move inland. The objective of capturing the Yontan airfield was given to the Sixth Division. The veteran First Marine Division, "The Old Breed," assisted in the attack on the airfield before moving across the island to the Katchin Peninsula on the opposite coast. Although this was its first operation as a division, the ranks of the Sixth were filled with veterans from other units. Okinawa marked the Old Breed's fourth operation. Veterans of Guadalcanal, New Britain and Peleliu, they were accustomed to hot spots and expected nothing less on Okinawa.

*designated landing day for "Iceberg."

To the right of the Marines was the Army's Seventh Infantry Division, veterans of Attu, Kwajalein and Leyte. The Ninety-sixth Division on the far right had also fought on Leyte. Okinawa was its second assault.

The Seventh Division was given the task of seizing Kadena Airfield before moving across the island to the east coast. The Ninety-sixth, meanwhile, would capture the high ground around the beaches and then proceed southward to capture the bridges near Chatan.

In order to accomplish Phase I of the operation, once the Marines completed their immediate objectives, they would have to gain control of the Ishikawa Isthmus thereby sealing off southern Okinawa. After the central portion of the island was secured, XXIV Corps would attack southward. Phase II would be set in motion after Buckner was convinced that Phase I was complete.

The American plan also called for the Second Marine Division, veterans of Guadalcanal, Tarawa, Saipan and Tinian, to play a diversionary role. The division would demonstrate off the eastern beaches of Minatoga in hopes of deceiving the Japanese into thinking that the main invasion was in that area.

The assault forces underwent intensive training. The logistical planners continued to organize while the intelligence groups pored over last-minute information. Nothing was left to chance. Okinawa's proximity to Japan made gathering information difficult at best. Interrogations of prisoners and former inhabitants along with old geographical studies were the principal tools the intelligence people had to work with.

In September, 1944, the first aerial photos were obtained when a B-29 flew over the island on a reconnaissance flight. Unfortunately, the weather was poor so the quality of the pictures left something to be desired. Additional aerial photos were obtained in October and from then on continually right up until March of the following year. Vital new information was gathered from the photographs and was incorporated into the planning. Intelligence correctly estimated the Japanese intention to organize their main defensive stand on the southern third of Okinawa and that this defense would be in depth.

The intelligence sources were capable of mounting heavy and multiple air attacks against the invasion forces. The use of suicide attacks, the dreaded kamikazes, was also a distinct possibility. As for the Japanese navy, the planners knew that the Battle of Leyte Gulf had all but destroyed its fighting ability, but they also knew that a threat from the few remaining naval forces still existed and that the Japanese would probably resort to the use of suicide motor torpedo boats and midget submarines.

The Seventy-seventh Division left Leyte on March 19 for the invasion of Kerama Retto. The Seventh and Ninety-sixth Divisions followed five days later. Meanwhile, the III Amphibious Corps organized itself for the departure. The leading elements of this force left the Solomons on March 12 followed by another one on March 17. The entire corps was sent to Ulithi where they would be transferred to LSTs and LSMs for the journey to their final destination. Finally, on March 25 the Second Marine Division Demonstration Group left Saipan.

From January onward Okinawa became a primary target for the American Air Force. Almost daily it was subjected to an intensive bombardment. One Japanese soldier had this to say about the bombing:

> While some fly around overhead and strafe, the big bastards fly over the airfield and drop bombs. The ferocity of the bombing is terrific. It really makes me furious. It is past 1500 and the raid is still on. At 1800 the last two planes brought the raid to a close. What the hell kind of bastards are they? Bomb from 0600 to 1800.[6]

The first of the American forces to arrive off Okinawa were the minesweepers. These began clearing operations off Kerama Retto on March 24. Task Force 58 had also commenced its preliminary bombardment of the assault area and Minatoga beach where the demonstration group was to feign a landing. At the same time, underwater demolition teams began their work in the actual assault area.

Okinawa was quickly isolated by the huge Allied force. To ensure early detection of approaching Japanese planes, radar picket vessels encircled the island from fifteen to one hundred miles off shore. If enemy planes were detected, the carrier combat air patrols would be dispatched to intercept and destroy them.

The first of many kamikaze attacks struck the forces making for Kerama Retto. Between March 26 and 31, six American ships, including the cruiser *Indianapolis*, flagship of Admiral Spruance, were damaged.

March 25 marked the beginning of the pre-landing naval bombardment reinforced by carrier aircraft attacks. On the twenty-sixth the Seventy-seventh Division assaulted Kerama Retto. 975 enemy troops defended the islands, only 300 of whom were combat-worthy. The balance were Korean laborers. Against little opposition, the Seventy-seventh secured its objective quickly. By the end of the first day three of the small islands were completely in American hands and the capture of the other two was nearly complete. The capture of the Kerama Retto islands was accomplished with the loss of 31 men killed and 81 wounded. The Seventy-seventh Division handled itself magnificently and expeditiously eliminated all enemy opposition. Admiral Nimitz sent a note to General Bruce, the divisional commander:

> My congratulations on the speedy and effective manner in which you accomplished assigned tasks in Kerama Retto. The present readiness of the Seventy-seventh Division to go again is characteristic of its spirit and comes up to the expectations I have learned to have for that fighting organization.[7]

An amphibious reconnaissance battalion of Marines, meanwhile, landed on Keise Shima where, by March 31, they positioned artillery to support the landings on Easter Sunday, April 1, 1945.

As morning broke on L-day, the sky was cloudy and the sea relatively calm with moderate surf conditions. To the veteran troops of the torrid jungle, the cool seventy-five degree temperature felt comfortable. Both GI and Marine prepared to disembark from their transports into the Hagushi beaches. Off Minatoga, a similar scenario was unfolding.

At 0406 Turner gave the order to land the landing force. A few enemy planes attacked the transports but were easily dealt with. Believing that the major American effort was to be at the Minatoga beaches, most of the enemy defenders were prepared to resist there instead of at Hagushi. Ironically, the first casualties were eight Marines killed and thirty-seven wounded from the Second Regiment, a unit not scheduled to land. A Japanese suicide plane crashed into a transport and LST carrying the demonstration troops.

By 0650 most of the troops had left their transports at the reef and boarded the waiting amphibious tractors for the final run into the beaches. Over their heads flew shells from the support vessels that were firing onto the beaches.

At 0830 the first assault waves began to land at their designated areas. To the surprise of the attackers there was very little in the way of enemy resistance, a rather unique experience for many of them. Veterans began to refer to L-day as Love Day. Within an hour, sixteen thousand combat troops were landed.

Wonder of wonders, the entire Okinawa landing had taken place with surprising ease, against little or no enemy gunfire, and no troop mines, or obstacles on the beaches.[8]

Most combat veterans were puzzled by this strange twist. What were the Japanese up to? Were they merely baiting a trap hoping to lure the invaders into it? Despite their amazement, once the beachhead was consolidated, the troops prepared to move inland according to the plan.

Meanwhile, at Minatoga, the Second Division continued its diversionary role. By 1500 the demonstration was over and the troops were re-embarked. The next day the charade was repeated but that evening the actors departed the stage.

The two primary objectives of the assault troops, the two airfields, were each about one mile from the beaches. At 1000 patrols from the Seventh Division were on the Kadena airfield and found it completely deserted. At the same time the Marines moved on Yontan Airfield with similar ease despite sporadic enemy machine gunfire. They found this field, too, devoid of Japanese.

By nightfall, the Tenth Army held a beachhead fifteen thousand yards wide and five thousand yards deep, with more than sixty thousand men ashore. Enemy resistance had thus far been negligible. In addition, a large portion of the Tenth Army's armor and artillery were also ashore.

The day's exploits brought a great deal of satisfaction to Buckner. Casualties were light; 28 killed, 104 wounded and 27 missing.

With the exception of some sporadic sniper and mortar fire, the first night on Okinawa was spent in relative quiet. At 0730 the next morning, with the weather perfect for combat, the Tenth Army resumed the attack. Once again resistance was light and the American advance moved steadily across the island. By the end of the second day, the Seventh Division had managed to gain the heights overlooking Nakagusuku Bay while a few patrols reached the coast. The Ninety-sixth Division found the terrain to be more of a hindrance than the enemy. Rugged hills, abandoned caves, mines and tank traps all combined to hinder progress. By nightfall the division's front line extended from Futema on the west coast to near Unjo on the east.

Commenting on the conduct of the Marine operations for the first two days Buckner signalled General Geiger:

> I congratulate you and your command on a splendidly executed landing and substantial gains in enemy territory. I have full confidence that your fighting Marines will meet every requirement of this campaign with characteristic courage, spirit, and efficiency.[9]

The virtually unopposed landings did not exactly work in favor of the Americans for they presented a logistical problem for the amphibious forces supporting the assault. The logistical plan called for a steady buildup of the beachhead for a subsequent slow advance against heavy resistance. Thanks to the light resistance encountered, however, the small craft originally assigned to move cargo were diverted for ferrying in more troops who were not scheduled to land until April 3. The result was a delay in the unloading of supplies. Nevertheless, with a superhuman effort the amphibians did manage to accomplish their task.

The end of L + 1 found Okinawa cut in twain by the advancing Americans, but the quiet was ominous. On the third the two corps continued to advance. The Seventh Division advanced into the Awashi Peninsula while the Ninety-sixth drove further south. Shortly thereafter, the Ninety-sixth met its first real opposition. As their advance moved steadily forward the volume of enemy fire increased, causing the attackers to reflect upon what lie ahead.

Meanwhile, the Marines were at the base of the Ishikawa Isthmus, a position they had not planned to reach until L + 12. Buckner gave Geiger the green light to accomplish Phase II of "Iceberg," the capture of northern Okinawa, even though Phase I was not yet accomplished.

In the next ten days the Sixth Marine Division gained more than twenty-five miles and reached the mouth of the Motobu Peninsula while the Twenty-second Regiment advanced to Hedo Misaki, Okinawa's northernmost point. Once that was reached, the Marines were free to concentrate on their main objective, Yae Take on the Motobu Peninsula, the main Japanese center of resistance in that sector (Map 23).

Yae Take was under the command of Colonel Udo. This strong point, a mountainous bastion, rose more than fifteen hundred feet above sea level. The ground approaching it was favorable for defense and Udo had organized the mountain into a superb defensive position. The Marines cautiously approached the most difficult position yet encountered. The enemy defenders were waiting with all their defensive skills to stop the American advance cold. Using every trick in the book, the Japanese lured the Marines into death traps. Snipers had a field day as they fired from high points into the ranks of the attackers.

Udo's force was comprised of fifteen hundred determined fighters made up of infantry, machine gun units, and light and medium artillery groups. The latter consisted of 75mm and 150mm guns along with two six-inch naval guns.

The Marine attack on Yae Take began on April 14 with a strike to the east of the position toward the west

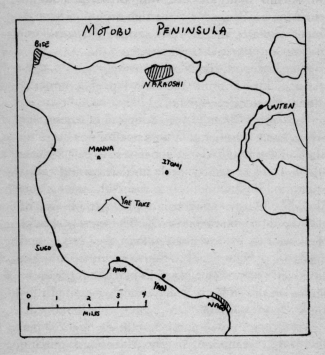

MOTOBU PENINSULA

BISE

NAKAOSHI

UNTEN

MANNA

ITOMI

YAE TAKE

SUGO

AWA

YABU

NAGO

0 1 2 3 4
MILES

coast at Tuguchi. Here the Marines managed to capture a seven hundred foot high ridge. From their elevated positions the Japanese poured heavy fire at the Marines but the dauntless troops continued to advance disregarding the danger. Meanwhile, two Marine battalions approached Yae Take from the north and managed to capture two high hills overlooking the Itomi-Manna road. At this point Yae Take was surrounded but the Japanese retained control of the high ground. Throughout the next day the Marines carried out small unit actions against enemy strong points.

By the sixteenth the Marines were ready to make their final assault against the bastion. The ferocious fighting, in many cases hand to hand, had resulted in high casualties. Over eleven hundred Japanese dead were counted. The fight on the sixteenth was bitter but by late afternoon the Marines managed to gain the crest of the hill. Around 1830 the Japanese counterattacked but were repulsed with heavy losses. Although his force was all but destroyed by now, the indominable Colonel Udo ordered the remnants to conduct guerrilla attacks.

Following their success at Yae Take, the Marines continued on to Motobu's northern sector which they cleared on the nineteenth. By the twentieth Japanese resistance on the peninsula had ceased to exist. In just fourteen days the Sixth Marine Division covered a distance of fifty-five miles. In the process they lost 207 men killed and 757 wounded. Six were classified as missing. The cost to the enemy was over 2,000 dead. Phase II was complete but Phase I was experiencing difficulty.

While the Sixth drove north the "Old Breed" advanced across the island's center, down the Katchin Peninsula and on April 6 managed to take the small island of Yabuchi Shima at the tip of the peninsula.

Meanwhile the XXIV Corps moved further south and reached the L + 10 line six days earlier than anticipated. On the sixth the corps commander, General Hodge, began to notice stiffer opposition as his troops approached the Shuri area. Once his forces started to move through Machinto, Kakazi and Tsuwa, the resistance deepened. It quickly became obvious that a long, drawn-out campaign was in the offing.

Admiral Turner, meanwhile, decided that the capture of the islands flanking Okinawa would be necessary to ensure the safety of the American forces and facilitate the amphibious support. Tsugen Shima, at the entrance of Nakagusku Wan, was assaulted on April 10 by the Twenty-seventh Division, veterans of Makin and Saipan. Ie Shima was secured between the sixteenth and twenty-first by elements of the Seventy-seventh Division.

The seizure of Tsugen Shima opened up the approaches to Nakagusuku Wan and ensured that XXIV Corps' units would be able to receive supplies from both east and west coast beaches. The capture of Tsugen Shima, however, was no easy venture. After a day and a half of fighting against determined enemy resistance, the Twenty-seventh did manage to take the objective. Their cost was 11 dead and 80 wounded. 234 Japanese bodies were found.

Ie Shima, on the other hand, was a far costlier battle. It was much larger than Tsugen Shima and its topography was ideal for airfield development. It already contained one good airstrip.

Prior to the main landing of April 16, a Marine reconnaissance force attacked Minna Shima on April 13 and captured it in two hours. Artillery batteries were then positioned so that they could provide supporting fire for the Ie Shima landing.

The Seventy-seventh Division's landing was relatively easy but as the GIs moved inland, resistance quickly grew stiffer. Hidden in caves and tombs, the Japanese contested every foot of Ie Shima. For six long days the division struggled and fought against an unyielding foe. With the Japanese having the advantage of high ground, the GIs were forced to battle uphill, exposed to the withering enemy fire. The Japanese positions were well sighted and contained many strong points. One of these was dubbed "bloody ridge" by the Americans. Eventually, on April 20, after a bitter bayonet and grenade attack, the Americans reached the top of the ridge and captured the main enemy defense structure known as "Government House." The following day the island was declared secure but the price had been heavy: 239 men killed, 879 wounded and 19 missing. Japanese losses were 4,706 killed and 149 captured.

One of the American dead on Ie Shima was the famous war correspondent Ernie Pyle who had come from Europe to observe what combat was like in the Pacific. Pyle was killed by a Japanese machine gunner while on his way to the front. From his position on LST 821 off the beach, a young radio operator, Merle Owen, could see the blockhouse near where Pyle perished. When the news made its way through the American lines, Owen said that everyone was deeply saddened. The sailors and GIs all felt that they had lost a good friend in Ernie Pyle.

The official history of the Seventy-seventh Division has this to say of the battle on Ie Shima:

Although overshadowed by the larger campaign on Okinawa, Ie Shima was an important battle in its own right. The airfield captured here was quickly developed into a huge B-29 bomber base from which American planes blasted Japan and swept the China Sea.[10]

Back on April 6, meanwhile, the Japanese mounted what turned out to be their only naval surface threat of the Okinawan campaign. The mammoth battleship *Yamato*, former flagship of the great Admiral Yamamoto, was sent on a suicide mission.

The objective of the *Yamato*'s sortie was for the battleship, escorted by a force of one light cruiser and eight destroyers, to assist the kamikaze attacks against the Americans in the Hagushi beach area. The *Yamato* carried only enough fuel for a one-way mission. Once it reached the beach area the *Yamato*'s orders called for it to shell the landing area with its huge eighteen-inch guns.

En route to Okinawa the Japanese ships were discovered by American aircraft. Planes from the carriers of Task Force 58 were quickly dispatched. The *Yamata* took a total of five bombs and ten torpedoes before sinking. The cruiser *Yahagi* and five destroyers were also lost. The surviving destroyers returned to Japan in despair.

The mission of the *Yamato* was but a small part of the overall suicide offensive against the Allied forces. The kamikazes were first experienced during the American invasion of the Philippines. It was an experience not easily forgotten.

In Japanese, kamikaze means "divine wind." The pilots believed that by crashing themselves and their aircraft into enemy ships they would achieve godhood.

Some even attended their own funerals prior to taking off. Their sacred vow said, "I am determined to destroy with my own body the enemy ships that menace our holy soil. I shall strike without returning."[11] The kamikaze effort represented a desperate bid by the Japanese to stop the Americans. 1,815 planes were assigned to the Special Attack Force. By April 6 the commander of the Japanese Combined Fleet, Admiral Toyoda, was ready to launch the first of ten major kamikaze flights, the last of which ended in June. A total of 1,416 sorties were flown and by the time the last kamikaze attack was over the damage inflicted was enormous:

> Twenty-eight ships were sunk and 225 damaged by Japanese air action during the campaign. Destroyers sustained more hits than any other class of ships. Battleships, cruisers and carriers also were among those struck, some of the big naval ships suffering heavy damage with great loss of life. The radar picket ships, made up principally of destroyers and destroyer escorts, suffered proportionately greater losses than any other part of the fleet.[12]

The reason for the heavy toll of the picket ships was understandable. They were usually the first American ships sighted by the kamikaze pilots. Impatient, the Japanese attacked the first ships they saw instead of continuing on to the beaches. Had they managed to reach the beaches in force, the result might have been disastrous.

From the deck of his LST 821 radioman Owen experienced the kamikaze menace first hand:

Almost every night the alarm sounded throughout the fleet. Transports, LSTs and other ships quickly weighed anchor in a hurry and moved out to gain room to maneuver. Many times it was a false alarm but often it was for real. Individual kamikazes or formations of them would arrive over the landing areas and begin firing on their targets. Every anti-aircraft gun in the fleet seemed to be firing at once. My own ship was never hit but we were attacked and managed to bring down a few of the enemy. I did, however, see other LSTs and a few cargo ships take hits. On one occasion a hospital ship was hit even though it was clearly marked with a big red cross.[13]

By April 7 it was clear to everyone in the XXIV Corps that the days of the fast-moving advances were over. The further south they moved, the stiffer the opposition grew. The Ninety-sixth Division attacked a Japanese strong point on Kajuzu Ridge and even though they were aided by the large guns of the battleship *New York*, the troops made only minor gains. Progress ground to a halt. Lashed by torrential rains on the eighth and ninth, the Ninety-sixth continued to push against the ridge but the heavy enemy fire and counterattacks forced the GIs to fall back to their jumping off point. On the tenth, despite a half hour bombardment by ships and artillery, the division managed to gain only three hundred yards (Map 24).

Over the next few days heavy Japanese counterattacks were repulsed but only with the greatest effort. On the thirteenth and fourteenth alone, 1,584 Japanese troops were killed and only 4 captured. The counterat-

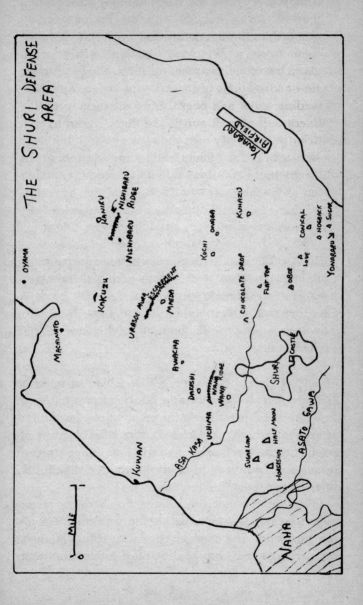

THE SHURI DEFENSE AREA

tacks proved to be wasteful in terms of Japanese dead.

To the men of the XXIV Corps, the Shuri stronghold began to resemble an impregnable fortress. If the Shuri stronghold was to be taken, additional artillery and troops were needed. Between the ninth and twelfth, artillery from the III Amphibious Corps and the First Marine Division were moved to the Shuri area. At the same time, the Twenty-seventy Infantry Division was brought into line.

On April 12, the soldiers, sailors and Marines heard of the death of President Franklin D. Roosevelt. Men reacted to the news in various ways:

> It was amazing and very striking how the men reacted. We held services, but services did not seem enough. The men were peculiarly sober and quiet all that day and the next. Plainly each of them was carrying an intimate sorrow of the deepest kind, for they paid it their highest tribute, the tribute of being unwilling to talk about, of leaving how they felt unsaid.[14]

General Hodge called for XXIV Corps to make a three division attack against the Shuri defenses on April 19. From the fifteenth onward preparations for the attack were made while the area was wounded by artillery, naval guns and planes. Tons of bombs, thousands of rockets and countless other shells were fired into the Japanese positions.

At 0600 on the nineteenth, the guns of twenty-seven artillery battalions opened up. At the same time, American planes flew low over the enemy and dropped their deadly explosives. One Marine pilot commented that

"He did not believe that we have ever exceeded or since equalled this magnitude of close air support on any given day."[15] To the troops anxiously waiting to jump off, the enormous bombardment was gratifying but being combat veterans, they were realistic enough to know from past experiences that somehow the Japanese would survive. The Japanese troops took refuge in their caves and concrete fortifications and, after the initial shock of the bombardment was over, moved out to man their positions. The American advance was stifled. Little if any progress was made all along the line that day.

At Kakuzu Ridge, the Twenty-seventh Division relieved the Ninety-sixth. It had no better luck in trying to take that strong point. The Twenty-seventh attempted a flanking movement by sending one battalion around the ridge to capture the village of Kakuzu. This attack proved successful but the enemy struck back with a fury and cut the infantry off from its supporting armor. With heavy losses, the Twenty-seventh was stopped dead in its tracks.

The Ninety-sixth Division, meanwhile, had been placed in the center of the XXIV Corps line and managed to push through Kaniku to the Nishibaru Ridge. But on the left flank of the corps, the Seventh Division made no progress at all against a rigid, fanatical resistance. The story remained the same from the twentieth through the twenty-fourth.

General Hodge, frustrated by his first attempt to break through the outer defenses of Shuri, renewed the attack on the twenty-fourth. Unbeknownst to him, however, was Ushijima's order to his front line defenders to fall back to secondary positions. Therefore, when the American attack was launched the entire corps made significant gains against enemy positions heretofore impregnable.

A few days prior to the launching of the XXIV Corps attack Buckner realized that Marine participation in the south was urgently required. On the twenty-seventh the III Amphibious Corps was shifted southward with the First Marine Division relieving the battle-worn Twenty-seventh division. On that day also the Seventy-seventh Division completed its transfer from Ie Shima to Okinawa. Its advance units were placed in the center of the American line where they began to relieve the weary troops of the Ninety-sixth. By the end of the day the Tenth Army was ready to continue the attack.

The American line now had the Seventh Division on the left, the Seventy-seventh in the center after relieving the Ninety-sixth, and the First Marine Division on the right with the Sixth Marine Division in reserve.

While the III Amphibious Corps took up its position, the XXIV Corps continued to apply pressure on the Japanese positions. Prior to its relief, the Ninety-sixth Division attempted to take the Maeda Escarpment, a vital high point with a dominating view of the surrounding territory. The area around Maeda witnessed some of the bitterest fighting yet encountered. On the twenty-ninth units of the Seventy-seventh continued the assault. Though new to the fighting on Okinawa, the division was still tired and understrength from its ordeal on Ie Shima and made little headway against a determined enemy.

On May 1, the First Marine Division completed its relief of the Twenty-seventh Division. With the Army units replaced by Marines, the III Amphibious Corps now took control of the west coast drive. The two corps, now side by side, prepared to eliminate the Shuri defenses.

That day the weather turned cloudy and rainy and remained that way for the next few days. Despite the inclement weather the Americans drove headlong into the Japanese positions. Gains were measured in yards and casualties were high. By evening of the second, after only two days of fighting, the First Marine Division had suffered 54 killed, 233 wounded and 33 missing. The Seventh Division registered no gains. Ushijima's defensive positions were proving a tough nut to crack. Hodge's dire prediction of two weeks earlier seemed to be fulfilling itself. He had said:

It is going to be really tough. . . . I see no way to get the Japanese out except to blast them out yard by yard.[16]

By then Ushijima no longer feared a landing in the Minatoga region and felt free to transfer troops from there to Shuri. General Cho attempted to convince Ushijima that now was the ideal time to mount a strong counterattack. Though General Kahara, the army operations officer, felt that a counterattack would result in a disaster and related his feelings to Ushijima, the latter was persuaded to go ahead with the attack. The scope of the attack was ambitious with the objective being the destruction of the XXIV Corps and the recapture of Futema which the Japanese erroneously believed to be the main headquarters of the Tenth Army. Tens of thousands of troops were deployed for the all-out counterattack. If successful, the homeland might yet be spared from invasion. The Japanese plan featured amphibious attacks in the east and west coasts with landings behind American lines in hopes of pinning the enemy in a vise.

American intelligence, though never in doubt that the Japanese possessed the capability for mounting a counterattack of great magnitude, believed the enemy would not do so. Despite the disclaimers, the XXIV Corps was not caught napping.

On May 3 and 4 the Allied ships were struck by the fifth mass kamikaze attack. Ninety-one sailors were killed, 280 wounded and 283 were reported missing. Damage to the vital radar pickets was extensive.

On the ground the Japanese counterattack struck at dusk on the third. The offensive opened with a mass bombardment. The Americans answered in kind. Added to the din were the fourteen and sixteen-inch shells from the naval support battleships. Soon afterward, the First Marine Division reported the presence of enemy barges making for shore at Kuwan. The Marines reacted to the threat quickly by firing mortars and machine guns at the crowded landing barges. Burning barges, flares and tracers lit up the coast. The Marines showed no mercy on those Japanese troops forced to jump from their burning barges. They raked the enemy as they bobbed in the water loaded down with combat gear. By the following morning the amphibious assault at Kuwan was an unmitigated failure. Additional landings further up the coast and on the opposite side of the island ended in the same dismal manner. But this was not the main offensive.

At 0430 thousands of Japanese mortars opened up on the American lines. With naval gunfire, artillery and air attacks the Americans responded and blunted the enemy thrust. By evening more than 77 tons of bombs, 450 rockets and 22,000 rounds of machine gunfire were fired at the attackers. Despite the ever-present threat of kamikazes, the ships continued to pour a hail of steel into the Japanese ranks. As a result, the counterattack was a failure. During the attack the Army units incurred 714 casualties, the Marines 649. 6,237 Japanese perished in the attack. The failure of the attack hurt the Japanese badly. Some of their division lost up to seventy percent of their original strength.

On the fifth the counterattack was called off and the Japanese resumed their defensive strategy. The failure of the attack weighed heavily on General Cho who:

> After the ill-starred action . . . abandoned all hope of a successful outcome of the operation and declared that only time intervened between defeat and the Thirty-second Army.[17]

That same day Buckner ordered both American corps to attack while the enemy was off balance. Once more the story was the same, however: savage resistance from behind highly fortified positions. The Marines ran into heavy opposition in a line running from Jichaku and Awacha. In two days only a few yards were gained. The blowtorch and corkscrew tactic, as Buckner called it, was the one most used by the Americans. This tactic combined the use of flamethrowers and explosives. One by one enemy caves were burned out and sealed up.

On the eighth the American troops were given the word that Nazi Germany had collapsed but the news gave little solace to the soldiers and Marines facing a savage enemy whose persistence seemed endless. Offshore, the ships of the fleet celebrated VE Day by firing a salvo into the Japanese lines precisely at noon. The resultant blasts shook the earth.

During the ninth and tenth the Sixth Marine Division took up positions along the Asa Kawa River in preparation for a full scale offensive aimed at destroying the defenses guarding Shuri. The attack that followed saw some of the bloodiest fighting yet on Okinawa.

Before the offensive could begin, however, the Marines had to capture the important positions guarding the path to Shuri: Dakeshi, Naha and Awacha. Here the fighting was extremely brutal. At the same time the XXIV Corps was embroiled in a desperate battle around a mass of hills north of Yonaburu that controlled the eastern approaches to Shuri. The main enemy defensive position in these hills was a feature called Conical Hill from whose heights the Japanese were able to observe any approach and could easily call down a murderous fire on any attackers. Advances in the hills were measured in yards and the casualties rose at an alarming rate.

On the eleventh the all-out American offensive began with the Marines moving toward Shuri from the northwest and the XXIV Corps from the northeast. By the twelfth the Ninety-sixth Division had gained a tenuous foothold on Conical Hill and systematically began reducing the enemy positions. From there the division advanced to Yonahuru. By now they were one step closer to the inner defenses of Shuri.

On the other shore the Sixth Marine Division captured the high ground north of their objective and quickly sent out patrols towards Naha.

At 0730 on the fourteenth the entire Tenth Army attacked with the intent of clearing the approaches to Shuri and surrounding the area. The Marines found the going extremely difficult as they attempted to break through the enemy line west and northwest of Wana. Small gains were registered and casualties continued to mount.

The Twenty-second Marine Regiment moved southward but found themselves stymied by a hill dubbed "Sugar Loaf." Japanese positions on the hill were designed so that they could cover an attack from any direction. Sugar Loaf appeared unconquerable. Since it was the western anchor of the Shuri line, control of Sugar Loaf was absolutely essential. At first the Marines did not realize the importance of the position but soon discovered that its capture would provide an opening into the very heart of the Shuri position.

From the heights of Sugar Loaf the Japanese rained a hail of death on the Marines huddling at the base of the hill. Twice on the fourteenth the Second Battalion of the Twenty-second Marines attempted to storm the objective but were repulsed both times. At 2300 under the cover of darkness the battalion commander, Maj. Henry Courtney, Jr., led his men up the hill. Tossing grenades as they charged, the Marines stunned the Japanese and were rewarded with the capture of the crest of the hill. The Marines quickly dug in to await the certain enemy counterattack.

From nearby positions, notably "Half Moon" and "Horseshoe" hills, the Japanese poured a withering fire into Sugar Loaf. All three positions were integral links in the Japanese defenses. The three hills were mutually supportive and connected by a network of tunnels which afforded the enemy the ability to reinforce each one as required.

Although Courtney and his men held the crest of the hill, whether they could hold onto it was another story. The Japanese counterattacked in force. Courtney had his men charge a nearby slope harboring many enemy positions. Throwing grenades before them again, he led his men forward in an effort to reduce the effectiveness of the enemy fire on his troops. Unfortunately, during the charge, Courtney was killed. For his inspired leadership and heroic action the major was posthumously awarded his country's highest award, the Congressional Medal of Honor.

By the morning of the fifteenth only twenty-five men of Courtney's original force remained on the hill where they continued to face enemy counterattacks. At 1130 the remaining few were pulled out and ordered to a hastily organized defense line on some high ground just in front of Sugar Loaf. The first of many attempts to take this strong point thus ended in failure. In fact, Tokyo radio broadcast a message in English to the American troops on Okinawa a few days later:

Sugar Loaf Hill . . . Chocolate Drop . . . Strawberry Hill. Gee those places sound wonderful! You can just see the candy houses with white picket fences around them and the candy canes hanging from the trees, their red and white stripes glistening in the sun. But the only thing red about those places is the blood of Americans. Yes, sir, those are the names of hills in southern Okinawa where the fighting's so close that you get down to bayonets and sometimes your bare fists. Artillery and naval gunfire are all right when the enemy is far off but they don't do you any good when he's right in the same foxhole with you. I guess it's natural to idealize the worst places with pretty names to make them seem less awful. Why Sugar Loaf has changed hands so often it looks like Dante's Inferno. Yes, sir, Sugar Loaf Hill . . . Chocolate Drop . . . Strawberry Hill. They sound good, don't they? Only those who've been there know what they're really like.[18]

The Twenty-ninth Marines were ordered to take Half Moon Hill on the fifteenth. They ran into the same stubborn resistance encountered by the Twenty-second Marines during their attack on Sugar Loaf the day before.

Throughout the fifteenth the battles raged. The following day the Sixth Marine Division experienced one of the bitterest days in the entire Okinawan campaign. After a full day of fighting had netted very little ground, one of its regiments, the ill-fated Twenty-second, recorded a combat efficiency of only forty percent. The division's commander, Major General Shepard, had no choice but to relieve the Twenty-second and place Sugar Loaf in the zone of the Twenty-ninth Marines.

On the seventeenth the Twenty-ninth attacked aided by the sixteen-inch gunfire of the support ships and a massive artillery barrage. Even that concentration of steel proved not enough. One company did manage to gain the crest of the hill but heavy casualties, added to a shortage of ammunition and a strong enemy counterattack, forced the battalion commander to order the survivors to relinquish their hard-earned positions. Sugar

Loaf was once more abandoned to the Japanese after a bitter fight.

During its futile attempts to take the hill, the Sixth Division learned one deadly lesson, the capture of that one objective was meaningless without the capture of the other two (Half Moon and Horseshoe Hills). At least two of the positions had to be taken simultaneously.

> If only one hill was seized with the others being neutralized or similarly captured, effective Japanese fire from the uncaptured positions would force the Marines to withdraw from the other two.[19]

On the eighteenth at 0946 the Twenty-ninth Marines managed to fight their way up Sugar Loaf once again in a little under two hours of fighting. Leaning on past experiences they subjected Half Moon to a deadly fire during the assault. The Japanese on Horseshoe, meanwhile, continued to pour mortar and machine gunfire into the ranks of the Americans. That position had to be eliminated.

By nightfall the fighting was still raging and by then the combat efficiency of the Twenty-ninth Marines was severely reduced. Since being committed to the battle nine days earlier the two regiments of the Sixth Division had incurred 2,662 battle casualties and 1,289 non-battle casualties. To bolster the weary regiments, the Fourth Marine Regiment was released from corps reserve and immediately sent to the relief of the battered Twenty-ninth Marines on Sugar Loaf.

The next day the Fourth Marines attacked Half Moon and Horseshoe Hills and by day's end had registered substantial gains. The Japanese were not about to take these losses sitting down, however, and at 2200 fired on the American positions. For the next two and a half hours they counterattacked the Americans. Most of the fighting was at close quarters and again much of it was hand to hand. In the morning the Marines still held their positions. Over five hundred enemy bodies were counted in front of their positions. The American attack resumed on the twenty-first with an attack down Sugar Loaf toward Horseshoe Hill. Once more stiff enemy resistance was encountered.

While the Sixth Division battled on the three hills, the First Marine Division was to the northeast and moving on Dakeshi and Wana. As they approached Wana it became obvious that they had entered the main Japanese defensive system. Using the rugged terrain to its best advantage, the Japanese blocked the Shuri approaches. The fight for Wana Ridge was particularly bloody. On the seventeenth some small gains were registered and Hill 55, an unusually strong position on the ridge, was captured by a platoon of Marines. The platoon soon found themselves isolated as Japanese counterattacks retook some of the newly acquired territory. Nevertheless, in spite of being cut off, the Marines clung to the hill.

By the nineteenth most of the ridge was in Marine hands. On the twentieth flamethrowing tanks burned and blasted Japanese strong points while Marines, advancing alongside the tanks, hurled grenades.

In an effort to stop the American attack, the Japanese shelled Wana Ridge from Shuri. Despite the intense barrage and strong counterattacks, by the twenty-first the ridge was captured. In the interim the weather turned sour and for the next week torrential rains soaked Okinawa forcing the American assault to grind to a halt.

XXIV Corps was also battling on hills and ridges. The enemy strong points in that sector were given bizarre names: Flat Top, Chocolate Drop, Hogback, Love, Dick, Oboe, and Sugar. Even with death staring them in the face at every step the American fighting man did not lose his sense of humor. Each of these strong enemy positions was reduced only after bitter and deadly fighting resulting in heavy casualties. Foot by foot the corps advanced to the Shuri line and, on May 20, the Seventy-seventh Division entered the outskirts of Shuri itself. Each yard covered was paid for in blood.

The rains that began on the twenty-first also affected the XXIV Corps' advance. Torrential downpours turned the entire countryside into a quagmire.

Weather notwithstanding, the Seventh Division continued its advance on Yonaburu. The rain continued unabated for the next nine days. Occasionally it came down as light sprinkles but most of the time it came down in torrents, turning the battlefield into one huge morass. The foul weather grounded aircraft and brought to a halt the vital supply drops. Consequently, all supplies for the front line forces had to be manhandled to the front. The combat engineers worked tirelessly in an effort to keep the roads open but in the long run the weather won out. The entire front became stalemated.

Ushijima remained confident that he had sufficient manpower to prevent the Americans from breaking into Shuri. He sent every available man to shore up a defensive line extending through Yonawa to Chan, southeast of Shuri. A few days later the general's hopes were shattered.

From one coast to another the Tenth Army was poised to break into Shuri. Using the cloak provided by the bad weather, Ushijima made preparations for a withdrawal from Shuri in the event the Americans somehow managed to break through. When the American attack did begin it made good progress. Facing a potential disaster, Ushijima ordered the withdrawal to begin. The movement was quickly discovered. Naval gunfire, artillery and mortars were concentrated on the retreating Japanese columns. The Tenth Army had hit the jackpot; the Japanese were caught in the open.

Taking advantage of the golden opportunity, Buckner ordered that unrelenting pressure be maintained on the retreating enemy to ensure that they would be unable to establish new positions further south. The horrendous weather, however, prevented making a full-scale attack.

Even though the Japanese had begun to withdraw from Shuri, the resistance they continued to put up belied the fact that they were pulling back. Shuri continued to bristle with death.

In the west the Sixth Marine Division secured the remainder of Naha. Then, when the Seventh Division moved into position southwest of Yonaburu, all was in readiness for the final assault on Shuri. On the twenty-ninth, the First Marine Division captured Shuri Castle, ancient seat of the rulers of Okinawa. Except for some Japanese rearguards who held out stubbornly, the majority of the formations defending Shuri escaped to the south.

Why had Ushijima abandoned the Shuri defenses?

The decision to do so was made at a conference held at the Thirty-second Army command post on the night of May 22. Originally, the Japanese planned to hold out around Shuri with a last-ditch stand in the vicinity of the castle. But Ishijima revised his plan after realizing that for the position to be held, fifty thousand troops would be crammed into a defensive perimeter measuring less than a mile in diameter. This confined area would not only preclude an effective defense, it would expose the troops like ducks in a shooting gallery. The general was faced with but two alternatives: retreat to the Chinen Peninsula, or to the Kiyamu Peninsula on Okinawa's southern tip. Since the Americans were already approaching Chinen, Kiyamu was considered the best sector in which to make the next decisive stand (Map 25). The dominant feature of the Kiyamu area was the Yaeju Dake-Yuza Dake escarpment. This area contained numerous natural and man-made caves ideal for conducting a prolonged defense and perfect protection from heavy bombardment. The area had already been prepared so that once the Japanese left Shuri, they had only to occupy the area and resume the deadly struggle.

The newest defensive position ran from Hanagusuku on the east coast through Yaeju Dake-Yza Dake escarpment to Kunishi and Nagusuku on the west coast. To enable Ushijima to have enough time to move his forces into position, the rearguard left behind at Shuri had to hold the Americans until May 31. The retreat would also have to be orderly with one force left behind to protect the one retreating. Temporary lines of defense needed to be established until the main lines were ready.

The severe weather, meanwhile, frustrated all American efforts to break through south of Shuri. Mud and

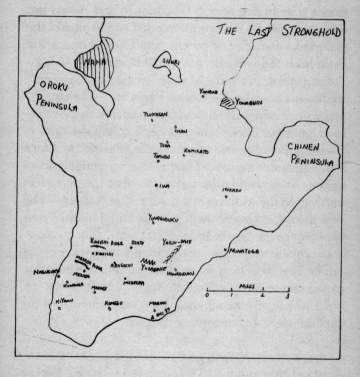

THE LAST STRONGHOLD

NAHA

SHURI

OROKU PENINSULA

Yonawa

Yonabaru

TSUKASAN

CHAN

CHINEN PENINSULA

TERA

KAMIZATO

TOMUSU

IWA

ITOKAZU

YUNAGUSUKU

KUNISHI RIDGE

OZATO

YAEJU-DAKE

MINATOGA

KUNISHI

MEZADO RIDGE

ARAGACHI

MEZADO

YUZADAKE

HANAGUSUKU

NAGUSUKU

KUWANGA

MAKABE

MEDEERA

KIYAMU

KOMESU

MABUNI

HILL 89

MILES

0   1   2   3

the enemy rearguard harassed the pursuing Tenth Army. It seemed that the horror at Shuri was no sooner ended than it was renewed with vigor as they moved south.

By June 1, it was estimated that the Tenth Army had killed a total of 62,548 of the enemy while capturing only 465. A mere eight square miles of Okinawa remained in enemy hands. Thus far, 5,309 Americans had perished, 23,909 were wounded and 346 had been reported missing. The butcher's bill for Okinawa was the largest of any Pacific battle and it was not over yet.

On June 4, the Sixth Marine Division made an amphibious attack on the Oroku Peninsula. The landing was unopposed thus allowing the Marines to move inland for about fifteen hundred yards before meeting resistance. For the next ten days the Marines fought a slogging match against a fanatical foe determined not to give an inch. Again the terrain favored the defenders and placed the Marines at a distinct disadvantage. The heavily tangled overgrowth provided the Japanese with excellent cover. Caves and bunkers were constructed in such a manner that each was mutually supportive of the other. The defenders were naval personnel under the expert leadership of Adm. Minoru Ota.

On the Sixth, the admiral sent a communique to his superiors in Tokyo regarding the battle:

More than two months have passed since we engaged the invaders. In complete unity and harmony with the army, we have made every effort to crush the enemy. Despite our effort the battle is going against us. My own troops are at a disadvantage since all available heavy guns and four crack

344

battalions of naval landing forces were allocated to army command.

I tender herewith my deepest apology to the emperor for my failure to better defend the empire, the grave task with which I was entrusted. . . . With my officers and men I give three cheers for the emperor and pray for the everlasting peace of the empire. Though my body decays in remote Okinawa, my spirit will persist in defense of the homeland.[20]

American superiority eventually won out. By June 13 the last of the naval base force was eliminated with some eighty-six of them surrendering. Others committed suicide or died defending their positions to the very last. At 1730 General Shepard reported to Geiger that all organized resistance on the Oroku Peninsula was at an end. Shepard noted:

The ten-day battle was a bitter one, from its inception to the destruction of the last organized resistance. The enemy had taken full advantage of the terrain which adapted itself extraordinarily well to the deliberate defense in depth. . . . Despite the powerful converging attack of three regiments, the advance was slow, laborious and bitterly opposed. The capture of each defensive locality was a problem in itself, involving carefully thought out planning and painstaking execution. During ten days of fighting, almost 5,000 Japanese were killed. . . . Thirty of our tanks were disabled, many by mines. . . . Finally, 1,608 Marines were killed or wounded.[21]

While the Sixth Division struggled at Oroku, the balance of the Tenth Army moved toward the southern defensive zone. On the evening of June 3, the Seventh Division reached Kakibana thereby isolating the Chinen Peninsula. The division then consolidated its position and prepared to move southwest against the Japanese positions in the Kiyamu Peninsula. The Ninety-sixth made easy gains in the center and captured Kamzato and Tera. At the same time, the Old Breed drove forward against only slight resistance. The weather, though, remained miserable.

The rains finally stopped on June 6 and the following day the sun shone for the first time in two weeks. That day the First Marine Division captured Itoman and regrouped before attacking a Japanese strong point on Kunishi Ridge. The ridge was a sheer coral escarpment bristling with defenses that formed the western anchor of the Kiyamu line. Because of the unlimited enemy field of visibility, the Seventh Regiment's attack on the eleventh was repulsed. Realizing that a day attack was suicidal, the regimental commander pulled his men back and prepared for a nighttime assault.

Before ordering the attack, Buckner made an effort to induce the Japanese to surrender. Thousands of leaflets were dropped on the enemy lines and Japanese language broadcasts were directed at them through loudspeakers. A message was also sent to General Ushijima from Buckner saying:

> The forces under your command have fought
> bravely and well, and your infantry tactics have
> merited the respect of your opponents. . . . Like
> myself, you are an infantry general long schooled

and practiced in infantry warfare. . . . I believe, therefore, that you understand as clearly as I that the destruction of all Japanese resistance on the island is merely a matter of days.[22]

Ushijima ignored the call for surrender. Buckner knew that he would but the effort had to be made.

At 0330 on June 12 the Seventh Marines launched their night attack. The attack took the Japanese totally by surprise and by 0500, the crest of the ridge was in American hands. It did not take the Japanese long to sense what was happening. They counterattacked immediately. For the next four days the Marines on Kunishi Ridge were isolated from all other American units. Despite repeated Japanese attempts to dislodge them, however, the Marines held on.

To the left of the ridge, the First Marines entered Ozato. Throughout the attack the Japanese lines were plastered with an enormous concentration of rocket fire from LCI gunboats ringing the peninsula.

By the sixteenth Kunishi Ridge was finally secured and the Marines moved forward to eliminate enemy resistance on the slopes of Mezado Ridge. This position was cleared on the seventeenth. The Marines then pushed into Kuwanga. The Japanese launched a strong counterattack against Mezado but it met with a bloody repulse.

The fresh Eighth Regiment from the Second Marine Division was committed to battle for the final thrust on Kujamu Peninsula. Incredibly, the Japanese commanders were still able to rouse their remaining troops to a fever pitch, convincing them that victory was yet possible.

Despite outward signs of imminent defeat and their impoverished condition, the confidence that Ushijima's army had in their ultimate victory was derived from deep-seated tradition, strongly enforced discipline, and the historically persuasive influence of Japanese military doctrine throughout the empire.[23]

Meanwhile, XXIV Corps faced a difficult task, the capture of the Yaeju Dake-Yuza Dake escarpment. For two solid weeks of violent, ferocious fighting, the GIs battled to eliminate the stiff resistance on their front. The Americans pushed relentlessly into the enemy defenses. Despite counterattacks, the Americans held onto the captured territory and continued to push ahead. By the seventeenth, the corps' hold on the escarpment was firm.

On the eighteenth, the battle integrity of the Japanese began to decrease noticeably. With the exception of a strong defensive position around Medeera and Mabuni, enemy resistance was decreasing. The First Marine Division attacked southwest from the Mezado Ridge toward an enemy line west of Makabe. Once it breached this line, the division continued right toward the sea.

That same day General Buckner travelled to the forward lines so that he could observe the recently committed Eighth Marines in action. Though cautioned about the hazards of such a trip, the general disregarded all warnings and proceeded to the front. Buckner went to an observation post on a ridge from where he could get a good view of the fighting. A few minutes after his arrival an anti-tank shell exploded near the post, followed in quick succession by five more. Buckner was mortally wounded. He died soon afterward.

On the nineteenth, General Geiger, promoted to lieutenant general, was appointed Tenth Army commander temporarily. This marked the first time in the history of the Marine Corps that one of their officers commanded a unit of this size. Four days later, on June 23, Gen. Joseph "Vinegar Joe" Stilwell succeeded to permanent command of the Tenth Army but only after Geiger had achieved the long sought after victory.

Also on the nineteenth, the "Deadeyes" of the Ninety-sixth Division lost their assistant divisional commander, General Easley. This event did not prevent the Ninety-sixth from launching its attack on Medeera. At the same time, the Seventh Division swept down to Komesu and Mabuni.

By now Ushijima knew that the end was near and started to prepare himself for a Samurai's death. In fact, as far back as June 16, he sent the first of several farewell messages to Imperial Headquarters in Tokyo:

> With a burning desire to destroy the arrogant enemy, the men in my command have fought the invaders for almost three months. We have failed to crush the enemy, despite our death-defying resistance, and now we are doomed.
>
> Since taking over this island our forces have, with the devoted support of the local population, exerted every effort to build up defenses. Since the enemy landing, our air and land forces, working in concert, have done everything possible to defend the island.
>
> To my great regret we are no longer able to con-

tinue the fight. For this failure I tender deepest apologies to the emperor and the people of the homeland. . . . I pray for the souls of men killed in battle and for the prosperity of the Imperial Family. Death will not quell the desire of my spirit to defend the homeland.

With deepest appreciation of my superiors and my colleagues in arms, I bid farewell to all of you forever.[24]

Three days later he sent another message to all survivors congratulating them on their tenacity and calling upon them to fight to the last and die for the emperor. But not all Japanese accepted his decision to fight to the last and forfeit their lives for the emperor. The American psychological warfare teams were experiencing more and more success in inducing Japanese soldiers to surrender.

On June 21, Ushijima and Cho composed a farewell poem. In many respects it was an epitaph for these two warriors.

> *The green grass of this isle*
> *Withers untimely before fall*
> *Yet it will grow again*
> *In the warm spring of the empire*
> *Smearing heaven and earth with our blood*
> *We leave this world with our ammunition gone*
> *Yet our souls shall come back again and again*
> *To guard the empire forever.*[25]

That same day General Shepard reported to corps headquarters that all organized resistance in the Sixth Division's zone had ceased. Only mopping up operations remained. Later in the day the First Division captured the few remaining enemy positions in its sector. By 1700 all resistance in the III Amphibious Zone was at an end.

In the XXIV Corps zone the story was basically the same. The GIs were involved in heavy fighting north of Makabe and around a major stronghold at Mabuni. Nevertheless, by day's end they too had secured their zone. General Geiger therefore gave the order to raise the flag. After eighty-two days of bloody fighting, Okinawa had fallen.

On the twenty-second Ushijima and Cho ended their lives in traditional Samurai fashion. Their bodies were buried secretly somewhere near the foot of Hill 89 south of Mabuni.

The new Tenth Army commander, General Stilwell, ordered an intensive mopping up program aimed at clearing up the isolated pockets of resistance still remaining. Enemy losses for the campaign were placed at 107,539 dead with another 23,764 presumed to be sealed up in caves. 10,755 Japanese were captured. Besides the loss of so many troops, the Japanese lost 7,830 aircraft and 16 warships.

American casualties totalled 49,151. Of this total, 12,520 were killed and 33,631 wounded. The rest were classified as missing. Included in the toll was 4,907 sailors killed and 4,824 wounded. 34 American ships were sunk, 368 damaged, a grim tribute to the effectiveness of the kamikazes, and 763 carrier aircraft were lost.

The battle for Okinawa resulted in the highest number of casualties sustained in the Pacific. If the capture of Okinawa was this costly, what would an invasion of Japan be like? In all:

more ships were used, more troops put ashore, more supplies transported, more naval guns fired against shore targets than in any previous campaign in the Pacific.[26]

The high price of victory was due to the fact that the battle had been fought against a capably led Japanese army of greater strength than anticipated, over difficult terrain heavily and expertly fortified. In addition, the battle lasted longer than expected, but the military value of Okinawa was well worth the price. It was large enough to act as a staging area for an invasion of Japan, it provided numerous airfields, and it furnished fleet anchorages right on Japan's doorstop. From its airfields fighter planes were able to escort the B-29s carrying out their attacks on Japan's cities from bases in the Marianas.

Teamwork was one of the key factors in the success of the Okinawan campaign. Interservice cooperation was at its finest there. In addition, the tank proved to be one of the greatest weapons on the battlefield.

Okinawa was also a model of amphibious operations. What had begun at Guadalcanal, had continued at Makin and Tarawa, been improved upon in the Marshalls, refined at the Marianas and Leyte and matured at Iwo Jima, was perfected at Okinawa. There, all that was previously learned in the art of mounting a seaborne assault against an enemy-held land mass culminated in the Americans' greatest Pacific victory.

Had Ushijima accomplished his task? Yes! He bought his homeland a precious three more months in which to prepare for an Allied invasion. Little did he know that an atomic bomb would end the war less than two months after his own life was over.

Introduction

NOTES

1. Kent R. Greenfield, ed., *Command Decisions,* p. 494
2. James F. Byrnes, *Speaking Frankly*, p. 259
3. Ernest J. King, *Fleet Admiral King,* p. 598
4. Ray S. Cline, *Washington Command Post: The Operations Division,* p. 344
5. Byrnes, *op. cit.,* p. 208
6. Greenfield, *op. cit.,* p. 510
7. *Ibid,* p. 51

BIBLIOGRAPHY

Bergamini, David. *Japan's Imperial Conspiracy.* Pocket Books, New York, 1972.

Byrnes, James F. *Speaking Frankly.* Harper & Bros., New York, 1947.

Churchill, Winston. *Triumph and Tragedy.* Houghton Mifflin Co., Boston, 1953.

Cline, Ray S. *Washington Command Post: The Operations Division.* Office of Chief of Military History, Washington, 1951.

Craven, Wesley and Cate, James. *The Army Air Forces in World War II, Volume V, The Pacific: Matterhorn to Nagasaki.* University of Chicago Press, Chicago, 1953.

Craig, William. *The Fall of Japan.* Dial Press, New York, 1967.

Feis, Herbert. *Churchill — Roosevelt — Stalin.* Princeton University Press, New Jersey, 1957.

Feis, Herbert. *Japan Subdued.* Princeton University Press, New Jersey, 1961.

Greenfield, Kent R. *Command Decisions.* Office of Chief of Military History, Washington, 1960.

Hoyt, Edwin. *Closing the Circle.* Van Nostrand Reinhold Co., New York, 1982.

King, Ernest and Muir, Walter M. *Fleet Admiral King.* W.W. Norton & Co., New York, 1952.

Leahy, William. *I Was There.* Whittlesey House, New York, 1950.

Stimson, Henry and Bundy, McGeorge. *On Active Service in Peace and War.* Harper & Brothers, New York, 1947.

Toland, John. *The Rising Sun.* Random House, New York, 1970.

Chapter One

NOTES

1. Arthur Swinson, *Defeat in Malaya,* p. 17
2. *Ibid,* pp.12-13
3. Stanley Falk, *Seventy Days to Singapore,* p. 45
4. *Ibid,* p. 45
5. Woodburn Kirby et al., *The War Against Japan,* Vol. I, p. 161
6. Winston Churchill, *The Grand Alliance,* pp. 587-588
7. Swinson, *op. cit.,* p. 39
8. *Ibid,* p. 74
9. A.J. Barker, *Yamashita,* p. 68
10. Falk, *op. cit.,* p. 104
11. Kirby, *op. cit.,* p. 197
12. Churchill, *op. cit.,* p. 620
13. Winston Churchill, *The Hinge of Fate,* p. 53
14. Charles Pfannes and Victor Salamone, *The Great Commanders of World War II, Volume IV: The Japanese,* p. 251
15. Noel Barber, *A Sinister Twilight,* pp. 216-217
16. Swinson, *op. cit.,* p. 140
17. Ronald Lewin, *The Chief,* p. 148
18. Barker, *op. cit.,* p. 68
19. Falk, *op. cit.,* p. 257

BIBLIOGRAPHY

Barber, Noel. *A Sinister Twilight.* Houghton Mifflin Co., Boston, 1968.

Barker, A.J. *Yamashita.* Ballantine Books, New York, 1973.

Churchill, Winston. *The Grand Alliance.* Houghton Mifflin Co., Boston, 1950.

Churchill, Winston. *The Hinge of Fate.* Houghton Mifflin Co.,

Boston, 1950.

Collier, Basil. *The War in the Far East 1941-1945*. William Morrow & Co., New York, 1969.

Connell, John. *Wavell*. Harcourt, Brace & World, New York, 1964.

Costello, John. *The Pacific War*. Rawson Wade Publishers, New York, 1981.

Falk, Stanley. *Seventy Days to Singapore*. G.P. Putnam's Sons, New York, 1975.

Kirby, Woodburn, et al. *The War Against Japan, Vol. I*. Her Majesty's Stationery Office, London, 1957.

Lewin, Ronald. *The Chief*. Farrar, Strauss & Giroux, New York, 1980.

Middlebrook, Martin and Mahoney, Patrick. *Battleship*. Charles Scribner's Sons, New York, 1977.

Pfannes, Charles and Salamone, Victor. *The Great Commanders of World War II Vol. IV: The Japanese*. Zebra Books, New York, 1982.

Reel, Frank. *The Case of General Yamashita*. Octagon Books, New York, 1971.

Swinson, Arthur. *Defeat in Malaya*. Ballantine Books, New York, 1969.

Taylor, Lawrence. *A Trial of Generals*. Icarus Press, South Bend, 1981.

Toland, John. *But Not in Shame*. Random House, New York, 1961.

Wigmore, Lionel. *The Japanese Thrust*. Australian War Memorial, Canberra, 1957.

Chapter Two

NOTES

1. William Manchester, *American Caesar*, p. 189
2. Ward Rutherford, *Fall of the Philippines*, p. 19
3. Hanson W. Baldwin, *Battles Lost and Won*, p. 117
4. Lawrence Taylor, *A Trial of Generals*, p. 43
5. *Ibid*, p. 66
6. Sydney L. Mayer, *MacArthur*, p. 89

7. Rutherford, *op. cit.*, p. 85
8. Mayer, *op. cit.*, p. 89
9. Gavin Long, *MacArthur as Military Commander*, p. 82
10. Rutherford, *op. cit.*, p. 109
11. Jonathan Wainwright, *General Wainwright's Story*, pp. 3-4
12. *Ibid*, p. 4
13. Louis Morton, *The Fall of the Philippines*, p. 442
14. Stanley L. Falk, *Bataan: The March of Death*, p. 187
15. Wainwright, *op. cit.*, p. 118

BIBLIOGRAPHY

Baldwin, Hanson. *Battles Lost and Won.* Harper & Row, New York, 1966.

Brereton, Louis. *The Brereton Diaries.* William Morrow & Co., New York, 1946.

Costello, John. *The Pacific War.* Rawson Wade Publishers, New York, 1981.

Falk, Stanley. *Bataan: The March of Death.* Modern Literary Editions, New York, 1962.

Knox, Donald. *Death March.* Harcourt, Brace, Jovanovich, New York, 1981.

Long, Gavin. *MacArthur as Military Commander.* D. Van Nostrand Co., New York, 1969.

Manchester, William, *American Caesar.* Little Brown and Co., Boston, 1978.

Mayer, Sydney. *MacArthur.* Ballantine Books, New York, 1971.

Morris, Eric. *Corregidor.* Stein and Day, New York, 1981.

Morton, Louis. *The Fall of the Philippines.* Office of Chief of Military History, Washington, 1953.

Pfannes, C. and Salamone, V. *The Great Commanders of World War II, Volume III: The Americans.* Zebra Books, New York, 1981.

Pfannes, C. and Salamone, V. *The Great Commanders of World War II, Volume IV: The Japanese.* Zebra Books, New York, 1982.

Rutherford, Ward. *Fall of the Philippines.* Ballantine Books, New York, 1971.

Taylor, Lawrence. *A Trial of Generals*. Icarus Press, Indiana, 1981.

Toland, John. *The Rising Sun*. Random House, New York, 1970.

Toland, John. *But Not in Shame*. Random House, New York, 1971.

Wainwright, Jonathan. *General Wainwright's Story*. Doubleday & Co., New York, 1946.

Chapter Three

NOTES

1. Herbert L. Merillat, *The Island*, p. 20
2. Robert Leckie, *Challenge for the Pacific*, p. 125
3. *Ibid*, p. 161
4. William Manchester, *Goodbye Darkness*, p. 211
5. Leckie, *op. cit.*, p. 181
6. Manchester, *op. cit.*, p. 218
7. Leckie, *op. cit.*, p. 265
8. Jack Coggins, *The Campaign for Guadalcanal*, p. 104
9. Leckie, *op. cit.*, p. 342
10. Joseph Collins, *Lightning Joe*, p. 147
11. William Halsey and J. Bryann, *Admiral Halsey's Story*, p. 148
12. *Ibid*, p. 148
13. Graham Kent, *Guadalcanal-Island Ordeal*, p. 158

BIBLIOGRAPHY

Blankfort, Michael. *Big Yankee-Carlson of the Raiders*. Little Brown & Co., Boston, 1947.

Collier, Basil. *War in the Far East*. William Morrow & Co., New York, 1968.

Coggins, Jack. *The Campaign for Guadalcanal*. Doubleday & Co., New York, 1972.

Collins, Joseph. *Lightning Joe*. LSU Press, Baton Rouge, 1979.

Costello, John. *War in the Pacific*. Rawson Wade, New York,

1981.

Dyer, George. *The Amphibions Came to Conquer.* Government Printing Office, Washington, 1969.

Ellis, John. *The Sharp End.* Charles Scribner's Sons, New York, 1980.

Gallant, Grady. *On Valor's Side.* Zebra Books, New York, 1980.

Halsey, William and Bryann, J. *Admiral Halsey's Story.* Curtis Publishing, New York, 1947.

Hoyt, Edwin. *Guadalcanal.* Stein & Day, New York, 1981.

Kent, Graham. *Guadalcanal-Island Ordeal.* Ballantine Books, New York, 1971.

Leckie, Robert. *Challenge for the Pacific.* Doubleday & Co., New York, 1965.

Manchester, William. *Goodbye Darkness.* Little Brown & Co., Boston, 1979.

Morison, Samuel. *History of U.S. Naval Operations in WW II, Volume V— The Struggle for Guadalcanal.* Little Brown & Co., Boston, 1975.

Oleck, Howard. *Heroic Battles of WW II.* Belmont Books, New York, 1962.

Pfannes, C. and Salamone, V. *The Great Commanders of World War II, Volume III: The Americans.* Zebra Books, New York, 1981.

Pfannes, C. and Salamone, V. *The Great Commanders of World War II, Volume IV: The Japanese.* Zebra Books, New York, 1982.

Pfannes, C. and Salamone, V. *The Great Admirals of World War II, Volume I: The Americans.* Zebra Books, New York, 1983.

Smith, S.E., ed. *The United States Marine Corps in WW II.* Random House, New York, 1969.

Steinberg, Rafael. *Island Fighting.* Time Life Books, New York, 1978.

Tregaskis, Richard. *Guadalcanal Diary.* Random House, New York, 1943.

Merrilat, Herbert L. *The Island.* Little Brown & Co., Boston, 1943.

Davis, Burke. *Marine — The Life of Chesty Puller.* Little Brown & Co., Boston, 1962.

Chapter Four

NOTES

1. Holland M. Smith, *Coral and Brass*, p. 134
2. Philip A. Crowl and Edmond G. Love, *Seizure of the Gilberts and Marshalls*, p. 156
3. Henry Shaw, Jr. et al., *Central Pacific Drive*, p. 27
4. Henry Shaw, Jr., *Tarawa: A Legend Is Born*, p. 21
5. *Ibid*, p. 25
6. Shaw, *Central Pacific Drive*, p. 37.
7. *Ibid*, pp. 55-56
8. Shaw, *Tarawa*, p. 57
9. Shaw, *Central Pacific Drive*, p. 66
10. *Ibid*, p. 71
11. Shaw, *Tarawa*, p. 88
12. *Ibid*, p. 96
13. Shaw, *Central Pacific Drive*, p. 79
14. Jane Blakeney, *Heroes*, p. 31
15. Shaw, *Central Pacific Drive*, p. 87
16. *Ibid*, p. 90
17. Smith, *op. cit.*, p. 125
18. Richard W. Johnston, *Follow Me*, p. 166
19. Crowl and Love, *op. cit.*, 156
20. Jeter A. Isely and Philip A. Crowl, *The U.S. Marines and Amphibious War*, p. 251
21. Andrieu d'Albas, *Death of a Navy*, p. 277
22. Hanson W. Baldwin, *Battles Lost and Won*, p. 255

BIBLIOGRAPHY

Baldwin, Hanson. *Battles Lost and Won*. Harper & Row, New York, 1966.

Blakeney, Jane. *Heroes*. Guthrie Lithograph Co., Washington, 1957.

Costello, John. *The Pacific War*. Rawson Wade Publishers, New York, 1981.

Craven, Wesley and Cate, James. *The Army Air Forces in World War II, Volume IV, The Pacific: Guadalcanal to Saipan*. University of Chicago Press, Chicago, 1950.

Crowl, Philip A. and Love, Edmund G. *Seizure of the Gilberts and Marshalls*. Chief of Military History, Washington, 1955.

d'Albas, Andrieu. *Death of a Navy*. Devin-Adair Co., New York, 1957.

Hough, Frank. *The Island War*. J.P. Lippincott Co., Philadelphia, 1947.

Hoyt, Edwin. *Storm Over the Gilberts*. Mason/Charter, New York, 1978.

Isely, Jeter A. and Crowl, Philip A. *The U.S. Marines and Amphibious War*. Princeton University Press, Princeton, 1951.

Johnston, Richard. *Follow Me*. Random House, New York, 1948.

Leckie, Robert. *Strong Men Armed*. Bonanza Books, New York, 1962.

Love, Edmund. *The 27th Infantry Division in World War II*. Infantry Journal Press, Washington, 1949.

Morison, Samuel E. *History of United States Naval Operations in World War II, Vol. VII: Aleutians, Gilberts and Marshalls*. Little Brown & Co., Boston, 1951.

Morton, Louis. *Strategy and Command: The First Two Years*. Chief of Military History, Washington, 1962.

Pfannes, Charles and Salamone, Victor. *The Great Admirals of World War II, Vol. I: The Americans*. Zebra Books, New York, 1983.

Russ, Martin. *Line of Departure, Tarawa*. Doubleday & Co., New York, 1975.

Shaw, Henry. *Tarawa: A Legend Is Born*. Ballantine Books, New York, 1968.

Shaw, H., Nalty, B., and Turnbladh, E. *Central Pacific Drive*. Historical Branch, U.S. Marine Corps, Washington, 1966.

Sharrod, Robert. *Tarawa: The Story of a Battle*. Duell, Sloan & Pearce, New York, 1944.

Smith, Holland M. *Coral and Brass*. Charles Scribner's Sons, New York, 1949.

Stockman, James. *The Battle for Tarawa*. Historical Section,

U.S. Marine Corps, Washington, 1947.

Wilson, Earl et al. *Betio Beachhead*. G.P. Putnam's Sons, New York, 1945.

Chapter Five

NOTES

1. M. Matloff, *Strategic Planning for Coalition Warfare 1943-44*, p. 36
2. George Dyer, *The Amphibions Came to Conquer*, p. 849
3. P. Crowl, *U.S. Army in WW II — Campaign in the Marianas*, p. 95
4. Edwin Hoyt, *To the Marianas*, pp. 190-191
5. *Ibid*, pp. 195-196
6. Holland Smith, *Coral and Brass*, p. 172
7. *Ibid*, p. 178
8. *Ibid*, p. 179
9. Hoyt, *op. cit.*, p. 207
10. *Ibid*, p. 261

BIBLIOGRAPHY

Buell, Thomas. *The Quiet Warrior*. Little Brown & Co., Boston, 1974.

Buell, Thomas. *Master of Sea Power*. Little Brown & Co., Boston, 1980.

Collier, Richard. *The Freedom Road*. Atheneum, New York, 1984.

Conn, Stetson, ed. *U.S. Army in WW II — Campaign in the Marianas*. Office of Chief of Military History, Washington, 1960.

Dyer, George. *The Amphibions Came to Conquer*. U.S. Govt. Printing Office, Washington, 1972.

Hoyt, Edwin. *How They Won the War in the Pacific*. Weybright & Talley, New York, 1970.

Hoyt, Edwin. *To the Marianas*. Van Nostrand Reinhold, New York, 1980.

Morison, Samuel. *History of U.S. Naval Operations in WW II:*

The Rising Sun in the Pacific. Little Brown & Co., Boston, 1948.

Pfannes, C. and Salamone, V. *The Great Admirals of WW II, Vol. I: The Americans.* Zebra Books, New York, 1983.

Smith, S.E., ed. *The U.S. Marine Corps in WW II.* Random House, New York, 1969.

Salmaggi, C. and Palvasini, A. *2194 Days of War.* Windward, London, 1979.

Shaw, H. and Nalty, B. *Central Pacific Drive.* Historical Branch, U.S. Marine Corps, Washington, 1966.

Smith, Holland. *Coral and Brass.* Zenger, Washingon, 1948.

Potter, E. B. *Nimitz.* Naval Institute Press, Annapolis, 1976.

Y'Blood, Jack. *Red Sun Setting.* Naval Institute Press, Annapolis, 1981.

Chapter Six

NOTES

1. J. Isely and P. Crowl, *The U.S. Marines and Amphibious War,* p. 475
2. G. Garand and T. Strobridge, *Western Pacific Operations,* p. 448
3. Richard Newcomb, *Iwo Jima,* pp. 8-9
4. Saburo Sakai, *Samurai,* p. 156.
5. Garand, *op. cit.,* p. 455
6. *Ibid,* pp. 459-61
7. Howard Conner, *The Spearhead,* Preface
8. Garand, *op. cit.,* p. 475
9. W. Craven and J. Cate, *The Army Air Forces in World War II, Vol. V: The Pacific — Matterhorn to Nagasaki,* pp. 584-585
10. Holland M. Smith, *Coral and Brass,* pp. 243-244
11. Conner, *op. cit.,* p. 53
12. Newcomb, *op. cit.,* p. 135
13. Robert Sherrod, *On to Westward,* p. 180
14. Conner, *op. cit.,* p. 57
15. Richard Wheller, *The Bloody Battle for Suribachi,* p. 108
16. Michael Russell, *Iwo Jima,* p. 59

17. Carl Proehl, *The Fourth Marine Division in World War II*, p. 153
18. Russell, *op. cit.*, p. 72
19. Isely and Crowl, *op. cit.*, pp. 489-490
20. Russell, *op. cit.*, p. 82
21. Isely, *op. cit.*, p. 497
22. Russell, *op. cit.*, p. 118
23. Whitman Bartley, *Iwo Jima: Amphibious Epic*, p. 176
24. Newcomb, *op. cit.*, p. 272
25. Russell, *op. cit.*, p. 156
26. Garand and Strobridge, *op. cit.*, p. 613
27. Isely and Crowl, *op. cit.*, p. 501
28. Samuel Eliot Morison, *Victory in the Pacific — 1945*, p. 73
29. Garand and Strobridge, *op. cit.*, p. 716

BIBLIOGRAPHY

Arthur, Robert and Cohlmia, Kenneth. *The Third Marine Division*. Infantry Journal Press, Washington, 1948.

Barity, Whitman. *Iwo Jima: Amphibious Epic*. Historical Branch, U.S. Marine Corps, Washington, 1954.

Buell, Thomas. *The Quiet Warrior*. Little Brown and Co., Boston, 1974.

Conner, Howard M. *The Spearhead: The Fifth Marine Division in WW II*. Infantry Journal Press. Washington, 1950.

Costello, John. *The Pacific War*. Rawson Wade Publishers, New York, 1981.

Craven, Wesley and Cate, James. *The Army Air Forces in WW II, Vol. V: The Pacific — Matterhorn to Nagasaki*. University of Chicago Press, Chicago, 1953.

Garand, George and Strobridge, Truman. *History of U.S. Marine Corps Operations in WW II, Vol. IV: Western Pacific Operations*. Historical Div., U.S. Marine Corps, Washington, 1971.

Henri, Raymond. *Iwo Jima: Springboard to Final Victory*. U.S. Camera Publishing Co., New York, 1945.

Henri, Raymond, et al. *The U.S. Marines on Iwo Jima*. Dial Press, New York, 1945.

Isely, Jeter and Crowl, Philip. *The U.S. Marines and Amphibi-*

ous War. Princeton University Press, Princeton, 1951.

Leckie, Robert. *Strong Men Armed.* Bonanza Books, New York, 1962.

Matthews, Allen. *The Assault.* Permabooks, Garden City, 1953.

Morison, Samuel. *History of U.S. Naval Operations in WW II, Vol. XIV: Victory in the Pacific 1945.* Little, Brown and Co., Boston, 1960.

Nalty, Bernard. *The United States Marines on Iwo Jima.* Historical Div., U.S. Marine Corps, Washington, 1970.

Newcomb, Richard. *Iwo Jima.* Holt, Rinehart & Winston, New York, 1965.

Pfannes, Charles and Salamone, Victor. *The Great Admirals of World War II Volume I: The Americans.* Zebra Books, New York, 1983.

Potter, E.B. *Nimitz.* Naval Institute Press, Annapolis, 1976.

Proehl, Carl. *The Fourth Marine Division in World War II.* Infantry Journal Press, Washington, 1946.

Russell, Michael. *Iwo Jima.* Ballantine Books, New York, 1974.

Sakai, Saburo and Cadin, Martin. *Samurai.* White Lion Publishers, London, 1957.

Sherrod, Robert. *On to Westward.* Duell, Sloane and Pearce, New York, 1945.

Sherrod, Robert. *History of Marine Corps Aviation in WWII.* Combat Forces Press, Washington, 1952.

Smith, Holland M. *Coral and Brass.* Charles Scribner's Sons, New York, 1949.

Smith, S.E., ed. *The United States Marine Corps In World War II.* Random House, New York, 1969.

Toland, John. *The Rising Sun.* Random House, New York, 1970.

Wheeler, Richard. *The Bloody Battle for Suribachi.* Thomas Y. Crowell, New York, 1965.

Wheeler, Richard. *Iwo.* Lippincott & Crowell, New York, 1980.

Chapter Seven

NOTES

1. Benis M. Frank, *Okinawa,* p. 19
2. Benis M. Frank and Henry Shaw, *Victory and Occupation,* p. 48
3. C. Nichols and H. Shaw, *Okinawa: Victory in the Pacific,* p. 49
4. Frank, *op. cit.,* p. 23
5. *Ibid,* p. 24
6. Frank and Shaw, *op. cit.,* p. 97
7. *Ours to Hold High, History of the 77th Infantry Division in WWII,* p. 239
8. Frank, *op. cit.,* p. 53
9. Frank and Shaw, *op. cit.,* p. 125
10. *Ours to Hold High, op. cit.,* p. 251
11. Henry Salomon, *Victory at Sea,* p. 237
12. Roy Appleman, et. al., *Okinawa: The Last Battle,* p. 364
13. Author's interview
14. George McMillan, *The Old Breed,* p. 368
15. Frank, *op. cit.,* p. 91
16. *Ibid,* p. 96
17. Frank and Shaw, *op. cit.,* p. 213
18. Appleman, *op. cit.,* p. 343
19. Frank, *op. cit.,* p. 119
20. Frank and Shaw, *op. cit.,* p. 321
21. *Ibid,* p. 324
22. Appleman, *op. cit.,* p. 463
23. Frank, *op. cit.,* p. 150
24. Frank and Shaw, *op. cit.,* p. 356
25. *Ibid,* p. 367
26. Frank, *op. cit.,* p.157

BIBLIOGRAPHY

Appleman, Roy, et al. *Okinawa: The Last Battle.* Dept. of the Army, Historical Div., Washington, 1948.

Belote, J. and Belote, W. *Typhoon of Steel: The Battle for*

Okinawa. Harper & Row, New York, 1970.

Cass, Bevan. *History of the Sixth Marine Division.* Infantry Journal Press, Washington, 1948.

Davidson, Williams and Kahl, *The Deadeyes: The Story of the 96th Division.* Infantry Journal Press, Washington, 1947.

Frank, B. and Shaw, H. *Victory and Occupation.* Historical Branch, Washington, 1968.

Frank, Benis. *Okinawa: Touchstone to Victory.* Ballantine Books, New York, 1969.

Hough, Frank. *The Island War.* J.P. Lippincott Co., Philadelphia, 1947.

Hoyt, Edwin. *Closing the Circle.* Van Nostrand Reinhold Co., New York, 1982.

Inoguchi, R., Tadashi, N. and Pineau, R. *The Divine Wind.* U.S. Naval Institute, Annapolis, 1958.

Isely, J. and Crowl, P. *The U.S. Marines and Amphibious War.* Princeton University, Princeton, 1951.

Love, Edmund. *The 27th Infantry Division in World War II.* Infantry Journal Press, Washington, 1949.

McMillan, George. *The Old Breed.* Infantry Journal Press, Washington, 1949.

Nichols, C. and Shaw, H. *Okinawa: Victory in the Pacific.* Historical Branch, Washington, 1955.

Pfannes, C. and Salamone, V. *The Great Admirals of World War II, Volume I: The Americans.* Zebra Books, New York, 1983.

Sledge, E.B. *With the Old Breed at Peleliu and Okinawa.* Presidio Press, California, 1981.

Salomon, Henry. *Victory at Sea.* Doubleday & Co., New York, 1959.

Sherrod, Robert. *History of Marine Corps Aviation in World War II.* Combat Forces Press, Washington, 1952.

Ours to Hold High: The History of the 77th Infantry Division in WWII. Infantry Journal Press, Washington, 1947.

McLEANE'S RANGERS
by John Darby

#1: BOUGAINVILLE BREAKOUT (1207, $2.50)
Even the Marines call on McLeane's Rangers, the toughest, meanest, and best fighting unit in the Pacific. Their first adventure pits the Rangers against the entire Japanese garrison in Bougainville. The target—an ammo depot invulnerable to American air attack . . . and the release of a spy.

#2: TARGET RABAUL (1271, $2.50)
Rabaul—it was one of the keys to the control of the Pacific and the Japanese had a lock on it. When nothing else worked, the Allies called on their most formidable weapon—McLeane's Rangers, the fearless jungle fighters who didn't know the meaning of the word quit!

#3: HELL ON HILL 457 (1343, $2.50)
McLeane and his men make a daring parachute drop in the middle of a heavily fortified Jap position. And the Japs are dug in so deep in a mountain pass fortress that McLeane may have to blow the entire pass to rubble—and his men in the bargain!

#4: SAIPAN SLAUGHTER (1510, $2.50)
Only McLeane's elite commando team had the skill—and the nerve—to go in before the invasion of Saipan and take on that key Jap stronghold. But the Japs have set a trap—which will test the jungle fighters' will to live!

Available wherever paperbacks are sold, or order direct from the Publisher. Send cover price plus 50¢ per copy for mailing and handling to Zebra Books, 475 Park Avenue South, New York, N.Y. 10016. DO NOT SEND CASH.

THE SAIGON COMMANDOS SERIES
by Jonathan Cain

SAIGON COMMANDOS #1   (1283, $3.25)

Here are the mysterious streets of a capital at war—filled with American men, adrift with deserters and orphans of war . . . and always the enemy, invisible and waiting to kill!

#2: CODE ZERO: SHOTS FIRED   (1329, $2.50)

When a phantom chopper pounces on Sergeant Mark Stryker and his men of the 716th, bloody havoc follows. And the sight of the carnage nearly breaks Stryker's control. He will make the enemy pay; they will face his SAIGON COMMANDOS!

#3: DINKY-DAU DEATH   (1377, $2.50)

When someone puts a price on the head of a First Cavalry captain, Stryker and his men leave the concrete jungle for the real thing to try and stop the assassin. And when the bullets start flying, Stryker will bet his life—on the SAIGON COMMANDOS!

#4: CHERRY-BOY BODY BAG   (1407, $2.50)

Blood flows in the streets of Saigon when Sergeant Mark Stryker's MPs become targets for a deadly sniper. Surrounded by rookies, Stryker must somehow stop a Cong sympathizer from blowing up a commercial airliner—without being blown away by the crazed sniper!

#5: BOONIE-RAT BODY BURNING   (1441, $2.50)

Someone's torching GIs in a hellhole known as Fire Alley and Sergeant Stryker and his MPs are in on the manhunt. To top it all off, Stryker's got to keep the lid on the hustlers, deserters, and Cong sympathizers who make his beat the toughest in the world!

#6: DI DI MAU OR DIE   (1493, $2.50)

The slaughter of a U.S. payroll convoy means it's up to Sergeant Stryker and his men to take on the Vietnamese mercenaries the only way they know how: with no mercy and with M-16s on full automatic!